INTERPRETING SEXUAL VIOLENCE, 1660–1800

The Body, Gender and Culture

Series Editor: Lynn Botelho

Titles in this Series

1 Courtly Indian Women in Late Imperial India
Angma Dey Jhala

2 Paracelsus's Theory of Embodiment: Conception and Gestation in Early Modern Europe
Amy Eisen Cislo

3 The Prostitute's Body: Rewriting Prostitution in Victorian Britain
Nina Attwood

4 Old Age and Disease in Early Modern Medicine
Daniel Schäfer

5 The Life of Madame Necker: Sin, Redemption and the Parisian Salon
Sonja Boon

6 Stays and Body Image in London: The Staymaking Trade, 1680–1810
Lynn Sorge-English

7 Prostitution and Eighteenth-Century Culture: Sex, Commerce and Morality
Ann Lewis and Markman Ellis (eds)

8 The Aboriginal Male in the Enlightenment World
Shino Konishi

9 Anatomy and the Organization of Knowledge, 1500–1850
Matthew Landers and Brian Muñoz (eds)

10 Blake, Gender and Culture
Helen P. Bruder and Tristanne J. Connolly (eds)

11 Age and Identity in Eighteenth-Century England
Helen Yallop

12 The Politics of Reproduction in Ottoman Society, 1838–1900
Gülhan Balsoy

13 The Study of Anatomy in Britain, 1700–1900
Fiona Hutton

Forthcoming Titles

Women, Agency and the Law, 1300–1700
Fiona Williamson and Bronach Kane (eds)

Sex, Identity and Hermaphrodites in Iberia, 1500–1800
Richard Cleminson and Francisco Vázquez García

The English Execution Narrative, 1200–1700
Katherine Royer

British Masculinity and the YMCA, 1844–1914
Geoff Spurr

INTERPRETING SEXUAL VIOLENCE, 1660–1800

Edited by

Anne Greenfield

LONDON AND NEW YORK

First published 2013 by Pickering & Chatto (Publishers) Limited

Published 2016 by Routledge
2 Park Square, Milton Park, Abingdon, Oxfordshire OX14 4RN
711 Third Avenue, New York, NY 10017, USA

First issued in paperback 2015

Routledge is an imprint of the Taylor & Francis Group, an informa business

© Taylor & Francis 2013
© Anne Greenfield 2013

To the best of the Publisher's knowledge every effort has been made to contact relevant copyright holders and to clear any relevant copyright issues. Any omissions that come to their attention will be remedied in future editions.

All rights reserved, including those of translation into foreign languages. No part of this book may be reprinted or reproduced or utilised in any form or by any electronic, mechanical, or other means, now known or hereafter invented, including photocopying and recording, or in any information storage or retrieval system, without permission in writing from the publishers.

Notice:
Product or corporate names may be trademarks or registered trademarks, and are used only for identification and explanation without intent to infringe.

BRITISH LIBRARY CATALOGUING IN PUBLICATION DATA

Interpreting sexual violence, 1660–1800. – (The body, gender and culture)
1. Sex crimes – History – 18th century. 2. Sex crimes in literature. 3. Sex crimes in art. 4. Sex crimes – Public opinion – History – 18th century.
I. Series II. Greenfield, Anne, editor of compilation.
809.9'33556'09033-dc23

ISBN-13: 978-1-138-66303-9 (pbk)
ISBN-13: 978-1-8489-3439-9 (hbk)

Typeset by Pickering & Chatto (Publishers) Limited

CONTENTS

Editor's Acknowledgements — ix
List of Figures — xi
List of Contributors — xiii

Part I: Overview and Scope
  Introduction – *Anne Greenfield* — 1
  1 Researching Sexual Violence, 1660–1800: A Critical Analysis
    – *Julie Gammon* — 13

Part II: Legal and Social History
  2 'For the Repressing of the Most Wicked and Felonious Rapes or
    Ravishments of Women': Rape Law in England, 1660–1800
    – *Mary R. Block* — 23
  3 From Rape to Marriage: Questions of Consent in Eighteenth-Century
    Britain – *Katie Barclay* — 35
  4 The Disordered Fundament: Sexual Violence on Boys and Sodomy
    Trial Narratives in the *Old Bailey Proceedings* – *Aparna Gollapudi* — 45

Part III: Drama
  5 The Titillation of Dramatic Rape, 1660–1720 – *Anne Greenfield* — 57
  6 Violently Erotic: Representing Rape in Restoration Drama
    – *Ann Marie Byrd* — 69
  7 'A Most Obedient Wife': Passive Resistance and Tory Politics in Eliza
    Haywood's *A Wife to Be Lett* – *Loring Pfeiffer* — 83
  8 Staging Rape in the Age of Walpole: Sexual Violence and the Politics
    of Dramatic Adaptation in 1730s Britain – *Jennifer L. Airey* — 95

Part IV: Fiction
  9 'What Do You Take Me For?': Rape and Virtue in *The Female Quixote*
    – *Robin Runia* — 107
  10 'Nothing But Violent Methods Will Do': Heterosexual Rape and the
    Violation of Female Friendship – *Dawn A. Nawrot* — 119
  11 Bringing Sentimental Fiction to its (Anti-)Climax: Laurence Sterne's
    A Sentimental Journey – *Nichol Weizenbeck* — 131

Part V: Other Genres
  12 'Violence that's Wicked for a Man to Use': Sex, Gender and Violence
     in the Eighteenth Century – *Lena Olsson*   141
  13 The Rhetoric of Rape: William Blake's *Visions of the Daughters of
     Albion* as Eighteenth-Century Rape Trial – *Misty Krueger*   149
  14 The Horror of the Horns: Pan's Attempted Rape of Syrinx in Early
     Eighteenth-Century Visual Art – *Melanie Cooper-Dobbin*   163

Notes   175
Index   215

EDITOR'S ACKNOWLEDGEMENTS

This book has benefited from the support of Chawton House Library, where I conducted research as a visiting fellow in summer 2013, and Valdosta State University's Faculty Research Seed Grant programme, which provided the funding and course-release time to complete this project. I am also grateful to Dr Jessica Munns for her excellent mentorship and encouragement over the years, and to my husband, Brett, whose conversation, encouragement and keen editor's eye proved invaluable at every turn.

LIST OF FIGURES

Figure 14.1: Jean-François de Troy, *Pan and Syrinx*, 1720   165
Figure 14.2: Pierre Mignard, *Pan and Syrinx*, 1688–90   169
Figure 14.3: Pierre Mignard, *Pan and Syrinx*, 1690   170

LIST OF CONTRIBUTORS

Jennifer L. Airey is Assistant Professor of English at the University of Tulsa, where she specializes in Restoration and eighteenth-century literature, theatre history and early modern gender studies. She is the author of *The Politics of Rape: Sexual Atrocity, Propaganda Wars, and the Restoration Stage* (2012), and has published articles on Wycherley and Dryden. Her article on the 1768 rape trial of Frederick, Lord Baltimore is forthcoming, and she is currently at work on a new book project, an analysis of gender and class violence in late eighteenth-century Gothic drama.

Katie Barclay is a postdoctoral research fellow at the ARC Centre of Excellence for the History of Emotions, University of Adelaide. She is the author of *Love, Intimacy and Power: Marriage and Patriarchy in Scotland, 1650–1850* (2011), winner of the Women's History Network (UK) book prize and the Senior Hume Brown Prize for Scottish History, which explores how couples negotiate meanings of both love and power within their correspondence. Barclay has written widely on emotional and marital relationships in Scotland and Ireland, with publications in *Cultural and Social History*, *Women's History Review* and the *Journal of Scottish Historical Studies*. She is the Lead Editor of the peer-reviewed journal, *Women's History Magazine,* and co-editor with Dr Deborah Simonton of *Women in Eighteenth-Century Scotland: Intimate, Intellectual and Public Lives* (2013).

Mary R. Block is an associate professor of history at Valdosta State University where she teaches courses in US Legal and Constitutional History and US in the Early National and Antebellum eras. She earned her PhD from the University of Kentucky. She has conducted extensive research in the history of Anglo-American rape law from the twelfth to the early twentieth century. Her publications on rape and the law include 'Rape Law in Nineteenth-Century America: Some Thoughts and Reflections on the State of the Field', *History Compass*, 7:5 (2009), pp. 1391–9 and '"Limited to Errors of Law": Rape Law and Adjudication in the Nineteenth-Century Kentucky Court of Appeals', *Ohio Valley History*, 11:3 (2011), pp. 44–64.

Ann Marie Byrd is Lecturer of Theatre at California State University, Fullerton. She has also taught at the University of Pittsburgh, the University of Notre Dame, the University of Colorado and Olivet College. She received her PhD from the University of Colorado at Boulder. Her research focuses on female dramatists across the centuries and particularly the English Restoration. She recently published a book-length study titled *The Ravishing Restoration: Aphra Behn, Violence and Comedy* (2010). Dr Byrd is a scholar, theatre critic, director and actor.

Melanie Cooper-Dobbin is a PhD candidate in the School of History and Politics at the University of Adelaide, Australia. Specializing in eighteenth-century art history, her studies are driven by a particular interest in the representations of mythology and gender. The present focus of her work is to reconsider the frequent appearance of masculine deities and satyrs in early eighteenth-century visual culture. Her Master's thesis was titled 'Wayward Wives and Deviant Mistresses: François Boucher's Mythological Women of the Rococo' (University of Adelaide, 2008).

Julie Gammon is a lecturer in history at the University of Southampton, UK. She completed her PhD research on narratives of sexual violence in England from 1640 to 1820 at the University of Essex where she also worked as a teaching fellow. She has also held a lecturing position at the University of Warwick. Her research is on gender and crime in the long eighteenth century with a particular interest in the treatment of marginal groups by the legal system including children, gypsies and homosexuals.

Aparna Gollapudi is an associate professor at Colorado State University, where she primarily teaches eighteenth-century literature. In addition to long eighteenth-century literature, culture, theatre, law and economics, her research interests include children's literature, especially the interactions of text and image in picture books. Gollapudi recently published *Moral Reform in Comedy and Culture, 1696–1742* (2011). She has also published on Penelope Aubin, Richard Steele, John Bell, Maurice Sendak and Peter Sis.

Anne Greenfield is an assistant professor of English at Valdosta State University, specializing in Restoration and eighteenth-century literature, especially drama. She completed her PhD at the University of Denver, and she is author of several articles on Restoration and eighteenth-century drama and Aphra Behn. She is editor-in-chief of *Restoration and Eighteenth-Century Theatre Research* and New Media Editor of *ABO: Interactive Journal for Women in the Arts, 1640–1830*. Her current book project deals with tragic depictions of rape and attempted rape in English theatre from 1660 to 1720.

Misty Krueger is Visiting Assistant Professor of British Literature at the University of Maine at Farmington. She received her PhD in English from the University of Tennessee. Her research specialty is in Restoration and eighteenth-century drama, and her secondary interests pertain to gender studies and women writers. Her publications include articles on playwrights Delarivier Manley, Sir William Davenant, John Dryden and Thomas Duffett. She is currently expanding her dissertation on revenge in Restoration tragic drama into a book project, and she is writing essays on Jane Austen's 'History of England' and *Northanger Abbey*.

Dawn Nawrot is a PhD candidate at the University of Wisconsin-Milwaukee. Her main interests include eighteenth-century women writers, the rise of the novel and feminist theory. She is currently working on her dissertation entitled, 'Female Betrayal and Rape in the Eighteenth-Century British Novel: Dangerous Narratives of Women as Consensual Liberal Subjects'. Her research evaluates how eighteenth-century literary representations of women's relationships, consent and subjecthood are participating in a larger political discussion about social contracts emerging in a liberal, individualist and capitalist society. She is also working to determine how female rape narratives construct women's role as subjects in the emerging novel and British society.

Lena Olsson is an independent scholar of English literature, formerly at Lund University, Sweden. She wrote her PhD thesis on John Cleland's *Memoirs of a Woman of Pleasure* (1748) and is the editor of Cleland's abridged *Fanny Hill* (1748) and the anonymous *The Genuine History of ... Sally Salisbury* (2004). Other publications include 'Idealized and Realistic Portrayals of Prostitution in John Cleland's *Memoirs of a Woman of Pleasure*', in Patsy S. Fowler and Alan Jackson (eds), *Launching Fanny Hill: Essays on the Novel and Its Influences* (2003) and '"A First-Rate Whore": Prostitution and Empowerment in the Early Eighteenth Century', in Ann Lewis and Markman Ellis (eds), *Prostitution and Eighteenth-Century Culture: Sex, Commerce and Morality* (2012). She is at present working on a study of the whore biography genre.

Loring Pfeiffer is a PhD candidate at the University of Pittsburgh and a faculty member in the English Department at Santa Clara University. Her research focuses on women playwrights, female sexuality and partisan politics in Restoration and early eighteenth-century England, and her article on Aphra Behn's *The Rover, Part II* (1681) is forthcoming in *Restoration: Studies in English Literary Culture, 1660–1700*.

Robin Runia is Assistant Professor of English at Xavier University of Louisiana. She received her PhD in literature from the University of New Mexico. Her research includes women's writing, development of the novel and gender and sexuality studies. She is a Mellon Faculty Community of Teaching Scholars fellow. Select publications include: '"Oppressed With My Own Sensations": *The Histories of Some of the Penitents* and Principled Piety,' *Religion in the Age of Enlightenment*, 4 (forthcoming); 'Prostitutes or Proselytes: Eighteenth-Century Female Enthusiasts,' *Eighteenth-Century Women: Studies in their Lives, Work, and Culture*, 7 (forthcoming); and '"The Breeches Are My Own, Henceforth I'le Rant": *The Widdow Ranter* and Cross-Dressed Politics,' *Restoration and Eighteenth-Century Theatre Research*, 26:1–2 (Summer 2012), pp. 5–21.

Nichol Weizenbeck is an ABD PhD candidate in literary studies and an arts, humanities, and social sciences fellow studying at the University of Denver. Her research focuses on British women's fiction of the early eighteenth century and the divergent movements of which early female British novels are comprised. In addition, the history of the novel, eighteenth-century studies, representations of sex, sexuality and gender, and women and gender studies comprise key components in her work. She has also served as the associate editor for *Restoration and Eighteenth-Century Theatre Research*.

INTRODUCTION

Anne Greenfield

Sexual Violence: A Favourite Subject

Few subjects were as frequently and as successfully inserted into the literary and artistic world of the Restoration and eighteenth century as was sexual violence. Depictions of sexual violence appeared regularly in novels, short fiction, tragic and comic plays, poems, the visual arts and more, with remarkable frequency during this era. In Restoration drama, this trope appears from 1662 onwards, beginning with the attempted rape of Bellmont in Thomas Porter's *The Villain*. Rape and attempted rape would become staples of tragic drama, with particular frequency during the 1670s and 1680s, and again at the turn of the eighteenth century. Older plays like William Shakespeare's *King Lear* (1606) were adapted and revived in the Restoration with newly-added scenes of sexual violence.[1] New tragedies that revolved around rape like Nathaniel Lee's *Mithridates* (c. 1678) were great successes, and were imitated widely. However, Restoration dramatists by no means confined these sexually-violent scenes to tragic drama. Even many of the liveliest and most mirthful comedies of the Restoration, like Aphra Behn's *The Rover I* (1677) and *II* (1681) and Thomas D'Urfey's *Trick for Trick* (1678) contain frightening scenes of attempted rape. Late seventeenth- and early eighteenth-century prose fiction was equally captivated by rape and seduction. In the short fiction of Eliza Haywood and Delarivière Manley, for instance, one is hard pressed to find a text that lacks female resistance to male sexual aggression. Likewise, as the English novel began to develop into its mature form it too was highly concerned with sexual violence. The victims of rape and attempted rape in these novels are surprisingly diverse, from Amy, the loyal servant in Daniel Defoe's *Roxana* (1724), to Clarissa, the middle-class, *nouveau riche* heroine in Samuel Richardson's *Clarissa* (1748), to Evelina, the unrevealed aristocratic heiress in Frances Burney's *Evelina* (1778). By the late eighteenth century, with the emergence of radical women writers like Mary Hays and Mary Wollestoncraft, one again finds great interest in the trope of sexual violence, this time in a way that redeems rape victims as socially productive figures who are able to survive their violations, even if not for long. In the visual arts, too, rape figured strongly. The myth of Lucretia alone was rendered and reproduced abundantly by painters in England and on the Continent, as seen in J. L. Gottfrid's *Historischer Chronik* (1674), G. B. Tiepolo's *Tarquin and Lucretia* (c. 1745–50) and Gavin Hamilton's *The Oath of Brutus* (early 1760s). Even in shorter-lived and less 'legitimate' genres like political pamphlets, broadsides, crime narratives, erotica and pornography, one finds no shortage of sexual violence. These sexually-violent representations found their way into every decade of the Restoration and eighteenth century, into nearly every genre and into the minds of many, many readers and viewers.

The remarkable prevalence of the trope of sexual violence is matched by its astonishing flexibility. In the hands of writers and artists of this period, sexual violence was used for a wide variety of, often seemingly contradictory, ends. For instance, Whig dramatists advocating the doctrine of resistance and social contract theory regularly depicted cruel tyrant-rapists whose sexually-violent crimes illustrated the need to overthrow unjust rulers. On the other hand, with an opposing agenda, Tory dramatists advocating the divine right of kings depicted cruel rebel-rapists whose sexual brutalities illustrated the atrocities that resulted when a monarch was overthrown. Taking yet another tack, writers of turn-of-the-century amatory fiction depicted 'seductions' that were (simultaneously and ambiguously) both welcomed and forced. These writers of amatory fiction used sexual violence to create narratives with strong political subtexts that grappled with the complex question of whether resistance to legitimate authority can ever be virtuous. With the rise of the novel, sexual violence was again depicted variously and unevenly: this trope was at times represented solemnly and centrally as in Samuel Richardson's *Clarissa* and *Pamela*, while elsewhere humorously and peripherally as in Henry Fielding's *Tom Jones* and *Joseph Andrews*. Not only did the trope of sexual violence vary from author to author, but even within single works, this trope could be put to opposing ends. Sexual violence could be used simultaneously to terrify and titillate audiences, or to make martyrs and whores out of the same female characters. Few other literary and artistic tropes were used for such antithetical purposes.

Part of the reason for the popularity and ubiquity of this trope lies in the importance of chastity in the seventeenth- and eighteenth-century collective imagination. When kept intact, a woman's chastity ensured that her husband reared his actual, biological children, and that her husband's inheritance was passed down to his legitimate successors. As a theft of chastity, rape was understood as a violation against men, as a theft of everything a man owned and achieved and as a fissure in the most basic structure of social order. When enacted upon a chaste woman (and, especially, a propertied chaste woman), sexual violence was theoretically believed to be a devastating crime to be prevented and punished at all costs. With such high stakes associated with the threat of lost chastity, writers of this era found a useful rhetorical device in the trope of sexual violence. Writers vilified their political enemies by painting them as rapists, they illustrated the breakdown of social order through the rapes of chaste wives and daughters and they terrified readers with the devastating losses that followed forceful 'seductions'. Because the threat of stolen chastity was believed to be a universally-detested crime, the trope of sexual violence could easily imbue a scene with power, suspense and gravity.

Another reason for the prevalence of sexual violence in art and literature of the period comes from sheer precedent. Eighteenth-century writers and readers were well aware of the long tradition of rape and attempted-rape depictions in Western literature. The anonymous poem, 'The Rape of the Bride' (1723) acknowledges this canon of rape depictions in its opening canto, which recounts a remarkable twenty-one mythical and historical acts of sexual violence in just two pages. These references span from sexual violations in classical Rome (such as Tarquin's rape of Lucrece) and Greece (for example, Agammenon's rape of Breseis), to accounts of fantastical sodomy (like the moon's rape of the young boy, Endymion), to metaphors of rape (the rape of the day by the night), to non-sexual injuries that are called 'rapes' (for example, the rapes of fruit, flowers and land by human cultivation). Rape, in this view, is not only a phenomenon that has, as the anonymous poet puts it, 'happen'd, on the Earth, / Since Mother Nature's early Birth',[2] but rape is also part of a long tradition of literary writing in the West. In an age when classical authors and their works were venerated and imitated widely, this literary precedent acted as a strong catalyst for English writers in appropriating the theme of sexual violence.

Doubtless, authors of this era adopted the trope of sexual violence for other reasons as well. For instance, a rape scene provided many a dramatist with the welcome excuse to display a beautiful actress, post violation, in a torn gown with unbound hair and a revealed bosom. Elsewhere, in the late eighteenth century, scenes of sexual violence served the purposes of radical women writers who wished to paint rape as a violation of a women's sexual autonomy, rather than as a mere property crime. In other hands still, the trope of sexual violence was turned on its head, as a topic of irreverence and wit, as in Henry Fielding's *Rape Upon Rape* or Alexander Pope's 'The Rape of the Lock' – both of which depended for their humour on the fact that rape was elsewhere treated as such a devastating and grave matter. Indeed, part of the appeal of the trope of sexual violence was that it could be used to grapple with and discuss a huge variety of issues. Writers found that their messages about gender, the legal system, inheritance, the passions, the body, resistance to authority, the family, social hierarchies – and so much more – could be discussed adeptly in stories that revolved around sexual violence. The usefulness and power behind this trope comes in large part from the ways in which sexual violence reflected so many other seventeenth- and eighteenth-century ideas, values and anxieties. Thus, not only does sexual violence stand out as a uniquely-prevalent and flexible trope, but it also acts as an important index to the underlying ideologies of this era.

This collection examines sexual violence in light of its striking complexity and flexibility, across a 140-year timespan and in a variety of genres. As this collection demonstrates, it is the malleability of the rape trope that made it such a success with so many authors, artists, readers and viewers at this time. Today, we often assume that rape and sexual assault have always been understood as universally-shameful and barbaric crimes. However, this trope abounded in literary and artistic communities, not because it was timelessly devastating but, because this trope was flexible enough to satisfy a variety of aesthetic, political and ideological purposes, all the while reflecting something destructive enough to ensure that readers would be intrigued, compelled or persuaded by its presence, whatever the form.

Sexual Violence in Context

Historical context, while important in interpreting literature of any variety from any era, is essential when investigating Restoration and eighteenth-century depictions of sexual violence. During this period, scenes of sexual violence mirrored and responded to mainstream ideologies of medical science, human sexuality, gender-relations, patriarchy, inheritance, violence, the law and much more. Without a proper understanding of how sexual violence was understood within these concurrent ideological contexts, a modern reader will likely be puzzled by the conventions used to represent this trope three centuries ago. For instance, one might wonder, why were raped tragic heroines always portrayed as virtuous and chaste? Why did they so often die after their sexual violations? And why did these characters receive so much attention and concern from their male kin, even though actual raped women had very little public sympathy and legal recourse at this time? It is only after one interprets depictions of sexual violence in light of contemporary ideologies that one can make sense of the above patterns. Historical context reveals, in answer to the above questions, that writers portrayed raped heroines as virtuous and chaste because they had to dispel contemporary assumptions that women accusing rape were promiscuous and untrustworthy. Likewise, writers often made their raped heroines die after their violations because, at the time, raped women were viewed as irreparably polluted, and, thus, letting a raped heroine die of grief or suicide was an excellent way of resolving her otherwise problematic future. Finally, raped characters garnered high levels of attention and concern from their male kin because, during this period, rape was largely conceived of as a property crime against fathers and husbands, and writers thus tended to emphasize the impact rapes had on victims' male relatives above the impact on the victims themselves. It is crucial, therefore, that one interprets Restoration and eighteenth-century representations of sexual violence in light of the contemporary ideologies that informed them.

In this vein, it is worth pausing at the outset to delineate how 'sexual violence' was understood by the English public of the Restoration and eighteenth century, as well as how the term will be used throughout this collection. The relationship between attitudes then and now is a complex one. On the one hand, many modern-day myths about rape carry a direct lineage to the eighteenth century. For instance, today's blame-the-victim attitudes towards female rape victims who are accused of 'asking for it' through their promiscuous attire or behaviour harkens back to the connection between rape and chastity seen so prominently during the eighteenth century and before. In one of many examples that could be cited, former US congressman Todd Akin's 2012 comments on the incompatibility of pregnancy with 'legitimate rape' bears a notable resemblance to the long eighteenth-century view that female orgasm was required for conception (and therefore 'true' rape could not result in pregnancy).[3] On the other hand, however, there are enormous differences between the ways sexual violence has generally been understood in the long eighteenth century and today. In fact, a look at the ways in which 'sexual violence' has been defined, responded to, tolerated and lamented over the last three hundred and fifty years reveals vast differences.

One of the greatest indicators of just how much attitudes towards sexual violence have changed over the centuries, lies in the changing definition of 'rape', the most salient and extreme form of sexual violence. Perhaps the greatest difference between definitions of 'rape' then and now lies in its breadth: the term 'rape' is far more heterogeneous and encompassing today than it was three centuries ago. In large part due to 1970s' efforts to protect more victims and to punish more assailants, we have expanded our understanding of rape to be more inclusive of both myriad victims and myriad sex acts. Today, rape victims can be chaste and unchaste, male and female, young and old. Likewise today, acts of rape can be committed by men and women, with or without penetration and ejaculation and they can be enacted on more than one area of the body. The greater inclusiveness of this term, however, has not led to greater concord. We can, perhaps, agree on a basic, modern-day definition of 'rape' such as, *sex without the consent of one party*. However, the ambiguities underlying such a definition are apparent. One has only to ask, for instance, whether rape requires penetration (and if so, are vaginal, anal and oral penetration counted equally?), or whether other forced sexual activity (such as violent fondling) can also be classified as 'rape'? What if the non-consenting party changes his/her mind during the sex act, is intoxicated, is unsure whether s/he consents, or isn't sure s/he was raped? Little consensus has been reached on these and many other questions – and, in fact, many of us hold ambiguous and even contradictory views on rape today.

Competing dictionary definitions of 'rape' reveal some of the ambiguities that underpin our modern-day understandings of this term. For instance, the *Oxford English Dictionary* defines rape as 'the act of forced, non-consenting, or illegal sexual intercourse with another person; sexual violation or assault'.[4] On the other hand, *Miriam-Webster* defines rape as 'unlawful sexual activity and usually sexual intercourse carried out forcibly or under threat of injury against the will usually of a female or with a person who is beneath a certain age or incapable of valid consent'.[5] Note that while *Miriam-Webster* defines rape as unlawful, the *Oxford English Dictionary* makes lawfulness a mere sufficient condition (rather than a necessary condition) of rape. Likewise, while *Miriam-Webster* assumes that this act is usually carried out against females, the *Oxford English Dictionary* makes no such stipulation. Little is settled even by these 'standard' definitions of the term.

While the meaning of rape has expanded in recent decades, the term was markedly narrow during the Restoration and eighteenth century. At that time, in order for a sex act to be understood as rape, it had to take a specific form (for example, heterosexual, penetrating), between specific sorts of people (for example, a chaste woman usually of equal or higher social status to her assailant) and accusations had to be made at specific times and in specific ways (usually within twenty-four hours of the sex act). Complicating scenarios that make it difficult for twenty-first-century thinkers to agree upon a definition of 'rape' (such as, when a victim changes her mind midway through the sex act) would have troubled no one during the Restoration and eighteenth century. Any sex act that failed to cohere with the above, highly-narrow definition of rape was decidedly understood as *not rape*.

Part of the impetus behind the narrowness of this definition during the seventeenth and eighteenth centuries was that rape, above all, was understood as the theft of a woman's chastity. Thus, any sort of forced sex that did not result in lost chastity (i.e. the rape of a woman who had already parted with her chastity) was almost never prosecutable under the law. William Blackstone makes this point clear in his 1765–9 observation that not all women were believed to be legally qualified to press charges for rape: 'The civil law seems to suppose a prostitute or common harlot incapable of any injuries of this kind [rape]'.[6] Trial transcripts from this period abound with female accusers whose claims of rape were promptly dismissed after they were found to be (or merely accused of being) unchaste. In fact, the association between rape and stolen chastity can be seen in nearly all definitions of 'rape' during these centuries. For instance, in *A Dictionary of the English Language*, Samuel Johnson defines 'rape' as the 'Violent defloration of chastity',[7] and John Brydall defines 'rape' as 'the violent deflouring [*sic*] of a Woman against her will'.[8] This equation of rape with lost chastity is reaffirmed again and again in the literature of this era: in tragic and serious works, rape victims are always female (a man has no chastity to lose), they are either virginal daughters or loyal wives (illustrating that their chastity was intact when the rape occurred), they are almost never wives raped by husbands (for a husband cannot steal what he already owns) and they are pristinely modest and pious (further emphasizing the claim that they would never have parted with their chastity before it was forced from them). Thus, even though the trope of rape was highly flexible and could be used in disparate ways, the prevailing understanding of 'rape' as stolen chastity meant that writers and artists were significantly limited in whom they could depict as rape victims and what sorts of violations they could classify as rapes. What mattered most during the Restoration and eighteenth century was, not whether sexual violence generally had occurred but, whether chastity had been compromised.

While this collection is firmly focused on the ways in which sexual violence was represented and understood during the Restoration and eighteenth century, it adopts an intentionally modern (and therefore inclusive) scope, examining a wide variety of sexually-violent acts, many of which would not have been grouped together by writers and thinkers during this era. For instance, the rape of a chaste heiress, the coerced 'seduction' of a semi-willing heroine, the sodomy of an adolescent male, and the sale of a wife were all believed to be abhorrent acts, yet not all would have been classified as 'rape' (especially since they did not all involve lost chastity), and certainly the modern expression 'sexual violence' would not have been used. However, this collection groups these acts together under the modern title 'sexual violence', not because eighteenth-century writers would have done so but, because we in the twenty-first century find this grouping to be useful and worthy of study. Similarly, modern-day scholars trace 'queerness' throughout the ages not because they believe that queerness was understood and defined then as it is now (which it certainly was not), but because they want to isolate, trace and call attention to the ways non-normative sexual acts have been understood over the centuries. While this collection's scope is intentionally modern, its scholarship is far from anachronistic. The collection is devoted to tracing Restoration and eighteenth-century ideologies and aesthetics as they responded to myriad sex acts and myriad victims – of all genders, ages, socio-economic positions and bearing any sexual history.

Collection Overview

Interpreting Sexual Violence: 1660–1800 analyses numerous forms of sexual violence as these acts were depicted in various mediums in a variety of genres across the whole of the Restoration and eighteenth century. In Chapter 1 Julie Gammon completes the collection's introductory section with a historiography of research conducted by recent scholars. As Gammon illustrates, the attention to the history of rape that 1970s' feminists began in isolation has since burgeoned into a considerable body of rigorous historical and literary scholarship generated by researchers in a variety of fields. This array of scholarship illustrates not only what the field has accomplished so far, but also the work that remains to be done.

The following section, 'Legal and Social History', interprets sexual violence as it was represented and understood in legal and medical treatises. Mary R. Block's essay, '"For the Repressing of the Most Wicked and Felonious Rapes or Ravishments of Women": Rape Law and Adjudication in England, 1660–1800' opens this section, providing a comprehensive historical overview of English rape law during this era. Block's analysis looks beyond the parliamentary statutes that address rape, of which there was a relative paucity, focusing instead on legal treatises that interpreted the law and that carried wide influence in judicial decisions. Block sheds important light on the enormous difficulty to be had in successfully prosecuting rapists, a difficulty that is particularly surprising for a legal system that was otherwise intended to favour the prosecution. This section of the collection continues with two, more specific, analyses of how sexual violence was treated and interpreted historically, legally and socially. Katie Barclay examines the roles of female consent and male force in courtship rituals. While eighteenth-century women had few opportunities to consent actively to sex, resistance was thought compulsory and the female will was believed to be something to be overcome by men – both in sex and marriage. The result, as Barclay shows, was a widespread toleration and expectation of physical force in courtship practices, and the normalization of sexual violence in heterosexual relations. The following chapter, by Aparna Gollapudi, analyses cases of sodomitical sexual violence against young men and boys as they were recorded in the *Proceedings of the Old Bailey*. As Gollapudi demonstrates, court officials tended to feminize the bodies of young male victims, in some ways figuring them as akin to raped underage girls. Gollapudi's analysis sheds light on a body of court cases that have been overlooked in recent scholarship, as well as on early eighteenth-century attitudes towards children, who are often figured in these cases as at once ignorant *ingénues* and cunning tricksters.

The remaining essays, comprising the majority of this collection, revolve around sexual violence as it was represented in the literature and art of the era. These essays illustrate both the range of literary and artistic genres within which we find depictions of sexual violence, and the common assumptions, values, narrative strategies and anxieties shared in these representations across all genres. The first two essays opening the 'Drama' section, my own essay, 'The Titillation of Dramatic Rape: 1660–1720', and Ann Marie Byrd's essay, 'Violently Erotic: Representing Rape in Restoration Drama', each examine the eroticism behind dramatic depictions of rape. My essay takes a cultural studies approach to the question of whether and to what degree rape scenes titillated viewers at this time, examining an array of Restoration and early eighteenth-century documents, including plays, pornography and erotica, rape trial transcripts (especially ones that were advertised and sold as erotica), popular journals from the period and engravings designed to accompany plays. I conclude that rape scenes were almost certainly titillating for many audience members. Yet, because tragic rape scenes did not depict culpably sexual women, they were customarily classified as part of high-tragedy rather than as base or offensive displays worthy of censorship. Byrd discusses the wide-ranging appeal of dramatized rape scenes as they were manifested in a variety of genres, both comical and serious. Byrd illustrates the extent to which sexual violence could be staged in a comedy of manners as 'a hilarious mockery of sexuality and female resistance', in a tragicomedy of intrigue as a sexual assault that is fully pardoned when the victim marries her rapist, and in a she-tragedy as a devastating act of sexual pollution that brings dishonour on an entire family. What ties these productions together in each of these genres, as Byrd demonstrates, is an abiding focus on the body of the actress.

Taking another tack, Loring Pfeiffer and Jennifer L. Airey examine the political, rather than the erotic, resonance of dramatic depictions of sexual violence. Pfeiffer takes up the topic of wife pandering, or the act of selling one's wife to another man, as seen in Eliza Haywood's *A Wife to Be Lett* (1723). Pfeiffer shows that the play's heroine, Mrs Graspall, faces an ideological challenge akin to the one facing Tories at the time. Mrs Graspall strives to remain a virtuous and obedient wife while, at the same time, resisting her husband's cruel designs to 'rent' her sexually to another man; Tories similarly sought to remain the 'party of obedience' while resisting the commands of the rising Whig majority. In Haywood's hands, the sexual becomes political, as Mrs Graspall's suffering illustrates the potential for sufferers to resist virtuously and passively such legitimate authorities. Airey's essay, 'Staging Rape in the Age of Walpole: Sexual Violence and the Politics of Dramatic Adaptation in 1730s Britain' focuses on far more explicit political propaganda found in 1730s dramatic depictions of sexual violence. Airey's chapter underscores the strong lineage between earlier uses of sexual violence as political propaganda (particularly by seventeenth-century Roundheads during the Civil Wars and Jacobites in the aftermath of the Glorious Revolution) and later, 1730s anti-Walpole rhetoric that likened political and economic corruption to ravishment. The longevity of sexual violence as a rhetorical tool serves as a reminder of just how adaptable this trope was, even when applied to a whole new series of complaints focusing on Walpole's economic and political corruptions, and personal profligacy.

The section that follows, focusing on sexual violence in fiction, shifts the discussion to the ways in which victims and assailants were portrayed. Robin Runia opens this section with her essay, '"What Do You Take Me For?": Rape and Virtue in *The Female Quixote*', which deals with the complex agency and culpability of heroines threatened with rape and seduction. While Charlotte Lennox mocks her heroine, Arabella, both for imagining too easily that the men around her are rapists and for failing to perceive real sexual dangers when she encounters them, she also grapples with serious questions about how and whether women can protect themselves against rape. As Runia argues, Arabella's position on this matter evolves throughout the novel: her initial assumption that a woman may preserve her virtue by having a highly-developed intellect, transforms into the view that female virtue, generally, should be measured not by chastity but by piety. This transformation in Arabella's thinking reflects a wider (if incipient) willingness, during this era, to question blame-the-victim attitudes. Dawn A. Nawrot takes up the question of female agency, not in victims of sexual violence, but in female accessories to these crimes. Nawrot examines Daniel Defoe's *Roxana* and Henry Fielding's *Tom Jones*, in which female characters assist (or attempt to assist) men in traumatic acts of sexual violence. These corrupted, mercenary female characters act as an important index to eighteenth-century attitudes towards women's participation in modes of patriarchy, as well as towards contemporary political anxieties about individuals' roles in social contracts. Lastly, in the final chapter of this section, Nichol Weizenbeck examines attitudes towards sexual violence as they appear in the eighteenth-century sentimental novel. As Weizenbeck illustrates, one of the surprising and often-overlooked features of the quintessential 'man of feeling' in novels like Lawrence Sterne's *A Sentimental Journey* (1768), is his harmless and impotent sexuality. Thus, an unexpected ramification of living a sentimental life – alongside experiencing sympathy, compassion, benevolence, humanity and pity – is experiencing sexual debilitation. As the chapters in this section demonstrate, even blame for the serious problem of sexual violence could be shifted widely from author to author, and it was far from settled whether and to what degree culpability lay with the victim or the accessory or the assailant.

The final section of this collection examines the trope of sexual violence in yet other genres and mediums. Lena Olsson opens this section with a discussion of the widely (if tacitly) held belief that it was very difficult to rape a woman who genuinely resisted the act. Olsson examines not only legal and medical texts that aver the difficulty and at times impossibility of raping an unwilling woman, but also works of eighteenth-century fiction and poetry that almost never depict rape through the force of a lone rapist (instead featuring accomplices who hold the woman down, or drugs used for sedation beforehand). While the myth of the 'unrapeable' woman seems to contradict commonly-held beliefs in women's inferior strength and lack of assertiveness, this myth also relies on widely-held blame-the-victim attitudes (i.e., the idea that women secretly welcome sexual violence, and that it is impossible for a man to force an unwilling woman). In the following chapter Misty Krueger turns to sexual violence in eighteenth-century verse, in an examination of Bromion's rape of Oothoon in William Blake's poetic slave narrative, *Visions of the Daughters of Albion* (*VDA*). Krueger analyses this poem alongside numerous testimonies from real-life court cases at the time, arguing that the text both mirrors the proceedings of a trial for rape and that it places blame on the injustices seen in such a patriarchal system that blames prosecutrixes for their own victimhood. While *VDA* does not offer a proto-feminist vision of female sexuality, the poem does offer a nascent concern for and rejection of many of the blame-the-victim attitudes that pervaded the literary and legal texts of this era. Lastly, in the final chapter of the collection, Melanie Cooper-Dobbin analyses yet another highly-popular medium for depicting sexual assault and rape: the visual arts. Cooper-Dobbin traces several images of Pan and Syrinx over the seventeenth and eighteenth centuries, showing a shift from earlier images that highlighted the male rapist as a dangerous sexual aggressor to later images that focus (humorously) on the female victim as a dangerous symbol of promiscuity. Cooper-Dobbin discusses the erasure of the disturbing side of sexual violence in these visual renderings, an effacement that aligned with the social mores and expectations of polite society during the early Enlightenment period.

With this multi-disciplinary, cross-genre, diachronic approach, *Interpreting Sexual Violence: 1660–1800* illustrates the variety, flexibility and complexity with which authors of the Restoration and eighteenth century appropriated the trope of sexual violence. Not only did these writers grapple with sexual violence as a serious problem for which there was no agreed-upon or singular source, let alone a solution, but they also used representations of sexual violence to discuss countless other problems and ideas. In this vein, this essay collection elucidates and interprets, not only the long-eighteenth-century fascination with sexual violence but also, the many purposes served by this trope in this era's literary and artistic imagination.

1 RESEARCHING SEXUAL VIOLENCE, 1660–1800: A CRITICAL ANALYSIS

Julie Gammon

'Rape myths not behind low conviction rate, says leading family lawyer' stated a headline from the *Guardian* newspaper in March 2013. Helen Reece (a lawyer and academic at the London School of Economics) argued that the rate of convictions for rape in England in 2011/12 (at less than seven per cent of prosecutions) should be attributed to the lack of independent witness evidence in such crimes. She acknowledged that certain 'myths' do exist in society that persist with 'victim-blaming': that is, alleging that the woman was at fault in her behaviour which led to the act of sexual violence. Instead of tying these myths to conviction rates, however, she contends that these myths are merely a convenient way of explaining the low number of guilty verdicts, as she believes that judges, lawyers and juries are in fact capable of distancing their arguments and decisions from such misconceptions. Reece fails to address, however, why these myths persist in society or, indeed, their origins, divorcing the potential for cultural exchange between wider social ideas and the courtroom environment. In discussing conviction rates she also completely ignores the reasons behind the low numbers of sexual crimes that are reported to the police, and even when they are reported, the limited odds that the case will reach a formal prosecution. As this collection shows, we must turn to history to fully investigate the roots of modern perceptions of sexual violence and to understand the significance of continuity and change in these ideas. The low prosecution and conviction rate for rape is certainly not unique to the twenty-first century and the ongoing prevalence of the myth of 'victim-blaming' requires deconstruction by historians so that it cannot be overlooked in the present (as Reece does).

No discussion of the history of writing about rape can ignore the overwhelming significance of Susan Brownmiller's *Against Our Will: Men, Women and Rape*, published in 1975.[1] Brownmiller's text was one of a tranche of feminist writings that sought to establish a patriarchal structure as the root cause of female oppression throughout history. Whereas Susan Griffin's earlier work identified the use of rape by men as a conscious threat to women, Brownmiller sought to contextualize this historically by considering rape as a tool of patriarchy.[2] The political agenda in such feminist writing was overt and indeed successful in creating public discourses about rape that had not previously existed. Brownmiller has been credited with transforming understandings of rape from a 'sexual' crime to a 'crime of violence'. Nonetheless, along with the plaudits, Brownmiller faced considerable criticism for being 'essentialist ... universalist ... and reductionist'.[3] For example, one particularly controversial review by Edward Shorter claimed that prior to the French Revolution rape can be better understood as a male release of sexual frustration than as a 'political' crime.[4] The main response to Brownmiller's influential work was the growth of studies that looked at the particulars of rape cases in specific times and places as social historians sought to redress the ahistorical nature of many feminist writings. Shani D'Cruze reminds us that the history of rape is not in fact a history of experiences of sexual violence but instead of historically specific discourses.[5]

Susan Edwards, writing in the early 1980s, claimed that nothing significant happened to the law of rape in England between its inception in the thirteenth century and the early nineteenth century.[6] Her view arguably reflected the perception of many historians that there was little value in studying the legal treatment of rape cases in early modern and eighteenth-century Britain due to the relative intransigence of the law during this period. Instead a number of key studies concentrated on the turn of the nineteenth century and the Victorian period as when most of the significant changes in the law of rape and cultural perceptions of the crime took place.[7] In addition, Gregory Durston has claimed an absence of a public discourse about rape throughout the eighteenth century.[8] He contends that any discussion that did take place in 'official' circles was little more than 'lip service' regarding something that was not considered an important issue at the time.[9] Roy Porter agrees that there is little evidence that rape was represented as a particular threat to women in the eighteenth century. Yet, Porter also points out that rape does not appear to have been presented as a specific 'problem' at any historical moment.[10] Therefore, the motives for ignoring the history of sexual violence prior to 1800 are no longer justifiable. Despite the undoubted importance of statute and medical changes in the nineteenth century for understandings of sexual violence, since the 1980s, a number of social and cultural historians have begun to address the role that legal and literary discourses played across the long eighteenth century in shaping accounts of rape. The richness of sources for the eighteenth century has enabled research projects that examine the interplay of official processes with voices from below. There is notably little consensus among scholars working on eighteenth-century sexual violence in explaining why the conviction rate for rape was so low, but this chapter highlights the divergences and main points of agreement within the historiography and identifies the key questions that have formed the areas of discussion. Which contexts shaped the eighteenth-century definition of 'rape' and to what extent did these change over time? Who were the victims of sexual violence? What were the motives of individuals in prosecuting for sexual violence? And, how did the legal treatment of sexual crime change across the eighteenth century? These are, arguably, the main themes identified in the core historiography and will therefore form the basis of the structure of this chapter as it considers how recent scholars have responded to these issues.

In order to understand how 'rape' was defined in eighteenth-century Massachusetts, Barbara Lindemann stresses the importance of also considering what was defined by contemporaries as 'normal' sexual behaviour.[11] In a cultural context where all sexual activity was interpreted as the possession of the woman by the man, Lindemann shows how rape was perceived as a natural extension of this, which signified a 'sexual assertion of authority'.[12] Similarly scholarship on early modern England has depicted the language of all sexual activity as a language of ownership of a woman by a man.[13] The perception of the female body as property meant that any violation would be regarded as a crime against a patriarchal figure and not against the woman herself. The association between rape and abduction is shown in the work of Nazife Bashar to have diminished during the seventeenth century so that by 1700 the legal focus had transferred to the individual female as a possible victim of an assault against her own body.[14] Historians of medicine and the body have made important contributions to understanding this shift in perceptions of victims through contextualizing contemporary beliefs about female sexual pleasure and the female body. Thomas Laqueur's study of changing knowledge of the body highlights how consent became the crucial issue in rape trials as medical theories engaged with the question of whether in fact an adult woman could be raped.[15] Likewise, Durston has shown that the general acceptance of violence within consensual sexual relations made defining 'rape' far more difficult and complex than the written legal codes acknowledged.[16]

Scholarship has indicated how the boundaries between rape and seduction were often blurred in popular discourse which in turn complicated accusations of rape. Anna Clark, in particular, has emphasized the role the 'forcible seduction' played as a normal part of courtship rituals. Her claims that men were expected to use a degree of violence in order to overcome female modesty have been echoed by other gender historians. Tales of non-consent in rape accusations were therefore extremely difficult to substantiate when an element of physical and mental coercion was an acceptable part of male–female courtship. Clark's chronology, however, is open to question. Whereas Clark regards the 'seduction myth' as having been a late eighteenth-century development, this myth can in fact be traced through much of the century. Research into the representation of rape in eighteenth-century literature has made a major contribution to challenging Clark's argument. Katherine Binhammer and Susan

Staves, among others, have emphasized how, in fiction, the boundaries between rape and seduction were frequently blurred.[17] Binhammer argues that Richardson's *Clarissa* (the key novel on rape in the eighteenth century) can be read as a failed attempt at seduction as much as a rape narrative. This confusion is largely attributed to the 'silence' surrounding the sexual act that took place in such novels. It is often not made explicit to the reader whether ultimately the woman gave in 'willingly' to attempts at seduction. In *Clarissa*, this is further complicated in that the victim/heroine never reports the sexual attack. This 'silence' has been interpreted by scholars in one of two different ways: on one hand, it has been portrayed as disempowering to Clarissa, that her silence and eventual death are her only options given the destruction of her honour through the act of rape.[18] Whereas, conversely this silence has been perceived more positively as a deliberate 'choice' by Clarissa to shift the reader's focus away from the shameful act of rape.[19] Much of the recent work on eighteenth-century literature has emphasized the necessity of silence by the victim as a way of reinforcing her chastity. To utter words about sexual conduct, even non-consensual, would immediately cast doubt upon her reputation.

As historiography has shown, for women in the courtroom trying to prosecute their assailant, silence was not an option. In order to prove her account, the prosecutrix, as Clark demonstrates, was expected to give detailed and explicit information about the attack. Cross-examination required women to explain fully what was done to them and how they responded. Historians have demonstrated how the language that such women were forced to use in the courtroom brought with it a large degree of shame and no compassion was shown for the ordeal that these women faced in the male, public space.[20] Legal requirements for evidence of penetration and emission from the assailant meant that remaining silent was an impossibility, even for victims as young as ten (as explained below), in the courtroom. A major contrast between literary and legal narratives of rape related to victims' claims that they fainted during the assault or were unable to remember the details. Clark demonstrates how a woman 'swooning' in literature was viewed by the readership as evidence of her non-consent as she had been unable to give consent actively. However, under the law, the trauma of a sexual assault that may have resulted in the woman failing to recall sufficient details, or as having fainted, was taken as a sign of consent.[21] Ordinary women, therefore, were unable to 'live up to' to the literary construct of the seduced maiden found in contemporary novels, arguably making it even less likely that their accounts would be believed. On the other hand, this perspective of the seduction myth most forcibly put forward by Clark has faced recent criticism in a doctoral thesis.[22] Stephen M. Constantine argues that the range of rape narratives in existence throughout the eighteenth century in fact served to provide a number of alternative ways for stories to be told and that literary texts were responsible for directly questioning and changing the attitudes towards sexual violence evident in the legal setting.

Fictional representations of the rape victim extended beyond the novel to the late seventeenth and eighteenth-century stage. A number of literary scholars, such as J. Pearson and E. Howe, have examined rape in Restoration dramas and point to its frequency as a theme from 1660 through the early eighteenth century.[23] Such narratives further complicated the plight of the victim in the courtroom by contributing to public discourse on whether rape could occur and if so, under what circumstances. As can be found in *Clarissa*, tragic stories of sexual violence on the stage inevitably ended in the victim's death, presenting a message that this was the only real solution for women faced with rape. Comedic representations of rape were rarer but played on ideas of the inherent lustful nature of women and the sense of 'no meaning yes' (not least in Henry Fielding's work), undoubtedly undermining the strength of 'real' women's claims of non-consent. As these scholars show, Restoration drama presented a view that rape could only be adequately dealt with through the woman's death. Research on the history of eighteenth-century erotica has in addition indicated that stories of rape frequently formed the basis of pornographic literature as such texts celebrated the perceived strength associated with masculinity rather than the plight of the victim.[24]

The relationship between conceptions of masculinity and the perception of sexual violence has raised a number of interesting questions for gender historians although, as yet, little attention has been paid in print to men accused of rape in the long eighteenth century.[25] Nonetheless it has been argued by Antony Simpson that women's abilities to articulate experiences of rape were shaped by an ethos of masculinity. This ethos served to justify male aggression as an inherent characteristic. As can be seen in the literature, it is claimed, the man who resorts to rape could be perceived as someone who had just 'lost self-control' rather than be regarded as a criminal.[26] In addition, Randolph Trumbach has somewhat controversially argued that a new definition of 'masculinity' during the eighteenth century emphasized a male heterosexuality that applauded male violence and therefore turned all women into potential victims. These perspectives contrast with Roy Porter's claim that increasingly through the eighteenth century the rapist was seen as a marginal figure. He argues that such men were vilified more and more in popular discourse as Enlightenment England constructed the civilized man as incapable of such barbaric behaviour.[27] Far from being a tool of patriarchy, Staves suggests that, by the later eighteenth century, sexual violence became regarded as incompatible with a functioning patriarchal structure.[28] There is, therefore, some disagreement between writers about how the men accused of rape were perceived by contemporaries. Nevertheless a consensus exists among historians that the judge and jury were predisposed towards believing in the 'innocence' of the accused. This meant that the main focus of the legal proceeding was on examining the veracity of the account given by the female 'victim' rather than that of the defendant. Historians continue to wrestle with the contradiction that existed in the eighteenth century between the centrality of the victim's testimony that emerged in the trial process and the requisite need for female silence as an indication of modesty and veracity, and how this restricted and shaped the story she was able to tell. Durston and others have illustrated how rape trials focused upon the behaviour of female accusers not just during the assault but before and after also. Her conduct as an employee, her personal associations and her sexual reputation were all scrutinized by the prosecution and defence in order to assess her as an 'unequivocal victim'.[29] The importance of establishing good character and the strategies for doing so was a focus of Clark's work, but again, other scholars have shown that similar concerns pre-existed her late eighteenth-century timeframe. Studies based on different archival sources have illustrated how stories by particular types of women were more likely to secure convictions than others. Lindemann shows that in New England, married women were the most credible victims of sexual violence and more guilty verdicts were passed in these cases.[30] In England, however, figures seem to indicate a somewhat different pattern with only cases involving juveniles carrying a slightly higher degree of success. Despite single female domestic servants making up the vast majority of prosecutrices in both urban and rural settings, the ease with which doubt could be raised about their good character reduced the likelihood of conviction.[31]

A major area of interest for historians working on trials for sexual crime in the long eighteenth century has been to investigate the motives of the alleged victims in pursuing a prosecution. A range of research illustrates that the numerical incidence of accusations remained low throughout the period which indicates the difficulty of forming general conclusions about the incidence of rape. As the fullest records survive for the Old Bailey, much of the material we have is centred upon London sources. For example, Durston states that forty-five men (and women as accessories) were convicted of rape between 1700 and 1799.[32] Statistical research beyond the metropolis remains limited due to the patchy survival of sources although John Beattie has carried out a valuable analysis of Surrey and Sussex records and the northern circuit Assize has also proved fruitful.[33] Trials in each region rarely reached more than one or two per year throughout the century suggesting the number of accusations remained consistently low. Indeed, once the significant hurdles to successful prosecution become transparent, then we might well ask why any women sought to have their attacker punished through the courts? The research carried out by historians of crime such as John Beattie, Robert Shoemaker and Peter King has influenced the historiography of sexual violence by identifying the difficulties the lower classes faced in accessing the courts, problems undoubtedly magnified therefore when the victims of this crime were young, single females. From the outset, the financial costs of prosecution were prohibitive and securing appropriate witnesses could be extremely difficult. We can assume, therefore, that such women were reliant upon patronage (from family, friends or employers for example) in order to access the legal process and/or cover the costs of a full criminal trial. For example, in his study of the 1730 trial of the infamous Colonel Charteris, Simpson shows how the victim, Anne Bond was able to turn to a former employer for personal and financial support.[34] The employer, Mary Parsons, possibly both engaged a lawyer for Bond and accompanied her in making the initial accusation of assault. Nevertheless, the actual source of financial support for prosecutors in most rape cases is a frustrating absence in the historical record, and historians are usually left to guess where this support came from.

An alternative suggestion has come from Simpson who has indicated that many victims did not wish to pursue their cases through the legal process but that there was an absence of alternative methods of resolving the offence.[35] Not only was the likelihood of conviction low, but also, if a man was convicted of rape or sodomy he would face the death penalty. This perceived harshness of punishment may indeed have acted as a deterrent to prosecution (contemporaries such as Henry Fielding believed that there was a mistaken 'softness' among victims of crime who did not want to see criminals sent to the gallows). Instead Simpson advances the argument that many women hoped to settle their cases through a process of informal negotiation – usually via compensation to make up for the injury caused – rather than go to court. Simpson believes that the initial step of approaching a magistrate was a central part of this negotiation process and only the minority of cases advanced to the trial stage. He adds that for lower-class women there was a lack of other opportunities: whereas higher class families might resort to 'criminal conversation' claims, working-class victims of rape could not resort to the civil law and, since the Restoration, the Church Courts no longer played an active role in policing sexual behaviour. Laurie Edelstein has been critical of Simpson's approach, arguing that there is little evidence that women wanted to settle their cases through a process of negotiation rather than pursue a criminal trial.[36] She instead claims that there were other options available to lower-class women who wished for a less formal outcome so that the women who 'chose' to go to trial must have done so in the pursuit of justice.

In summary, Edelstein claims that accusations of blackmail emerged in rape trials as a deliberate strategy by the defendant to discredit the victim's claims. In contrast, Simpson argues that the disparity between legal and lay understandings of the 'making it up' process meant that attempts to resolve a case through compensation prior to the trial could be wrongly perceived by the court as a malicious prosecution. More recent research has shifted focus from the debate between Edelstein and Simpson to instead examine the basis of the contemporary concerns that sexual crime cases were often falsified for financial gain.

Matthew Hale's famous seventeenth-century dictum 'rape ... is an accusation easily to be made and hard to be proved, and harder to be defended by the party accused, tho never so innocent' has formed the basis of investigations into whether eighteenth-century claims of sexual violence were treated with scepticism due to a long-held belief that women would invent accusations of rape in order to extort money from 'their victims'.[37] Simpson's research demonstrates that there is very little evidence to show that malicious accusations were commonplace but certainly a prejudice existed in society that women were capable of making false allegations. Clark argues that this perception was exacerbated by a judicial intolerance towards the veracity of rape claims.[38] Given the clear picture that has been established in the historiography about the hurdles involved in pursuing any rape prosecution and the evident suspicion from within the legal system towards women who accused men of sexual violence, we should perhaps be considering not why so few women pursued their assailants through the courts in the long eighteenth century, but instead why *so many* opted to prosecute given how greatly the odds were stacked against their chances of success.

One initial answer to this question lies in the different types of 'victims' of sexual violence who told their stories in the long eighteenth century, as these differences could have a significant bearing on how they were treated in the legal environment. In particular, the preponderance of child victims of violence has been the focus of studies that try to ascertain why they made up such a high proportion of victims in rape and sodomy trials.[39] The abuse of young children, it has been argued, was more likely to result in a criminal trial as the question of consent was irrelevant if the victim was below the age of ten and therefore proving the felony charge was thought to be more straightforward. It has also been claimed that the public was more horrified by accusations of child rape and would more willingly convict the accused. Historians have identified, however, that the legal situation involving female victims between the ages of ten and twelve was often complicated by a misapplication of the law of rape which led to courts insisting upon evidence of non-consent even from those in this age category. There is, however, some disagreement among scholars regarding the severity with which child rape was treated, whether it was perceived as a considerable social problem by contemporaries and if it was thought of very differently to other crimes of sexual violence. Simpson argues that concerns about a 'defloration mania' in the mid-century capital led to a prevalence of child rape cases reaching court.[40] In contrast, my own research indicates that a recognizable public hostility towards child abuse was not so evident in a legal environment where most victims in fact fell into the problematic ten-to-twelve age category and were therefore treated as adult women. It is interesting, however, that such studies are using accounts of sexual violence to shed further light on how ideas about childhood and innocence were changing in the eighteenth century as well as exploring the themes of crime and sexuality.

The study of sodomy as a crime of sexual violence in the eighteenth century has been largely overlooked by historians; the notable exception to this being the doctoral research carried out in the early 1990s by Simpson.[41] Even the book-length study by Netta Murray Goldsmith, *The Worst of Crimes: Homosexuality and the Law* (1999) follows the pattern of using sodomy records as a way of exploring 'gay' history in the eighteenth century.[42] There certainly remains space within the existing historiography for a detailed investigation of the treatment of sodomy as a sexual crime. While there have been some studies of the prevalence of accusations of extortion by the defence in male–male sexual violence cases which can be related to fears of blackmail in trials for the rape of women (see above), historians have otherwise so far learnt remarkably little about the victims and perpetrators of acts of sodomy as it was legally defined.

The final area of research for historians of eighteenth-century sexual violence has been to consider how both criminal trials were operating and how standards of proof were changing during the period as a result of new legal precedents, even if statute law remained static. The eighteenth century witnessed the emergence of new standards of forensic medical evidence which had a significant impact on how trials for sexual violence (both rape and sodomy) developed. Thomas Forbes has shown how surgeons became crucial witnesses in trials for sexual crime as the burden of evidence swung increasingly towards the need to prove that violent sexual intercourse (including both penetration and ejaculation) had taken place.[43] In addition the question of whether the transmission of venereal infections constituted proof of sexual relations between the defendant and prosecutrix developed over the course of the century. The work of medical historians has been fundamental in emphasizing how the increasing 'professionalization' of medicine in the eighteenth century significantly influenced the law. In turn, gender and social historians have shown how narratives of sexual violence became shaped by this developing medical knowledge.[44] If a conviction was at all hoped for, so-called medical experts testifying for the prosecution arguably became crucial by the mid-eighteenth century. Indeed it is possible to argue that the 'silencing' of the female rape victim in the courtroom had as much to do with the replacement of her character testimony with 'scientific proofs' as it did with ideas about gender. A parallel development in legal practice was the presence of the defence counsel in the courtroom, which became increasingly common in felony trials. John Langbein and Peter Linebaugh have used the varying status of different forms of evidence and the establishment of new processes in rape trials to debate the significance of the changing power structures in the eighteenth-century courtroom (for example the relationship between the judge and jury and the status of hearsay evidence).[45] Their discussion has helpfully informed historians of sexual violence regarding the wider legal context to the development of new procedures in trials for sexual crime.

In 1971 Susan Griffin stated that 'the obscurity of rape in print exists in marked contrast to the frequency of rape in reality'.[46] The historiography of eighteenth-century sexual violence has developed from the assumption that accounts of rape during the period had been silenced. In fact, studies have shown that even though the numbers of incidents of rape that would have reached trial were very low, it remains possible to explore a range of questions linked to eighteenth-century perceptions of gender. The absence of statistically significant numbers of rape cases has led researchers to employ strategies of language and discourse analysis in trying to uncover meaning and in particular the field of literary studies has contributed vastly to understandings of contemporary perceptions beyond the legal framework. A consensus has not been reached, and probably never will be, about the reasons for the scepticism underlying the stories of rape victims in the eighteenth century. Nor has consensus been reached on the motives of the women who prosecuted men for rape. And critical 'silences' also remain unexplored. The historiography of rape has yet to give serious consideration to the men accused of rape. And, more importantly, the metropolitan bias to the existing research needs to be redressed where possible. How different were the stories told and the experiences of rape outside the capital? In addition, our understanding of sexual violence remains, somewhat unsurprisingly, dominated by legal narratives. Some attempts have been made to uncover accounts of sexual violence told in other situations (such as petitions to the Foundling Hospital Governors) but far more needs to be done.

Acknowledgements

With thanks to Sarah Pearce, Mark Cornwall and Mark Stoyle for their invaluable support and advice in the preparation of this chapter.

2 'FOR THE REPRESSING OF THE MOST WICKED AND FELONIOUS RAPES AND RAVISHMENTS OF WOMEN': RAPE LAW IN ENGLAND, 1660–1800

Mary R. Block

Writing a history of rape law in early modern England is no simple feat. Arguably the most sustained and consistent grievance with English rape law is that it did not adequately define 'rape' or explain what was necessary to prove it, a conundrum exacerbated by the fact that legal authorities commonly conflated the crime of rape with the quasi-crime of ravishment. This conflation has made it exceedingly difficult to separate one from the other and thus to interpret the law of rape in and of itself. Further, the period was one of significant social and economic change that affected the legal system. Despite these hindrances, an analysis of English rape law in the early modern period is both possible and important. Lawmakers, legal authorities, judges, jurors, defendants and complainants did not exist in a vacuum, but lived in a culture in which they were both producers and consumers. A historical analysis of rape law in early modern England reveals a legal culture that tolerated inordinate levels of male violence against women, even from men they did not know. The doctrines and criteria that constituted the common law of rape created extraordinary standards that, when coupled with popular attitudes towards women, made conviction for rape exceptionally difficult.[1]

When a woman accused a man of rape, she asserted that he had broken a law, but locating that law was complicated. In their historical examinations of English rape law, several historians have argued that we need to examine the law in action as revealed in court cases because there was great disparity between the law on the books and the law in practice. Inherent in this assertion is the assumption that England had 'rape statutes', that is, a law on the books. That assumption is not entirely accurate. Corrine Saunders in her important history of English medieval rape law noted that scholars could not find from the extant record a single fixed law that controlled rape trials in that era. The same may be said for the early modern period. Where then is this law on the books? While parliament enacted several statutes prohibiting the quasi-crime of ravishment between the twelfth and sixteenth centuries, scholars typically cite only three pertaining specifically to rape: the First (1275) and Second (1285) Statutes of Westminster and an Elizabethan statute (1576). Of those three, the 1275 law proscribed ravishment, not rape, and should not be counted. The 1285 statute does qualify because the first part is couched in the language of rape law. Chapter thirty-four is titled, 'It is Felony to commit Rape', and provided, 'That if a Man from henceforth do ravish a woman Married, Maid, or other, where she did not consent, neither before nor after, he shall have Judgment of Life and Member'.[2] The rest is a ravishment law. The Elizabethan statute is largely, though not exclusively, a rape law, especially its fourth section, which created a prohibition against child rape.[3] As sources of law, these rape statutes are useful only to a point, in part because there were so few of them, and in part because they did not define 'rape' or explain what was necessary to prove it.

The paucity of statutes means we have to look elsewhere for an exposition of rape law. For the early modern period most English rape 'law' was articulated not in statutes but in legal treatises. Treatises are not laws but explanations of them. They not only clarify the meaning of the statutes, they interpret case law. In a very real sense, treatises are both the law on the books and the law in action. Treatises are an important source that scholars should consult for an analysis of rape law in early modern England. Treatise writings reflected cultural sentiments about sex, violence, women and women's natures and they merged those sentiments rather seamlessly into the law. Judges relied heavily on these writings when adjudicating rape cases. The result of this juridical deployment of the legal discourses in the treatises was the establishment and implementation of doctrines that made rape convictions practically unattainable. An analysis of the law in those books is vital to an understanding of the common law of rape. The difficulty lay in extricating the legal concept of rape from that of ravishment. All too often, scholars have produced muddled interpretations of rape law because they, like their sources, conflated the two crimes. This essay attempts painstakingly to cull only the rape law from the treatise writings to glean the history of this most serious crime.

Recent scholarship has made great strides towards clarifying the differences between rape and ravishment. Rape referred to the forcible violation or defilement of a female. Ravishment was more complex. Ravishment was a crime, a public wrong against the king's peace, especially when the king held guardianship rights to the lands or marriage of an heir or heiress, and it was a 'trespass', a private wrong against an individual. Ravishment referred to abduction or elopement. Both rape and ravishment entailed a seizure or taking of a person, but unlike rape, ravishment was not gender-specific. While either a male or a female could be ravished, only a female could be raped. More importantly, unlike rape, ravishment did not necessitate a sexual violation or even sex. To be sure, someone could abduct an heiress and force her into a marriage, the consummation of which constituted a rape. This seemed to be what treatise writers and lawmakers had in mind when they conflated the two crimes. *Glanvill*, the earliest known treatise on English common law, began with the statement, 'In the crime of rape a woman charges a man with violating her by force' and ended with a declaration that the 'wrongdoer' could not escape his fate after conviction by offering,

> to marry the woman he has defiled. For if he could it would frequently happen as a result of a single defilement that men of servile status disgraced forever women of good birth, or that men of good birth were disgraced by women of low estate, and thus the fair repute of their families would be unworthily blackened.[4]

Glanvill began by discussing rape and violence against a woman, and ended by pondering ravishment, the abduction of an heiress to profit from a marriage with her. Male heirs were also ravished, but the writer was unconcerned with that. The treatise illustrates the difficulty legal historians face as they try to parse the common law denotation of rape.

With regard to rape law in the early modern period, Parliament enacted a statute in 1576, 'For the Repressing of the most wicked and felonious Rapes or Ravishments of Women, Maids, Wives and Damosels ... ', that stood as England's 'rape law' until the nineteenth century. Section one defined 'rape' as a felony, which meant it was punished with death, and denied benefit of clergy to anyone convicted of it. Section four of the law created a new felony, the crime of carnal abuse of an infant female, and established a uniform age of consent for females at ten years old. Any man who had coitus with a female younger than ten years had carnally abused her and the law barred him from claiming her consent as a defence.[5] Still, the Elizabethan statute yielded neither a legal definition of 'rape' nor an enumeration of what was necessary to constitute the crime. Researchers must look to the treatises for that.

In employing the phrase 'rapes or ravishments', the Elizabethan statute attempted to distinguish between the two crimes. Members of Parliament made no effort to separate them in previous statutes and treatise writers habitually blurred them in their commentaries, which has proven problematic for researchers attempting to deconstruct the common law definition of 'rape' and has resulted in no end of confusion and consternation for anyone attempting to analyse it. Legal historian J. B. Post was absolutely correct in lamenting that the 'problem with the common law of forcible rape is that it was placed in the same statute as ravishment, the abduction or elopement of an heir or wife'.[6] He concluded that the 'law conflated the two distinct crimes and the courts blurred them even more until the distinctions between a sexual assault and a consensual or collisional elopement or abduction was virtually obliterated'.[7] We shall try to separate them here and focus as narrowly on rape as the sources allow.

Legal writings consistently described rape as a crime of violence against the body of an individual woman and not as a property crime. From *Glanvill*'s treatise produced in the late twelfth century to William Blackstone's, published in the mid-eighteenth century, legal writers portrayed rape almost exclusively as a forcible violation of a woman. Henri de Bracton wrote that rape was 'a crime imputed by a woman to the man by whom she says she has been forcibly ravished against the king's peace'.[8] Henry Finch defined 'rape' as 'the carnal abusing of a woman against her will' while Edward Coke defined it similarly as the unlawful carnal knowledge of a woman against her will.[9] Throughout the early modern era, English legal authorities employed comparable language. William Hawkins called it an 'assault upon a woman in order to ravish her'.[10] Thomas Wood referred to it as one of the 'Private Felonies [that] may be [committed] against the *Body* of the Subject without taking away [her] life'.[11] Blackstone, characterized rape as 'the carnal knowledge of a woman forcibly and against her will', and discussed it in a chapter titled, 'Offenses against the Persons of Individuals'. Perhaps attempting to clarify the confusion previous writers created in conflating rape and ravishment, Blackstone explained that English law had once understood the crime of ravishment as including 'both the offense of forcible abduction, or taking away a woman from her friends ... *and also the present offense of forcibly dishonoring them*'.[12] By the mid-eighteenth century, authorities were making a discernible effort to distinguish between the two crimes. Nonetheless the historical record reveals that from the twelfth through the mid-eighteenth century, authorities understood 'rape' as a violent act against a woman's person.

Coinciding with their understanding of rape as the violent defilement of a woman, legal experts made her body the primary site of evidence for the crime. The guidelines writers devised to establish proof of rape reflected a cultural distrust of women and their claims of non-consensual sex. Treatise writings required that officials or respectable persons in the community witness the marks of violence 'done to her, and any effusion of blood there may be and any tearing of her clothes' to ensure the women's body was actually damaged.[13] Physical evidence was not the exclusive source of proof, however, as they also emphasized the woman's behaviour following an alleged assault. From *Glanvill* to Blackstone, authorities developed criteria women had to meet. Between the various treatises we can delineate several elements that constituted proof of rape. They included the requirement she make immediate complaint. The reason for this, Blackstone observed, was 'to prevent malicious accusations'.[14] Failure to make an immediate complaint, wrote the eminent Matthew Hale, 'carries the presumption that her suit is but malicious and feigned'.[15] Suspicion of rape charges and of the women who brought them pervaded the legal literature. Hale's admonition that 'rape was an accusation easily to be made' derived from popular depictions of women as conniving and excessively carnal and manifested the law's conception of a universal female.[16] All women were sinister, vengeful and prone to lying. No woman should be trusted. Women instigated trouble and in the case of rape complaints they either sought retribution for having been jilted or discovered shame and guilt after having been seduced and then decided they had been forced. Requiring proof of violence, including effusive bleeding and torn clothes, and requiring evidence that she made complaint at the first opportunity helped to ensure that something more than mere seduction had occurred.[17]

In addition to marks of violence and an immediate complaint, the criteria mandated that a woman cry out in case someone was nearby who could intervene. Officials believed that a woman who failed to cry for help likely had not been forced. Blackstone affirmed that the complainant could testify and the jury determined her credibility. Blackstone cautioned jurors only to believe a woman 'of good fame'.[18] Many felony trials hinged on a litigant's character, the general reputation one had in one's community. Jurors could believe a reputable woman's testimony, but 'if she be of evil fame, and stands unsupported by others' jurors should be wary that 'her testimony is false or feigned'.[19] A woman had to perform each of these requirements to demonstrate her claim of rape was real. Her body and her behaviour served as vital evidence of the crime. She had to prove all the criteria. Failure to demonstrate even one of these was detrimental to a successful prosecution.

Historians observed a dramatic transformation in the social construction of womanhood between Enlightenment and modernity. The shift corresponded to economic changes from a mercantilist and barter system to a cash and credit capitalist system that allowed for the creation and expansion of a middle class. A significant consequence of this economic change was the separation of home and work. Concomitant to the economic changes was a cultural revolution in which the social construction of womanhood transformed from that of demonic spawn of Satan to angelic maker of hearth and home. The notion that women had ungovernable sexual appetites attenuated and eventually yielded to a concept of a less passionate female, especially with regard to middle-class women.[20] Yet English legal authorities clung tenaciously to the ancient ways of thinking about femininity and womanhood when it came to women who accused men of rape. Legal literature continued to depict women alleging rape as lying harpies, conniving wenches and spiteful indicters of innocent or rakish men.

Courts of Assize constituted England's primary criminal courts for felony and high crimes cases. They conducted virtually all rape trials in the early modern period. London had its own tribunal, the Old Bailey Sessions Court, which heard cases of felony perpetrated there. To set the criminal process in motion, a woman made a formal complaint of rape to a justice of the peace or magistrate who also served as law enforcement officer and detective. He had the authority to examine witnesses, take depositions, compel witnesses and prosecutors to appear at court, arrest and detain the accused and, perhaps most important of all, decide whether the case would proceed.[21] Felony trials in the first half of the early modern era were essentially lawyer free, but judges modified that beginning in 1730 after the Old Bailey was rocked by a series of corruption scandals. Before this modification, the individual who brought the suit prosecuted it, unless the charge was murder or homicide, in which case the next of kin or the local coroner prosecuted. In rape trials, the complainant prosecuted her own case, unless she was a minor, in which case her next male kin handled matters. She also acted as the pre-trial investigator, gathering witnesses and information. If the cause proceeded, the justice of the peace or magistrate ordered the arrest and confinement of the accused. Bail was available but financially impractical for most men accused of rape. As a prisoner, the accused was not informed of the charges until the trial when he got the indictment. An indictment for rape stated the formal charge, the name of the accuser and the details of her allegations. Most defendants had not devised a defence strategy or gathered information before being led into court. The element of surprise was an important component of the common law criminal system. The defendant did not have the time or opportunity to concoct an alibi. He had no choice but to tell the truth because it was all he had to defend himself.[22]

At trial, the prosecuting witness gave sworn testimony where she stated the details and presented the facts and corroborating evidence she had. Her witnesses also testified under oath. Throughout the process, the prisoner, as trial summaries called him, challenged and rebutted the prosecutor's statements, evidence and her witness's testimony. There was one vital difference between prosecutor and prisoner statements in these trials: the prisoner did not give sworn testimony nor did his associates. It was an important aspect of common law criminal trials. In felony cases, the accused could not testify in his own defence. Even though he faced his accuser in court and responded to her allegations, he did so unsworn and technically was not a 'witness'. The courts did not consider his statements 'testimony'. The prisoner's allies also gave unsworn statements. Defendants in felony trials faced other discriminations. Prosecutors had the power of compulsory process, and could compel their witnesses to appear in court. Prisoners did not. Neither side had a lawyer during the trial, but in pre-trial preparations the prosecutor had the benefit of a solicitor who gathered information and subpoenaed witnesses.[23]

The system was skewed to favour the prosecution, which could well be and often was the Crown or the Crown's representatives. As prosecutor, a woman who charged rape ostensibly benefited from this. Remarkably, even though the system was intended to favour the prosecution, this did not help females who prosecuted for rape. Gregory Durston examined records from London's Old Bailey Court from 1700 to 1800 and found only forty-five convictions out of 281 indictments for rape.[24] This conviction rate was significantly lower than for other felonies. What is more, if the jury found a prisoner not guilty of rape, he could turn around and bring a malicious prosecution suit against his accuser.

Edward I (r. 1272–1307) commissioned his own expert to produce a treatise that included explication of the laws enacted during his reign. In the midst of his rather mundane recapitulation of rape and ravishment, the writer, called Britton, declared that where a prisoner confessed to 'the fact [of coition], but says that the woman at the same time conceived by him, and can prove it, then our will is that it be adjudged no felony, because no woman can conceive if she does not consent'.[25] Clearly, Britton meant that if a woman prosecuting for forcible defilement begat a child as a consequence, the Crown rejected her suit. The notion that pregnancy indicated consensual sex derived from ancient Greek theories about conception. From the ancient Greeks, the idea found its way into Roman law through the Justinian Code and into English law through medieval canonists who drew heavily from Roman law. From canon law it meandered into the ostensibly secular common law and, shortly after Britton published his treatise, criminal courts started implementing it in rape cases as a matter of doctrine. According to Saunders, judges from the Eyre of Kent may have rendered the first official decision on the matter when they dismissed a rape suit in 1313 because the complainant was pregnant. The judges ruled that conception required orgasm and orgasm strongly indicated consent. A woman who consented to coition, had not been raped.[26]

Not all legal experts thought the idea sound science or good precedent. While a few courts implemented it, other jurisdictions rejected it and even judges who sat on the same bench disagreed about it. As medical knowledge regarding the functions of the reproductive organs improved more and more the notion came under attack. The debate between legal experts themselves and between legal and medical experts was important. It matters what legal experts in the early modern era wrote about rape law. Treatises grew in importance over the course of the seventeenth and eighteenth centuries as the body of law grew and became more complex and more important to English society and the economy. Over the course of the seventeenth and eighteenth centuries most, though not all, legal authorities came to reject the premise that conception proved consent and invalidated a rape accusation. Hale employed the double negative declaring, 'that it can be no rape, if the woman conceive with child, seems to be no law'.[27] Hale saw no connection between pregnancy and an accusation of forcible defilement. Edward Coke did not even broach the subject. Wood proclaimed that, 'It is no excuse that the Woman Consented after the fact ... or that she Conceived'.[28]

The debate over whether pregnancy was a tell-tale sign the sex was consensual continued into the eighteenth century. By then, the question seemed relatively settled so far as English legal writers were concerned, but medical authorities kept it alive. In his *Treatise of the Pleas of the Crown*, William Hawkins presented one of the more interesting and thoughtful legal commentaries on the question of pregnancy and rape. Acknowledging that some of his contemporaries believed conception indicated consent, Hawkins deemed the opinion 'very questionable'.[29] He reasoned that 'the previous violence is in no way extenuated by such a consent', and moreover, 'if it were necessary to show that the woman did not conceive, the offender could not be tried till such time as it might appear' she was or was not pregnant.[30] It seemed a lot to ask either party to wait so long, 'likewise because the philosophy of this notion may very well be doubted of'.[31] Two influential treatise writers of the late eighteenth century, Blackstone and Edward Hyde East, did not address the matter, suggesting they thought it settled as well with regard to the law.

Men of medicine seeking respectability and an opportunity to expand their influence established a new field of study called medical jurisprudence. A prime goal of medical jurisprudents was to insinuate medical expertise into legal practice. Samuel Farr, an early proponent of the new field published one of the first English language books on the subject in 1788. Farr included a section on rape law. Invoking the ancient Greek natural philosopher Galen who gave us the two-seed theory of conception and the idea that conception necessitated orgasm, Farr wrote, 'it may be necessary to enquire how far her lust was excited, or if she experienced any enjoyment' during her rape.[32] Here the doctor deployed the age old idea that women were prone to lust and naturally inclined to enjoy sex, a lot. This construction rendered rape virtually impossible because even though a woman might start out resisting, at some point the sex would excite her lust and she would ultimately give in to her carnal nature and consent. At this moment, the woman could conceive. Farr professed that 'without an excitation of lust or the enjoyment of pleasure in the venereal act, no conception can probably take place. So that if an absolute rape were to be perpetrated, it is not likely she would become pregnant'.[33]

The more legal authorities ignored or rejected the relationship between consent and conception, the more rigidly and incessantly medical jurisprudents insisted on it. In his early nineteenth-century book on medical jurisprudence, O. W. Bartley, declared that 'pregnancy supervening such a connection, is an irrefragable proof of the woman's acquiescence'.[34] Farr at least had qualified his language. Continuing, Bartley wrote, 'I am persuaded that when a person or persons are *in coitu*, under the control of depressing passions, as terror, apprehension, excessive grief, fear, alarm, and the like, conception cannot be the result' because 'these passions suspend (or if I may be allowed the expression) paralyze every energy, mental and corporeal'.[35] Because conception depended on 'the exciting passion' that a woman naturally experienced and the '*mutual* orgasm' so vital to impregnation, Bartley concluded, 'if any desponding or depressing passion presides', pregnancy was impossible.[36] Therefore, 'if a woman becomes pregnant subsequent to and in consequence of the alleged rape, it may be presumed, she not only acquiesced but was "particeps criminé"', meaning a participant to the crime. The invention of medical jurisprudence and the insinuation of doctors into the courtroom did not bode well for women who charged men with rape.

Following the passage of the Elizabethan statute in 1576, legal authorities adopted the language of the child rape law and deployed it in their observations on the rape of adult women. The result was the semblance of a legal definition of 'rape'. The more precise descriptor originated in 1613 when Finch published his disquisition, *Law, or, a Discourse Thereof*, which defined 'rape' as 'the carnal abusing of a woman against her will'.[37] Gradually, this more precise definition caught on among legal writers. As it did, some of them raised the question of what constituted carnal abuse. Most writers asserted that for purposes of law, carnal knowledge meant both penetration and ejaculation. The complainant not only had to swear her assailant had penetrated her but also that he had climaxed inside her. A few authorities, however, maintained penetration alone sufficed to make the crime. This stirred disagreement as to whether a woman had to swear to one proof, penetration, or two proofs, penetration and seminal emission, to secure a rape conviction.

Edward Coke adopted the newer definition of 'rape' as the unlawful carnal knowledge of a female against her will. This was significant because Coke's *Institutes* was one of the most consulted legal works in the early modern period. Coke proclaimed that evidence of both penetration and ejaculation was 'required for carnal knowledge'.[38] One without the other was not complete coition, so if a man ejaculated but never penetrated the woman that also was not carnal knowledge under the law.[39] Coke was in the majority on this issue. Wood and Hawkins concurred. Wood stated, 'There Must be Penetration and Emission, otherwise' it was 'an Assault only'.[40] Hawkins wrote, 'that no assault upon a woman in order to ravish her, however shameless and outrageous it may be, if it proceed not to some degree of penetration, and also of emission, cannot amount to a rape'.[41] Most of Hawkins's contemporaries believed the legal definition of carnal knowledge required both elements.

However, not every esteemed legal expert agreed. Hale was the odd man out in this debate. He argued that proof of ejaculation was indeed evidence of rape, but that both elements need not have occurred in order for the act to constitute rape. The woman need only swear that the accused penetrated her and 'the least penetration maketh it rape or buggery yea altho there be not *emission seminis*'.[42] The jury could infer from the fact of penetration that the accused had ejaculated inside the complainant. Legal expert Edward Hyde East, who sided with the majority view, recapitulated the debate and summarized the case that established the rule.

In 1781, an Assize Court established the precedent mandating proof of both penetration and seminal emission in rape trials. Mary Portas prosecuted Samuel Hill for rape. At trial, Portas swore positively Hill had penetrated her, but admitted she was unsure whether he had ejaculated inside of her. Judge Buller, the presiding judge, asked the trial jury for a special verdict and they found Hill guilty of penetration, but not ejaculation. This finding rendered a felony conviction impossible and raised the issue of what if any crime the Crown could convict. Unsure how to proceed, Judge Buller decided to wait until the next session when the full court could determine the matter. When the court convened, three judges, Buller included, thought penetration alone sufficed and Hill should be executed. Seven jurists, however, ruled that both elements were necessary, 'but thought the fact [of whether the defendant ejaculated] should be left to the jury'. *Hill's Case* ostensibly settled the matter: the complainant had to swear to both elements and the jury would determine whether she was convincing. English criminal court judges readily adopted the rule and made it a controlling principle in rape trials.[43]

Before this precedent, East stated that proof of penetration alone typically sufficed to convict. The rule requiring two proofs ultimately made convictions for rape so difficult it compelled the national legislature to act. A man had only to withdraw before ejaculation and he could not be convicted of rape under the new standard. Parliament passed a law in 1828 decreeing, 'Offenders frequently escape by reason of the Difficulty of the Proof which has been required' in rape trials.[44] Therefore, 'for Remedy thereof be it enacted, That it shall not be necessary ... to prove the actual Emission of Seed in order to constitute actual carnal knowledge, but that the carnal knowledge shall be deemed complete upon Proof of Penetration alone'.[45]

Examination of the disquisitions of treatise writers shows that, if we focus on rape law alone, we find that from the late twelfth century through to the early modern era, rape was defined as a crime of violence against a woman. However, the social construction of femininity rendered the idea that a woman could be raped problematic. Even a change in this social construction failed to affect the way the law viewed women who accused men of rape. In addition, treatise writers promulgated standards of evidence that made proving rape difficult. Despite the fact that the English criminal system was skewed to favour the prosecution, women rarely secured convictions against men they accused of rape. These standards coupled with prevalent notions that women were habitual liars gave judges and jurors a reason not to convict. English treatise writers in the early modern period developed a more precise definition of 'rape' and rejected the ancient notion that conception invalidated a charge of rape. As legal experts rejected outmoded science, men of medicine intervened to continue its implementation in the courts. As treatises clarified the definition of 'rape', authorities devised new criteria of proof that made it harder still for women to convict men of rape. Parliament had to intervene because the new standard allowed too many men to go unpunished; it enacted a statute in 1576 signalling that the Crown stood to protect English women and minor females from sexual depredations. Yet treatise writers established the criteria the courts implemented which made conviction for rape difficult and thus undermined this Parliamentary protection. What is clear from this analysis is that the law in the books matters.

3 FROM RAPE TO MARRIAGE: QUESTIONS OF CONSENT IN EIGHTEENTH-CENTURY BRITAIN

Katie Barclay

> If Maidens are ravished, it is their own choice,
> Why are they so wilful to struggle with Men?
> If they would but lie still, and stifle their voice,
> No Devil or D— could ravish 'em then.[1]
> 'An Excellent New Ballad from Ireland', *c.* 1780

Taken from a 'humorous' ditty sold alongside the trial of a man for abducting an heiress, the above quotation highlights one of the seeming paradoxes of rape: that the same act of sexual intercourse can have very different implications depending on whether the woman involved consented. From the rather sexist perspective of the ballad singer, this paradox could be resolved if women stopped being so 'wilful' and subordinated themselves to male desire. The 'humour' of the song lay in the fact that, in the context of eighteenth-century Britain, women were expected to refuse sexual advances (at least from men who were not their husbands) and that, increasingly, their resistance to such advances was the central marker of their virtue and character, particularly for non-labouring women.[2] As Simon Dickie notes in the context of portrayals of rape in eighteenth-century literature: 'at every level of society men seem to have expected a show of resistance from any woman who was not completely abandoned'.[3]

The importance placed on female resistance to sexual activity before marriage shaped both men and women's sexual behaviour and, in particular, put women in a position where their will was something to be overcome, rather than sexual intercourse being a mutually-negotiated experience. Men became the aggressors in courtship, seeking to woo and win their sweethearts. As a result, the line between consensual sexual intercourse and rape became blurred, as the level and nature of the force men should use to overcome the female will became an area of debate. This chapter explores how expectations of female resistance shaped women's and men's experiences within courtship and, in particular, how it created a context where violence, and so rape, became just another form of 'force' used by men to overcome the female will. To do this, this chapter contrasts the eighteenth-century concept of the 'rape of seduction' with violent sexual assaults and forced marriages and demonstrates how they existed on the same explanatory continuum.

Rape of Seduction

The imagining of seduction as a form of rape was a popular trope of the era. *A New and Complete Dictionary of the Arts and Sciences* (1764) provides the legal definition of rape as 'the carnal knowledge of a woman by force and against her will', but also notes that: 'The civilians make another kind of rape, called rape of subordination or seduction; which is seducing a maid either to uncleanness or marriage, and that by gentle means'.[4] The English divine, Henry Gally, noted in his treatise on clandestine marriage, that 'There are two kinds of Rapes, the one by Force, and the other by Seduction or Subornation', in his case noting that the latter was an offence 'not in respect to the Persons ravish'd, who in this case are Consenting, but in respect to their Parents'.[5] It was an idea found both in popular culture, with a letter by 'Mary Mouthwater' in the *Newcastle Courant*, noting that seduction was 'a Rape of Our [women's] Minds, a forcing our Consents by a thousand Perjuries', and in trials such as that of Elizabeth Linning, who raised a suit for seduction in the Scottish courts in 1749, on the grounds that her lover 'robb[ed] a woman of her virtue, by debauching her mind'.[6]

The 'rape of the mind' that occurred during seduction literally referred to the process of falling in love. Mary Mouthwater described the process of seduction as a 'strong Artillery of Love, [that] forced the tender Virgin's Heart', while the Scottish author Jean Marishall described it as a woman '[giving] up her heart, unsuspecting of [men's] base design'.[7] The best-selling advice author John Gregory noted the force inherent in even honorable courtship, arguing that when a woman realizes she is in love, 'she feels a violence done both to her pride and her modesty'.[8] Eighteenth-century authors imagined falling in love as a form of violence, because they understood love to require the subordination of women to their male lovers, reflected in the promise 'to obey' in the wedding vows. The act of falling in love for women involved overcoming the female will, an inherently violent act, preparing her for the loss of identity expected within marriage.

While the significance of 'union' had always been central to marriage, the growing importance of romantic love and the cult of sensibility redefined 'union' to incorporate an 'emotional coverture', where women were expected to mould their minds, desires and wills to that of their spouses.[9] As a result, marriage was not just imagined as absorbing female property into that of the male, but as incorporating their very identities as well. As Julia Rudolph and

Leslie Richardson have astutely noted, even as women were increasingly given the agency to consent (or not) to sexual activity and so recognized as people (rather than property), that same agency was not extended to other aspects of their lives. As a result, their power to consent was offset by their loss of personal identity once they married (or through marriage negotiations between parents and spouse), reinforcing the social status quo of women as subordinate to men.[10] In this, women's sexual autonomy reflected their economic positions, where unmarried adult women were able to contract out their own labour, sign contracts and dispose of their own property, but where married women's abilities to dispose of their own labour and property was subject to their husbands' consent, if not subsumed entirely into their estates.[11] Likewise, as women were granted property in their person, they were increasingly expected to cede, or merge, that property into the identity of their spouse.

This merging of the two selves was increasingly believed to be a part of courtship, and courting became a form of uniting that metaphorically mirrored the union of sexual intercourse and so conflated both sexual and emotional unions. As a result, women who had been 'courted' were understood to have been joined to their suitors in a similar way to women who had been coupled through the act of sexual congress; correspondingly, their virtue was similarly 'tainted', damaging their attractiveness on the marriage market, and giving rise to the growth in breach of promise of marriage suits across the United Kingdom, which operated on the premise that the wronged woman would find it difficult to find another suitor.[12]

Marriages that went ahead without an emotional connection were viewed as a form of rape for operating against the will of the woman, a topic of central concern during a period where the importance of parental consent to marriage was a question of lively debate.[13] Samuel Butler observed that

> Wedlock without love, some say,
> Is but a lock without a key,
> It is a kind of rape to marry,
> One that neglects or cares not for ye;
> For what does make a ravishment,
> But being 'gainst the minds consent.

Indeed this verse was quoted widely across the period.[14] Daniel Defoe argued that to force a woman to marry without affection was 'a Rape upon her Mind; her Soul, her brightest Faculties, her Will, her Affections are ravished', while one writer to the *Spectator* observed of his origins in 1712, 'The Match was made by Consent of my Mother's Parents against her own; and I am the Child of the Rape on the Wedding-Night'.[15]

The importance placed on the female will as determining rape can undoubtedly be construed positively as key to recognizing a woman's right to consent to sex and marriage. However, it also downplayed the manner in which that consent was gained. The conflation of courting rituals with seduction, which became 'a rape of the mind' only when the suitor abandoned his lover, and of sexual and emotional intimacy (where sex without love was rape, unless the woman was a prostitute), reduced female agency through making her vulnerable to male choices. In doing so, eighteenth-century culture tied female identity to sexuality.

Moreover, by focusing on the mind as the location of rape, eighteenth-century culture reduced female bodily autonomy. This was particularly evident in the growth of sentimental rape literature and the narrative of the 'virtuous whore', where women maintained their mental virtue, despite the loss of their physical chastity.[16] *The Memoirs of Arabella Bolton* (1770), nominally based on a 'true story' but owing a considerable debt to the seduction literature of the period, featured a virtuous woman, whose two rapes (several years apart by different men) followed her being drugged. In the first instance, Arabella is raped by a man who claims to be courting her for marriage and, at least initially, marriage is presented as the honourable solution to her problem. When her suitor refuses to marry her, she lives virtuously, refusing offers both of marriage and of being a kept mistress, before being raped a second time during a job interview and eventually dying in poverty with a pure mind.[17] In an almost identical narrative to Arabella's first rape during the seduction trial, *Fenton* v. *Seigh*, Miss Fenton described how her suitor had drugged her before he 'effected his purpose'.[18] She noted that she was not unconscious, but 'deprived of her power of resistance, with a sort of stupor that had seized all her faculties, and which she could not express'.[19] Thinking that he would marry her, she continued to sleep with him subsequently.

This trope of the drugged or, occasionally, swooning rape victim was a central feature of later eighteenth-century literature, especially following Samuel Richardson's *Clarissa*, allowing women to be physically, but not mentally, violated. While such narratives nominally emphasized female consent, by pointing to the strength of the female will in resisting seduction (mental or physical), increasingly such narratives not only effaced the female self through rape, but through removing her ability to resist. Women no longer refused or consented to sex, but were made utterly passive to male desire. In doing so, late eighteenth-century writers 'solved' the problem noted by feminist historians that through actively resisting their rapes (screaming or physically fighting), early modern women portrayed themselves as 'active' and so 'unfeminine', negatively influencing how their rapes were interpreted by all male juries and the judiciary.[20] Yet, in doing so, such writers prioritized female innocence at the cost of female sexual agency.

This absence of active female consent can also be seen in other contexts. Numerous accounts of female seduction that appear in trials use silence to symbolize female consent. In 1747, Alexander Hamilton understood his sweetheart's silence to mean consent, describing their first sexual encounter where, 'he said to her will you make me happy, to [whi]ch she returned no answer, & thereupon the deponent enjoyed her for the first time'.[21] Moreover, legal treatises also advised that female silence could stand for consent in certain contexts, such as 'when the Father or Mother do contract Sponsals, or promise Marriage for their Child; for the Childs silence in this case (being present and hearing the same) is taken for a consent and approbation therof'.[22]

As a result, the opportunities for active female consent to sex were rare, with marriage vows perhaps being the most explicit articulation of the female will. Ironically, this was reinforced through rape trials of the period where women were expected to demonstrate their active physical, and particularly vocal, resistance. Women who did not 'cry out' during their rapes were assumed to have consented. This redirected the focus conceptually from active female consent towards female resistance, or non-consent. It was not whether a woman said 'yes' to sex that was important, but whether she said 'no'. Moreover, as some form of resistance was expected of women within courtship, in practice 'no' was always ambiguous. Female consent was eroded to the extent that it became a 'crying out', an act of resistance, to be ultimately and ideally overcome.

Courtship Practices and Rape

The construction of female consent as a form of resistance created a context where 'force' was a requisite part of courtship, informing how 'rape' was interpreted. As Anna Clark has noted in her study of rape at the end of the eighteenth century, physical violence was considered to be a normal part of courtship by many people.[23] This was illustrated across the period in a wide range of literary sources, where sexual access to women was presumed, sexual violence was deemed entertaining, often used as a popular plot device, and repeatedly depicted as harmless to all involved in the longer term.[24] Perhaps one of the most evident examples of violence within courtship is the practice of bride abduction.

Bride abduction, where women were taken from home and raped and/or forced through a marriage ceremony, was particularly common in Ireland. Between 1700 and 1836, over 400 abductions came to public attention; given that many, if not most abductions, were settled privately by marriage, this was probably only a fraction of the true number.[25] While such reports were less common in Scotland and England, cases consistently appeared across the century in both jurisdictions, and there was a small flurry of trials for abduction in England at the beginning of the nineteenth century.[26] It is also worth noting that abductions, seductions, breached promises of marriage and rapes often contained very similar accounts of sexual violence, but were tried under different 'headings' in court both in the same and in different national jurisdictions, making it difficult to make quantitative comparisons.[27]

The motivations behind bride abductions were complex and varied. Some were consensual elopements to overcome parental refusal; many were effectively property theft where men abducted women to access their dowries or personal estates; occasionally women were abducted and raped during familial or community disputes in order to 'punish' their families for some real or perceived wrongdoing.[28] As all of these examples make clear, bride abductions ultimately located female consent as secondary to the consent of other family members and to the men who wished to marry or rape them. Even in cases where women consented to their abductions, such acts were necessitated by the limited cultural authority of women and their inability to choose their marriage partners. Moreover, while the law formally abjured the validity of forced marriage across the United Kingdom, in practice such marriages were often upheld. Despite William Gordon of Holm, in Dumfriesshire, Scotland, being prosecuted and imprisoned for forcibly abducting and marrying Margaret Tait in 1750, their marriage remained valid and they went on to cohabit and raise a family.[29] In many cases across the kingdom, this was because the women involved appear to have consented to the marriage, either at the time of the abduction or subsequently.

Female consent appears to be particularly important in the English context, where abduction suits increasingly became a forum for negotiating the balance of parental and child rights when choosing a spouse.[30] This may be partly informed by the legal context, where most evidence for abductions in England appears in the criminal courts, rather than in the civil courts as in Scotland. In such cases, as in Ireland and Scotland, female consent or refusal became central to determining whether abductors were found guilty. In Scotland, however, where abductions also appear in the Commissary Court in suits to free victims from their purported marriages, the court proceedings suggest a greater ambiguity towards female consent. Despite Jacobina Moir's successful criminal prosecution of her abductor and his sentence of transportation, Thomas Grey still tried to declare their marriage valid and the court allowed him to bring proof. Whilst Jacobina concentrated on the force inherent in the abduction, the court spent considerable time on his claims of her consent during the ceremony and, particularly, her signature on a marriage certificate. Even though, after a year of hearing evidence, the court found for Jacobina, the issue of force had become secondary to the legal proof of the ceremony of marriage.[31] This negation of violence can be seen in other cases where marriages were upheld after abduction, and in the examples of both Mary Gainer and Elizabeth Duncan who desired their marriages to be declared valid after their abductors subsequently abandoned them.[32]

That some anxiety around the validity of marriages following abduction also existed south of the border can be seen in the response to Edward Wakefield's abduction of Ellen Turner. Despite Edward being found guilty of abduction and imprisoned, Ellen's family pursued and received an Act of Parliament to declare their 'marriage' void, suggesting some unease over whether force itself was enough to annul it.[33] Edward himself argued in court that, despite the abduction, the marriage was valid, and so Ellen could not testify against him, her husband.[34] Similarly, the numerous other men who abducted women for marriage across the period did so on the belief that the force used to overcome 'female', or indeed 'familial', will was not a problem if consent for marriage was ultimately gained.

Rape could even be understood as a legitimate part of courtship. Across the century, ballads, folk songs and chapbooks provided detailed accounts of courtships and marriages that originated in, or were consolidated by, rape. Such violence was not viewed as ultimately problematic, drawing heavily on the belief that women desired sex but required men to overcome their natural modesty.[35] As one woman was imagined saying, following her rape by her suitor: 'Read in my eyes my grief, my Jewel, / But in my Heart my coming Joy'.[36] Descriptions of courtship accounts that appear in seduction, breach-of-promise-of-marriage and declarator-of-marriage (to prove a marriage) cases and other similar trials often feature women whose initial sexual encounters with their suitors had been violent. Clark's study found that seventeen per cent of English seduction suits involved women who claimed their suitors had used violence against them.[37] In 1782, Mary McLauchlan, a servant, asked the Scottish Commissary Court to declare the validity of her marriage to her employer, Alexander McDonald, describing her 'marriage' thus:

> [Alexander] called the said Complainer into his room and having locked the Door upon her, he Seized the said Complainer by the hair of the head, threw her to the ground and by violence had Carnal knowledge of her, after this he requested the s[ai]d Complainer to Conceal what had passed, and that he w[oul]d make a publick declaration of her being his Wife.[38]

After this, Mary allowed him 'every priviledge of a husband'.[39] Despite being to modern eyes a violent rape, Mary understood this sexual encounter as a form of marriage and sought to maintain her relationship. If Mary's account is accurate, Alexander also accepted this construction of events, at least at that time. The court disagreed and found no marriage proven, but this is as likely to do with class disparity (few servants successfully proved marriages with employers) as the nature of her testimony.[40] In 1822, Marion Meikle described walking in the garden with her suitor, Robert McGhie, when 'he seemed to be seized as with a sudden frenzy and laid hold of the Pursuer in a very improper and unbecoming way'.[41] She protested, but after he promised her marriage she 'yielded to the treacherous solicitations'.[42] Far from disbarring marriage, sexual violence in these cases was used as central evidence in proving these relationships.

The normality of violence within courtship informed how eighteenth-century observers responded to the sexual violence they encountered. The

Caledonian Mercury described a London case, where a girl of thirteen was taken by a family friend to a brothel and, despite her protests, treated 'with great brutality', under the headline of 'Seduction' and, moreover, noted that her mother was 'enraged' on being told and 'threatened to send her to gaol'.[43] Eleanor Master's suitor was found not guilty of rape after she admitted that she had sex with him on a subsequent occasion, despite the fact that only days after meeting him, he came to her home when she was alone, tied her hands behind her back, stuffed her mouth with a handkerchief and raped her on a chair. After he had completed his attack, he informed her that, if she told no-one, he would marry her. On his acquittal, the court sternly warned him that:

> The seduction of these young women, under pretence of marrying, is not a crime of much less criminality than that which you have been tried for; and you will some time or another get your neck into the halter, if you do not leave off these practices.[44]

Moreover, the construction of sex in seduction suits required resistance from the seduced women to prove that the woman was virtuous, thus implicating sexual violence in 'normal' courtships. Andrew McDowall argued in 1796 that he was not guilty of the seduction of Margaret Kennedy because he 'laid her down on the bed, where he found no resistance'.[45] Robert McGhie replied negatively when asked by the court whether Marion Meikle 'made any resistance to the accomplishment of his wishes'.[46] Alexander Walker disowned marrying Janet Colquhoun by arguing that she never:

> endeavoured to resist the liberties he took with her; and so far from supposing there was any intention of marrying her, or even indulging such an idea, She herself has repeatedly declared that the freedoms she permitted were too great ever to lead to that expectation.[47]

Perhaps because of the cultural ubiquity of sexual violence within courtship rituals, rapes were rarely prosecuted. In England, they made up about one per cent of indictable felonies across the early modern period, so that, between 1660 and 1800, Surrey Assizes prosecuted one rape per year and Sussex only one every four years. For those that were prosecuted, the conviction rate was around sixteen per cent.[48] In Ireland, rape prosecutions were similarly rare; one study showed forty-one prosecuted across Ireland between 1797 and 1799 during a period of particular social and political upheaval (when the number of reported rapes tends to increase).[49] The majority of cases that came to court in both jurisdictions featured young girls under the age of consent for both sex and marriage.[50]

In Scotland, only a handful of cases of rape and sexual assault came to the High Court of Justiciary, which was meant to have exclusive jurisdiction for rape, across the century.[51] In practice, rape was prosecuted in the lower criminal courts, and it continued to be regularly dealt with in the Kirk sessions as a 'sin' alongside fornication, rather than as a crime – reflecting the difficulty of distinguishing rape from consensual sexual behaviour within the imaginary of the Scottish church.[52] This conflation of sin and crime, consensual and non-consensual sex, can also be found in the case of Matthew Foulden of Jedburgh, whose charge of rape on a sixteen-year-old girl was legally 'aggravated' by the fact that 'he was married at the time'.[53] Unlike in England and Ireland, adultery remained a crime in Scotland throughout the eighteenth century, potentially punishable by death in serious cases. As a result, immoral but consensual sexual acts and non-consensual sexual acts were all viewed as equally problematic, reducing the focus on 'force'.

The ultimate consequence of such a conflation of consensual sex and rape was the cultural acceptance of women marrying their rapists. Like bride abductions, this practice was associated with Ireland, with one British politician wryly describing an 'Irish marriage' as one 'where the rape was committed first, and the marriage concluded afterwards'.[54] Examples of marriage following rape appeared in the press across the period, but they received particular publicity towards the end of the century.[55] Some historians have questioned the legitimacy of the claims of women in such cases, seeing rape accusations as a method of pressuring men to fulfil marriage promises.[56] Yet, evidence from the trials themselves suggests a much more complex picture.

As seen in the examples above, some women simply thought that marriage was an acceptable resolution to rape; other women were reluctant to marry their rapists, but found their wishes overridden. In one case, a young Irish woman was asked by the judge overseeing the trial of her rapist, 'would you rather marry the prisoner or hang him?' She replied: 'I would like to give him the benefit of the law, Your Lordship'.[57] The judge retorted 'A pretty benefit indeed!', before asking her father the same question to which he replied 'married'.[58] The judge then explicitly asked whether he consented to the match, and the father agreed. The judge told him to speak to his daughter and after a whispered conversation between them, the father informed the judge: 'She consents my Lord'.[59] The prisoner's consent was then sought and they were immediately married by the chaplain of the court.[60] Despite the woman clearly saying that she wanted 'the benefit of the law', she found herself married to her rapist.

In English and Scottish contexts where, at least superficially, the idea of marriage following rape was presumed to be, at best, distasteful, it was rare to find a rape trial that ended in the marriage of the two parties. Rather, women who desired this outcome used alternative legal suits to force marriage or gain compensation. The main difference between Ireland and the rest of the United Kingdom, however, was not that women married their rapists, but, that in Ireland, women were willing to use the criminal courts to pursue this conclusion.

While this may suggest that eighteenth-century commentators saw marriage as the solution to rape, there was some debate around this issue.

Clearly, as demonstrated by the number of women who continued to sleep with their rapists after being attacked as well as those who pursued marriage with them in the courts, the cultural acceptance of sexual violence within courtship was such that many women did not believe that it should operate against future marriage. However, that many commentators placed emphasis on the importance of an emotional union in marriage meant that, for some, a prosecution of rape and a life of virtuous singleness was preferable to the ongoing violence of an unloving marriage. The Scottish feminist and advice writer, Jean Marishall, took this further arguing that the seduced woman who convinces her lover to marry her,

> looks on her husband as her lord and master, who reminds her that he has conferred upon her an honour which she had no right to expect. Fearful of offending, she becomes a timid, spiritless soul all the days of her life.[61]

Yet, while condemning marriage as the solution, she provided no alternative for such women, offering them only 'sympathy'.[62] In practice, even where women resisted men's sexual advances, mental virtue did not remove the social stigma of their rapes; if they could not marry their seducers (either due to his refusal or because they wished to remain true to their feelings), they found they must remain single and become social outcasts, prostitutes or, in fiction, die tragically. In all of these outcomes, the act of becoming sexual beings removed or restricted female autonomy, opportunity and, in the case of marriage or death, even the female self.

Conclusion

While eighteenth-century British society increasingly respected a women's right to consent to sex and marriage, it also limited the nature of that consent to a form of resistance to male desire, where the female will was something to be overcome to allow the female self to be fully submerged into that of her husband. In conceiving of the female will as a form of resistance, courtship became a place of struggle, where men were expected to use force, and female consent became not an active expression of female desire but a lack of 'no', and so found even in silence. As a result, force was considered a normal part of courting behaviour and so sexual violence was located alongside wooing as methods to overcome the female will. This resulted in rape being normalized within courtship and many women and men understanding marriage as an acceptable resolution to rape and abduction.

4 THE DISORDERED FUNDAMENT: SEXUAL VIOLENCE ON BOYS AND SODOMY TRIAL NARRATIVES IN THE *OLD BAILEY PROCEEDINGS*

Aparna Gollapudi

On 13 July 1757, William Williams was indicted for 'making an assault on Thomas Smith, an infant about twelve years of age' and 'committing upon him that detestable crime call'd sodomy'.[1] The boy's mother and a neighbour woman deposed that the 'prisoner and the child used to lie together in one bed', and one day, 'the child made much complaint' so they 'examined his fundament, and found it disorder'd and in an extreme bad way'.[2] However, because they could 'say no more than what they heard the child say' and the boy, when 'examined as to the nature of an oath', seemed to have 'no knowledge of the consequence of false swearing', the accused, Williams, was acquitted.[3]

The scenario presented above, with the child complainant, the accused sodomite and the disconcertingly graphic glimpse of the boy's sexually wounded body in the mother's testimony, is not atypical of some sodomy trials brought to court in the eighteenth century. Twenty-five cases of sodomy were tried at London's Old Bailey between 1730 and 1780; of these, eight were cases that involved children, which in the eighteenth-century courtroom meant boys under the age of fourteen.[4] The trials were published for the profit and delight of eighteenth-century readers in the *Proceedings of the Old Bailey* (*OBP*),[5] a periodical that appeared after each of the eight annual court sessions and featured accounts of all the cases tried there. These published accounts, now digitized and easily accessible, offer new ways of considering how charges of sodomy were treated in the London courtroom when the accusers were young boys. Though legal terminology did not distinguish these eight indictments for sodomy from cases brought against mutually consenting adult males or unsuspecting men who were entrapped into expressing same-sex desire and then dragged to court, they *are* different due to the age of the prosecutors. Not only was such sodomy always legally non-consensual because it involved boys below the age of discretion, it also often included scenarios of sexual coercion and violence. Unlike the misleading phrase 'sodomitical assault', in many charges brought by one adult male against another, where the 'assault' could refer to little more than 'giving some unnatural Kisses, and shewing several beastly Gestures',[6] trial accounts featuring young boys frequently represented sodomy as a sexually violent crime that leaves the sodomized body wounded. In this, they are closer to the *OBP* narratives of sixty-four rape cases involving underage girls in the period, than to the sodomy prosecutions of adult men.

While trials brought on behalf of children, whether for rape or sodomy, have many similarities, the role of the violence represented in the two is slightly different. Rape always connotes coercion while sodomy does not; but when boys brought cases against men, they were routinely expected to prove that violence had been perpetrated. Though both sodomy and rape were capital crimes, the former was clearly considered more heinous, vile and unnatural.[7] When a boy accused a man of sodomy, it was treated as a more serious charge because it was more destructive of the adult's social and moral respectability. In the absence of any clearly defined discourse of paedophilia to trigger immediate indignation, and the familiar presence of Ganymede figures from Graeco-Roman history to model socially integrated pederasty, trials in which boys accused men of sexual assault became a synapse between two powerful emergent discourses in the period – that of sodomy and childhood. These trial accounts reveal that when a boy called a man a sodomite in court, he also often set in motion a complex of discursive and institutional violence, as intent on conscripting the child accuser as punishing the alleged assaulter.

The *OBP*'s accounts of sodomitical sexual violence against children, stark and graphic as they often are, expose other kinds of aggression against the boy accusers coded into the trial process itself. On the one hand, the disproportionate burden of proof that children bear as plaintiffs implies a kind of legal, institutionalized violence, played out in the practices and procedures of the courtroom, which brutally truncates the boy's access to the law's power of redressing grievance. On the other hand, the boy in these sodomy trial narratives is trapped between two competing discourses of childhood – that of the Lockean, Enlightenment rational subject *in progress*, and that of the child as an innately sexual being with animal-like energies – both of which disempower him as a speaking subject in the court, thus inflicting a kind of discursive violence. The inextricably intertwined strands of physical, legal and discursive violence in these trial accounts offer useful insight into the cultural politics and anxieties implicit in the contest between the sodomite and the child.

However, despite the detailed and mostly clinical descriptions of sexual violence in the *OBP*, it would be incautious to treat these trial records as having unproblematic historical 'truth value'. The *OBP* was essentially a commercial publication, printed by private booksellers with varying degrees of oversight by court officials through the eighteenth century. Aimed primarily at the middling and upper echelons of society, though also permeating into the lower classes, the *OBP* was clearly published with an eye to its readership's interest in the most sensational cases. Robert Shoemaker has also noted that despite its pretensions to accuracy, the reportage of cases often served ideological ends, 'represent[ing] the court as an accessible and impartial source of justice' through its narrative choices.[8] Sodomy cases would, of course, be especially vulnerable to such ideological tailoring for publication. After all, court records of sodomy trials from this era are fundamentally homophobic texts, capturing the socio-legal condemnation of homosexual acts. In addition to ideological pressures, the trial records were also shaped by convention and the exigencies of print. Even the most detailed accounts present only a fraction of the words spoken in a courtroom. Judges' summaries, juries' questions, character-witnesses' testimony and even the few words defendants spoke to clear themselves were routinely excluded from the published trials. The sodomy trials from the *OBP* focused on here are, in all probability, similarly 'distorted and fragmentary'.[9] However, they are valuable as popular representations of the interface between criminalized sexual behaviour and discourses of childhood. As such, the trial accounts in the *OBP* are culturally significant plots in which the alleged sodomite's testimony is pitted against the child's. Within such an ideologically laden discursive environment, the boy's sexually coerced body becomes his own 'voice', a crucial but disputed evidentiary sign.

The sensational representations of sexually injured bodies in the *OBP*'s sodomy trial accounts probably helped sell copies, but they also had some important functions in the narrative arc from indictment to verdict. For instance, violence or pain was often the starting point of inquiries into whether a crime had actually been committed. Thus, the exceptionally brief account of the case against William Williams included above plots two main narrative points: (1) Thomas Smith complains to his mother; and (2) she examines his anal passage to confirm his story. Turning the reader's attention to an inspection of the child's body after an accusation of sexual assault might seem a natural progression, but it also indicates the primary concern of the law in cases of sodomy. In a sodomy trial, the letter of the law demanded proof of both penetration and ejaculation inside the body to convict the accused. In this, sodomy was akin to rape, which also required evidence of penetration as well as emission. In general, though, as Anthony Simpson argues, 'a much different and much more relaxed interpretation of proof of the fact was required in sodomy cases', as compared to rape trials, thus ensuring that it was easier to convict men involved in homosexual acts than rapists who had violated women.[10] It was often enough evidence for a witness to see two men acting suspiciously 'with their breeches down' for them to be convicted of sodomy,[11] while a woman could find it very difficult to prove rape despite strong evidence.

However, while Simpson's observation about the differential burden of proof might be true of sodomy and rape cases in general, the situation shifts when the focus is narrowed to trials involving children. Unlike the lower bar of proof in sodomy cases involving adults, indictments for sodomizing an underage boy usually attend as rigorously to proving penetration and ejaculation as do prosecutions for rapes of girls within the age of consent (which was ten in the law books but in practice was often taken to be twelve).[12] When Paul Oliver, an apprentice to Gabriel Laurence, and a 'Male Infant of the Age of fourteen Years', accused his master of buggering him, the court was particular about ascertaining that both penetration and emission had taken place. The account reconstructs this exigency thus:

> He [Oliver] being asked what he [Laurence] did to him? He answered, He put his Pr—y M—r [Privy Member] into his Fundament a great way. Being ask'd If he perceiv'd any Thing come from him? He reply'd, Yes; there was Wet and Nastiness which he wip'd off with the sheet, and what he was ashamed to tell; that he had tore him so, that he could not tell what to do, and could not do his Needs.[13]

Through the modern pathologizing lens of paedophilia, the apprentice boy's deposition about the anal injury inflicted on him by his master is deeply disturbing, but eighteenth-century trials dealing with sexual assaults on children – both boys and girls – were primarily intent upon confirming that the crime was indeed completed in all its technicalities, i.e., both penetration and emission had taken place. Indeed, Netta Goldsmith says of eighteenth-century Judge Page, very much a man of his times, that he 'took a sterner view of a homosexual act between two consenting adults than he did of pedophilia'.[14] The physical hurt and difficulty in defecating Oliver mentions are thus important but somewhat incidental to the 'main fact' the court is attempting to ascertain.

This also means that certain kinds of violence are more visible than others in the transcripts. Oliver also says, for instance, that at 'about Two O'Clock in the Morning [Laurence] jump'd upon him, and held him down, that he was almost stifled, his Breath being almost gone; that he strove what he could, but he kept him down'.[15] Such a violent struggle would probably leave some marks on the boy's body; however, there is absolutely no mention of any other injury sustained while Oliver 'strove what he could' except for that which he sustained in his anus. This silence about injuries while resisting sexual assault follows a pattern of absence in almost all trial accounts involving underage boys and girls. In a particularly gruesome narrative, for instance, in which the accused rapist, Christopher Graff, has to sop up blood from his room and the stairs after assaulting twelve-year-old Sarah Pearse, the focus is still only on vaginal injury, though the child deposes that 'she cry'd out, and held by the Door, but he loosed her Hands, and told her it would signifie nothing to cry out for no body could hear her, and then [tied] a Napkin about her Head to prevent her making a Noise'.[16] Any bruises she might have sustained in this struggle are erased by the narrative focus on the marks of violence that specifically confirm penetration.

The *OBP* reveals, though, that the trial narrative genre did have its own iconography of sexual violence when it came to child victims. Just as rape was denoted on the stage by 'ravished hair' or on a novel's page by a line of asterisks, a cluster of images haunts the process of proving the act in the *OBP* – soiled linens, transmission of venereal distemper, difficulty in walking but most importantly, of course, wounded sexual organs. The sharpened and selective focus on signs of genital or anal injury meant that reliable, *expert* interpretation of corporeal signs was needed in many of these cases. Thus, in trials for sodomy where the prosecutor was an underage boy, the figure of the surgeon becomes an important presence in the courtroom. Following a trend towards the increasing medicalization of crime, the judges often asked whether the child had been examined by a surgeon, thus setting up a sort of protocol to be followed when a child complained of sexual assault. While William Williams's fundament seemed only to have been examined by his mother, frequently, parental inspection – or, in the case of rape, a midwife's testimony – was deemed inadequate. The surgeon's voice, on the other hand, had more authority and was expected to offer an objective interpretation of a child's orificial peculiarities.[17] Indeed, Arthur Gilbert notes that in the eighteenth century, 'It was held in medical circles that sodomy left various signs – stigmata may be the better word – on the fundament' and treatises expounded the anal signs to look for in order to discover penetration.[18] Though the surgeons testifying in trials were probably no experts in this emergent science of sodomy-detection, their observations in the courtroom are a part of the new specular medical regime that Michel Foucault articulates so convincingly in his *History of Sexuality* (1976–84). In trial narratives, the allegedly sodomized body of the child is an object of investigation with ambiguous signs requiring expert interpretation. In the 1729 case against Henry Hambleton, the surgeon examined the sphincter of fourteen-year-old prosecutor John Wynn and concluded: 'That he found the Parts enrag'd, the Muscles extended, and a Caceration about the Anus, yet he could not discover any thing but what might possibly proceed from the Piles, or other natural Disorders'.[19] The doctor's testimony was very agreeable to Hambleton, of course, who insisted that the boy recently had 'a Boyl on his Fundament, which was the Cause of his Disorder'.[20] The interpretation of John Wynn's posterior orifice as symptomatic of piles rather than violent penile penetration ensured Hambleton's acquittal.

Even in cases where the marks of violence on the body are read as reliable proofs of sodomitical assault, the court's gaze, fixed intently on the child's bared behind, can be as penetrative as the act it seeks to confirm, a form of legal-procedural violence which almost mimics that which it is meant to punish. In the trial against Gilbert Laurence, accused of sodomizing his apprentice, the surgeon deposed:

> That upon examining the Lad, he found his Fundament quite open; that it had been penetrated above an Inch, and much lacerated; that there was a Hole, in which a Finger and Thumb might be put, and that the Fundament was Black all round, and appear'd like that of a Hen after laying an Egg.[21]

The surgeon's visually evocative description of the boy's anal cavity using inches, finger widths and pictorial analogy is a memorable mix of mathematical precision, empirical 'hands on' observation and fanciful imagery. It also indicates the extent to which trial narratives resisted the increasing sentimentalization of children in the period, translating violence or pain into scientifically observed empirical phenomena marked on the body, rather than a provocation to moral-emotional displays of sensibility or sympathy. Such moments also suggest that in the eighteenth-century courtroom the spectacular centrepiece of these sodomy trials was often the body of the child accuser, held up to public scrutiny in the most intimate way possible. The voyeuristic potential of such trial accounts is implied in Peter Wagner's study of the market for sexually explicit courtroom narratives that included, but was not limited to, the *OBP*. Wagner notes that 'the "physician's account" was frequently mentioned on the title page and made obvious in the text by special print'.[22] While such proliferating representations of criminal sex and violence point to new tastes in the reading public, the heightened importance of children's bodies in sodomy trials also reveals that the discourses of childhood brought to bear upon the boy plaintiff could constitute a sort of violence which severely injured his credit as a reliable historian of his own experience in the courtroom.

All the cases hitherto discussed involve accusations of violence inflicted on a child. Significantly, though, the only violence that 'matters' legally is that which proves the sodomy did actually occur. The injuries suffered by the child are relevant only insofar as they contribute towards proving that a man is indeed a sodomite. But, the sodomite *as a perpetrator of violence* is legally invisible. He is not on the dock for having hurt a child but for having committed 'the detestable and abominable crime (among Christians not to be named)'.[23] The evidence of violence so carefully set out in these trials seems more concerned with corroborating the boy's story than with the sodomite's crime. This approach to sodomitical violence, which turns away from the boy as a suffering victim to scrutinize cautiously his reliability and veracity, reveals a rather different construction of the child than that associated with the eighteenth-century 'cult of childhood'. The child here is not the promising, quintessential representative of Enlightenment human educability and perfectibility, a Rousseaustic product of uncorrupted nature or an innocent who must be shielded from his own and adults' sexuality. Instead, the young boy in the sodomy trial transcript suggests that alternative notions of the child – which highlight his potential guilt as a fabricator of false accusation rather than his potential gifts of purity and innocence, his mental puerility rather than his promise – continue to thrive in eighteenth-century culture. As Anja Müller has shown in her study of the child figure in the period's prints, children are often 'characterized by lack and inferiority' and represented as fully immersed in 'an underworld of crime and illicit sexuality'.[24] While the eighteenth century did witness the invention of childhood as a desexualized space of cherished innocence, discourses constructing the child as 'unequivocally a sensual child' also flourished.[25] Egan and Hawkes have shown the pervasiveness of Comte de Buffon's construction of the child as 'a stranger to thought or reflection' who 'amuses himself as a young animal' in the period.[26] In sodomy trials, these conceptions of the child as an unthinking creature subject to sexual as well as criminal impulses are frequently the norm. All sorts of doubts about the intellectual, moral and sexual nature of the child are unleashed in these trials when a young boy dares impugn the rectitude of a respectable and economically productive adult male by accusing him of the most heinous of crimes. And often, ironically, the indisputable marks of sexual violence on his body prove to be an important advantage for a boy facing his alleged attacker. Though the 1697 law treatise, *Infants' Lawyer*, claimed that 'our Law hath a very great and tender Consideration for Persons naturally disabled ... especially for Minors' and 'protects their Persons' as well as 'preserves their Rights', the reality of courtroom contests was quite different.[27] As Simpson states, after an extensive survey of rape and sodomy cases in the period, 'It is generally thought that eighteenth-century society saw the progressive development of ... more protective attitudes towards children. If this is so, this development is [not visible] in criminal law', as prosecuting sexual crimes against children became more difficult than ever through the century.[28]

One reason for this difficulty was that as the adult rational individual gained stature in political and philosophical Enlightenment discourses, the value of the child's word in court depreciated. The Lockean model of human understanding, which privileged men's capacity for rationality, also confined the child as a subject to be moulded through correct pedagogy because he was *not yet capable* of rational behaviour and judgement. Similarly, with the emergence of 'consent based political ideology' which argued that rational adult males can be governed only by their own sanction, the name of 'child' became one of the 'names differentiated from "men"' (others being women, slaves, lunatics, etc.) as 'lacking in reason' and therefore unable to consent.[29] These shifts permeated into eighteenth-century legal discourses as well. Holly Brewer illustrates that it was only in the late seventeenth century that serious attempts were initiated to encode formally an age limit on who could testify in court and law treatises began to debate earnestly the validity of a child witness's words. Children of six or seven were even compared to 'a lunatick or a madman' in point of 'reason and understanding', by a judge in 1726.[30] Similarly, in 1760, Sir Geoffrey Gilbert wrote in more tempered words that all children suffer from 'want of skill and discernment' and are 'perfectly incapable of any Sense of Truth'.[31] William Blackstone says specifically about underage boys: 'A male infant, under the age of fourteen years, is presumed by law incapable to commit rape ... [as] the law supposes an imbecility of body as well as mind'.[32] While Blackstone's statement protects young boys from criminal responsibility, it also constructs them as pre-rational 'imbeciles', thus undercutting the validity of their testimonies and accusations. The legal notion of an age of discretion is based on the idea that children cannot participate in certain adult things – sex, moral responsibility and rational judgement, for instance. On the one hand this shields them from being exploited by manipulative or violent grownups. On the other hand, however, it safeguards adults from their juvenile accusations. The acquittal of William Williams because Thomas Smith seemed to have 'no knowledge of the consequence of false swearing', shows how new attitudes towards the child as a *tabula rasa* subject who does not yet have rational discernment could translate into a kind of legal violence against children, in which court outcomes favour adults.

Even in cases where the child proved that he understood the nature of an oath, as did ten-year-old Thomas Read when accusing Charles Atwell of sodomy, the reliability of his testimony is suspect. Read, quite an articulate boy for his age, is grilled rigorously in the courtroom about each date he forgets and about each detail in his testimony that he alters in an effort to detect if he is lying. For instance, much is made of his changing his testimony about his position on the bed during the sodomy:

> You [were] lying your full length and he lying his full length? – No, we could not lie our full length for my knees were up.
>
> ...
>
> Why do not you? – No, my knees are always so (bending them) I was obliged to put up my legs when he put his c—k into me.
>
> Did you say that, till the surgeon made the observation that it was impossible for him to commit this crime if you lay in the manner you described, now I want to know whether you did not say before the justice that you lay side by side with this young man and that you laid quite straight; did you or not say that before the justice? – Yes, I did and I contradicted it at the same time.
>
> ...

> How came you to alter it afterwards by saying you did not lie straight? – I said I lay straight, my legs were down straight but my knees were bent in this manner (bending his knees a little).[33]

The court's meticulous focus on Read's exact posture and the precise angle of his limbs in order to investigate the fault lines in the child's testimony suggests the law's trust in the story his body tells rather than his mouth. The detail of bending his knees is especially important because it also becomes a point of contention in the all-important medical examination of the boy's fundament. Three of the four surgeons testifying at the trial agree that they 'could see no appearance of any laceration having happened there; the part was strongly contracted, was small, and in a healthy state as it should be; if any thing had happened there, it must have been a long time before, for there was no appearance of such a thing, or of any laceration'.[34] The fourth, however, opines that penetration could 'undoubtedly be without laceration if his knees were as he has now described'.[35] His is the minority opinion, however. Atwell is acquitted in the absence of any concrete physical evidence except the testimony of a boy who is constructed in the trial narrative as eloquent but probably cunning and deceptive. If a boy's lacerated body is crucial for convicting the accused sodomite, the absence of any unequivocal marks of violence is the evidence that damns the child accuser.

Indeed, if the allegedly sodomized body does not show corresponding signs of forceful penetration, the child's self-narrativization seems to be of little value in the courtroom. For not only were children perceived as being simple-minded, but their 'lack of discretion' also meant they were deficient in moral sense, without full awareness of proper ethical or religious consequences of their actions. Children's amoral nature meant the stories they told in court were viewed with considerable suspicion, especially when they were accusing an adult male of a capital crime. Blackstone urges that courts be very cautious in prosecuting cases brought by underage accusers, especially when the charge is sodomy because, 'it is an offence of so dark a nature, so easily charged, and the negative so difficult to be proved'.[36] Also, he cautions that 'where the evidence of children is admitted, it is much to be wished, in order to render their evidence credible, that there should be some concurrent testimony'.[37] The discursive violence implicit in the persistent construction of children as radically unreliable narrators in the courtroom means that often it is a boy's disordered fundament that becomes the clinching 'concurrent testimony' that Blackstone demands in such cases.

The complex role of anal violence as the test of a boy's veracity in a sodomy indictment becomes evident if we consider a case in which a man of fashion with links to high society was convicted *without* categorical medical proofs of sexual violence. Captain Robert Jones was sentenced to death for sodomizing thirteen-year-old Francis Hay in 1772, but he was granted a royal pardon at the last moment, due to the intercession of his influential friends.[38] His conviction and pardon provoked what Rictor Norton calls 'the first public debate about homosexuality in England'.[39] The account of the trial published in the *OBP* was widely circulated and frequently summarized in the slew of pamphlets, newspaper reports and editorials that were written to argue for or against Jones's guilty verdict and his eventual reprieve. Hay's testimony in the trial had mentioned pain in his legs and thighs, causing him to 'straddle as [he] walked', but because he did not confide in an adult about the sodomy until a fortnight later, there was no definitive medical testimony to confirm anal penetration of the child. Hay, who went to Jones's apartment thrice on behalf of his uncle, a jeweller, from whom the captain had ordered some trinkets, was questioned closely about his long silence regarding his attack and his voluntary return twice to the abode of his attacker, but his detailed and steady deposition seemed to convince the jury who deemed the defendant guilty.

In the print wars discussing this case, Jones's supporters argued that he was convicted on very flimsy grounds without adequate proof. Much of their indignation stemmed from what they perceived as the dangerous precedent of condemning a man to death simply on the basis of a young boy's testimony. In questioning the basis of Jones's conviction, his supporters make manifest a plurality of cultural anxieties about children's natures. In these accounts, the child is either ignorant, dishonest or sexually suspect, and thus cannot be relied upon. The 'tenderness of [Hay's] age' makes his 'evidence insufficient' without proper adult corroboration of the case's specifics.[40] The veracity of his accusations is doubtful and though 'the Matter rests merely upon the Boy's Evidence ... it may as well be a Calumny as not'.[41] Not only does the boy deal in false slander, his sexual morals too are far from unimpeachable. Hay's 'repeated return' to Jones for getting payment and to ensure his uncle keeps getting business from him is continually termed 'prostitution' in the pamphlets and newspapers. He is, thus, a '*Voluntary* patient' in criminal sexuality rather than a victim.[42] Significantly too, writers who support Jones's conviction and strongly critique his pardon have comparatively little to say about the child accuser. Most of their anger is directed to what they see as a morally lax attitude towards the terrible Christian sin of sodomy and a corrupt socio-political system in which you can get away with any crime as long as you have powerful friends. On the whole, the silhouette of the child that emerges from this print debate is far from idealized or even sympathetic. No significant concern is voiced about any possible harm to the child or even any potential moral and sexual corruption he might have suffered.

Instead, writers supporting Jones's pardon are frequently indignant and irate about the absence of any symptoms of sexual violence the boy suffered. So entrenched is the expectation of medical testimony of violence in such cases that its lack is seen as a serious drawback in this newspaper report:

> It has been observed by many that no surgeon was evidence on the trial of Capt. Jones, as to examining whether the boy appeared to be injured, and that it would have been a very important circumstance to elucidate the truth of the charge.[43]

Indeed, there seems to be an active reimagining of the scene amongst the debaters where the child appears injured, pained, crying and completely transparent to the adults around him. As one writer says:

> Have we had Witnesses in the Captain's Case? No: Have we any probably [*sic*] Arguments of a Violence committed to the prejudice of the Boy? No: Has any Body heard his Cries, or seen his Tears? No. Had I heard his Cries or Seen his Tears I might have asked him why he cried and wept.[44]

Another writer similarly scripts what a 'real' victim would do, noting that if a boy 'comes running to his relations immediately ... bitterly complaining', with 'all marks of distress, violence, and despair in his countenance' so that they take him to the justice where the 'surgeons find him in a shocking condition, *penetratio, &c.* is visible' then *that* would be a convincingly sodomized boy victim.[45]

Without all these proper signs of violence, the worth of a child's testimony is ambiguous at best. Even if Hay is able to convince the jury of his veracity, morality and judgement like a rational would-be Lockean adult, he is put on trial in the print media. The fear a figure like Hay generates is captured by this emotional appeal in one of the pamphlets: 'Horrible to think! The Law which allows a Boy to swear away any Life is not the Law of a free Nation; 'tis the Law of a slavish Nation; nay 'tis an infernal Law'.[46] In this account, a legal system that values a child's word over that of an adult, giving him power over the adult men of a 'free Nation', upends natural hierarchies, condemning them to the 'infernal' realm. In their insistence on clear signs of sexual violence in cases where boys accuse adult men of sodomy, eighteenth-century culture and law betray deep anxieties about children, their nature and their ability to rule the life of adults who are reduced to a 'slavish' state. As these cases show, in sodomy trials, the sodomite was not the only figure perceived as a threat to patriarchal power systems; sometimes the boy could surpass him in the anxieties he evoked.

Signs of sexual violence thus become one of the most important forms of 'concurrent testimony' supporting a boy's story of sodomitical attack in court. In the *Smith* v. *Williams* case that opens this chapter, for instance, less ink is spent on the child's words – we only know that he 'made much complaint' – compared to that used for describing the effects of violence on his body as his mother 'examined his fundament, and found it disorder'd and in an extreme bad way'. The child's speaking body, especially when its signs are properly interpreted by medical experts, is more valuable than the narrative of even the most eloquent boy. Of course, as in Smith's case, sometimes even the disordered fundament cannot withstand the 'imbecility' of the child which prevents him from having the rational and moral capacity to understand the nature of an oath to tell the truth. Simpson observes after his comprehensive scrutiny of sexual crimes in the eighteenth century that 'courts were influenced much more by the [perceived] social threat posed by a particular crime', than by abstract legal principles, so that conviction often depended upon which crime was seen as 'an especially worrisome problem' rather than upon the law itself.[47] Sodomy cases involving underage boys reveal that often, the young boy could compete with the potential sodomite as being a particularly 'worrisome' figure, frequently provoking another bout of aggression when he reaches the courtroom, only this time it is legal-institutional and discursive violence. The comparative invisibility of the sodomite as an agent of corporeal violence in trial narratives, along with the hyper-visibility of the signs of violence he leaves behind reveal the court's priorities of upholding the status quo of heterosexual patriarchal hierarchies in the face of threats not only from the subversive masculinity of the sodomite but also from the accusations of impudent boys.

Acknowledgements

I am very grateful to my friend, Prof. Ellen Brinks, whose brilliant suggestions enriched this essay immensely.

5 THE TITILLATION OF DRAMATIC RAPE, 1660–1720

Anne Greenfield

Between 1660 and 1720, there were remarkably over fifty tragedies depicting rape and/or attempted rape produced on the London stage. These scenes of sexual violence flourished in each of the patent theatrical companies; they were written by members of both of the major political parties; and they were authored by male and female dramatists alike. Never before in English dramatic history were there so many representations of sexual violence, and never before were representations of sexual violence so successful with audiences.[1]

Despite this abundance, recent scholars have reached little consensus as to how, specifically, theatregoers responded to these scenes of sexual violence: whether viewers understood them as pathos-driven spectacles of female victimization, as topical political allegories and/or as titillating displays of sexual scenarios. The last of these possibilities – that audiences (rather perversely) enjoyed tragic scenes of rape as erotic spectacles – has been a matter of scholarly debate over the last decade and a half, and to date this issue remains unresolved.

Jean Marsden and Elizabeth Howe have argued that rape depictions of the Restoration were interpreted as titillating erotic performances, made popular by the advent of professional actresses (and the sexual potential associated with them) on public stages in 1660. Marsden argues that, 'As the joint appearance of actresses and scenes of rape indicates, rape becomes possible as theatrical spectacle only when visible signs of the female are present: breasts, bare shoulders, and loosened or "ravished" hair'.[2] However others like Derek Hughes and Susan J. Owen disagree, interpreting scenes of rape and attempted rape as far more aligned with Restoration politics than Restoration eroticism. As Hughes contends, the most significant increase in rape depictions came about in the late 1670s and 1680s, nearly two decades after the 1660 advent of professional actresses. Thus, according to Hughes, the prime concern of most tragic rape depictions is 'not sex, but power'.[3] Without a vast and extant body of first-hand responses to these plays (and an especial dearth of responses from women), scholarship on this issue has not resolved the question of whether and to what degree Restoration and early eighteenth-century rape depictions actually titillated their original viewers.

Part of the reason it is so difficult to determine whether these rape depictions were sexually-arousing to their original viewers, is that sexual desire and arousal are fluid, culturally-constructed and culturally-dependent phenomena. One cannot assume that audiences three centuries ago would have been sexually excited by the same visual displays and subject matter that excite audiences living today. As historians of human sexuality widely acknowledge, the study of sexuality and representations of sexuality in history must take into account ideologies from those eras, including those towards gender, the body, medicine, procreation, pleasure and patriarchy. Thus, it is fruitless to project backward our modern-day intuitions about the eroticism or, conversely, repulsiveness of Restoration and eighteenth-century rape depictions. One must turn to ideologies towards and responses to rape, at that time, if one is to determine whether these scenes were sexually-arousing to viewers during that era.

As we shall see in examining an array of documents – including plays, erotica, trial transcripts, journals and engravings – rape, very probably, did titillate many Restoration and early eighteenth-century theatregoers. First, sexual violence occupies a prominent place in texts that were chiefly designed for erotic consumption at this time, indicating that the trope of rape and attempted rape was compatible with sexual titillation. Secondly, a man's desire to rape a woman was understood at this time as natural and masculine, rather than wicked and perverse – which increases the likelihood that men would have indulged in fantasies of sexual violence when encountering such depictions on the stage. Lastly, tragic rape scenes of this era were not seen as base or offensive displays worthy of censorship, but rather as beautiful components of high art – making this dramatic trope seem elevated and wholesome, rather than obscene and indecent. When considered as a whole, this evidence indicates not only that tragic rape scenes were almost certainly the source of erotic pleasure for many viewers, but also how and why these scenes were able to titillate audiences without being censured for doing so.

Representations of Sexual Violence in Erotica

During the Restoration and eighteenth century, there was a strong market in erotica for depictions of male sexual aggression, female submission, violence and even rape.[4] This market for sexual violence is, in many ways, our best source of evidence in determining whether, and to what extent, dramatic depictions of sexual violence were sexually titillating to their original viewers. After all, few late seventeenth- and early eighteenth-century theatregoers recorded their reactions (let alone their sexual reactions) to depictions of rape and attempted rape in theatrical productions. One of the best indications, then, that scenes of sexual violence elicited sexual responses in theatregoers, comes from the fact that sexual violence was regularly and successfully used to elicit sexual responses in readers of erotica at this time.

Historians of sexuality have long recognized the preponderance of forced sexual activity in seventeenth- and eighteenth-century erotica. As Karen Harvey explains, female submission to male desire – sometimes freely given, other times coerced – was ubiquitous in these texts, and the underlying ideology of these pieces 'championed male sexual aggression against defenseless women'.[5] Even works of erotica that feature willing, lustful heroines regularly insert scenes of male aggression and female resistance. For example, in the anonymously-written erotic text, *The Practical Part of Love* (1660), even though Helena is full of 'immoderate and impatient lust' and is eager to part with her maidenhead,[6] the scene leading up to her loss of virginity is imbued with sexual assault, struggle and resistance (between Helena and several men):

> the wine and her excellent Beauty had intoxicated them all, so that from kissing and admiring they began to mend their pace, and fall a snatching and groping, and after two or three bustlings, and wrinches of hands, & a displeasant wry look or two invade the botto[m] of her Petticoat ... while she tugs and struggles to let down her coats and cries, *fie Gentlemen*.[7]

Helena's resistance, we are told, 'flusters and animates the Gallants' even more,[8] and they take liberties with her until she willingly departs with them to a nearby lodging (where she consummates unnamed 'lewd practices').[9] Such scenes blend sexual pleasure with sexual violence, painting the heroine's resistance as congruent with and even a catalyst for sexual titillation.

Not only was sexual violence a common component of erotica, but depictions of rape on the stage and depictions of sexual activity in erotica also share several prominent motifs, further evincing the erotic appeal of these sexually-violent scenes. For instance, both the seduced heroines in erotica and the raped heroines in tragedies are regularly depicted with unbound, dishevelled hair. Hair, as Gill Perry demonstrates in *Spectacular Flirtations*, was associated with night-time, the bedroom and sex, and this visual display was a strong signifier for sexual activity at the time.[10] In fact, the association between a heroine's loose hair and sexual violence was so strong that in William Mountfort's *The Injured Lovers* (1688), the raped Antelina conveys to Rheusanes (her betrothed) that she has been raped, not by stating it explicitly but, by pointing to her ripped dress and dishevelled hair. She asks him,

> Do these torn Robes and hair look well, Rheusanes ...
> Should you meet one thus Ruffled on a Road,
> Stretcht on the Ground or fastned to a Tree,
> Would you not judge they had been Rob'd [i.e., raped], Rheusanes?[11]

This link between disordered hair and sexual violence was so common, in fact, that one finds a great many stage directions, in Restoration and early eighteenth-century plays, that point to a raped heroine's 'loose' or 'dishevelled' hair (a fact that is especially significant in light of the overall rarity of stage directions in plays at this time).[12]

Numerous other motifs were common to both dramatic rape scenes and erotica, including bound women, phallic stakes and posts, torn apparel and revealed white bosoms. For instance, the engraving designed to accompany John Dryden's 1735 edition of *Amboyna* reveals several of these elements, including a bound rape victim, a phallic tree, an exposed bosom (and displaced gown), dishevelled hair and an uncovered leg with stocking showing. If the staging of this scene in *Amboyna* was anything like Hubert-François Gravelot and Gerard Vandergucht's 1735 rendering of it, then this scene would have had a great deal in common with the motifs found in erotica at this time. Even the emphasis on female modesty in both rape scenes and erotica may be indicative of the potential for erotic titillation in both of these venues. As Harvey points out, female modesty was a trait that had long been understood as one that 'increased women's attractiveness and heightened men's desires'.[13] The fact that the same motifs of sexual violence found in dramatic rape scenes were also commonly found in concurrently-published erotica is a fairly reliable indication that rape scenes were titillating for certain viewers. As Sarah Toulalan explains, 'Pornography may not necessarily be reflective of a society's actual practice, but it must be sufficiently in tune with its contemporary audience's desires and understandings to find a market prepared to spend both time and money on its consumption'.[14] Thus, the violence that seems to have titillated so many readers of erotica and pornography would have, very probably, also titillated many theatregoers who viewed scenes of rape on the stage.

The fact that dramatic rape scenes were depicted in similar ways to sex scenes in erotica is a strong indication that tragic rape scenes on the stage would have been interpreted as titillating spectacles to be enjoyed, in part, for their sexual appeal. Yet, on the other hand, these shared motifs do not necessitate that rape was seen as an erotically-pleasing action, in and of itself. In fact, dramatic rape depictions may have been thought erotically titillating, above all, not because viewers had already-present fetishes for rape but, because rape could be represented in such suggestive and arousing ways. One must not underestimate the sex appeal that would have been associated with actresses on the stage generally. After all, the only other time that many male viewers would have seen a woman with her hair down and in various states of undress (as tragic rape victims were displayed) would have been in a bedroom, prior to sex. Thus, regardless of whether or not an audience member indulged in fantasies of rape before entering the auditorium, that audience member would have likely found it difficult to witness a rape scene without interpreting it, in part, as a sexual spectacle.

Many English viewers, however, may have possessed already-present fetishes for sexual violence at this time. One source of evidence for this comes from the sale of rape trial transcripts as pornography. As Harvey points out, descriptions of rape in erotica were markedly similar to those found in trial transcripts: 'In court, women might described [*sic*] how an assailant "came into the bedroom [and] threw her down and attempted to be rude with her" ... and such depictions were virtually indistinguishable from those in erotica'.[15] During the late seventeenth and early eighteenth centuries in particular, there were several, highly-popular publications of transcripts for trials revolving around rape – most of which were sold by known publishers of erotica.[16] Examples include *The Tryal and Condemnation of Mervin, Lord Audley Earl of Castle-haven* (convicted in 1631, published in 1699) and *The Case of Seduction* (1726).[17] Tellingly, the title pages of these manuscripts prominently advertise 'rape' as one of the crimes committed.[18] For instance, the description on the title page of *The Case of Seduction* promises a case involving a man 'Committing Rapes upon 133 Virgins'.[19] Unfortunately for readers who sought to hear about these episodes of rape, the promise of rape is part of a 'sucker-trap title', as this book describes no rapes and only two accusations of 'seduction'.[20] Sexual violence, of course, is far from the only source of titillation in these trial transcripts (these texts also capitalize on the market for sex scandals involving Catholic priests, spousal murder, sodomy, bestiality, 'penitent' prostitutes and much more). Yet, it is evident from the prominence with which rape was advertised in these manuscripts marketed by known publishers of erotica, that rape was not only congruent with mainstream erotic interests at this time, but that it was also, very probably, a source of arousal for many readers.

One sees other acknowledgements, in popular journals from the period, of the English public's appetite for displays of combined sexuality and violence towards women. Edward ('Ned') Ward, in *The London Spy* (1703), for instance, complains about the high degree of pleasure taken by spectators when a female prisoner was stripped to the waist and whipped publically at Bridewell. He recounts,

> she was ... forc'd to shew her tender Back, and tempting Bubbies to the Sages of the Grave Assembly, who were mov'd by her Modest Mein, together with the whiteness of her Skin, to give her but a gentle Correction. Finding little knowledge to be gain'd from their proceedings, and less Pleasure and Satisfaction from their Punishments; my Friend and I thought it better to retire, and leave them to be Flog'd on till the Accusers had satisfied their Revenge, and the Spectators their Curiosity.[21]

This manner of stripping prisoners to the waist and beating them was commonly inflicted on both men and women.[22] Not only was there a high level of tolerance for such sexualized violence against women, but, as Ward's report reminds us, there was a high degree of sexual satisfaction taken in response to these visual displays.

Rape, of course, was far from the only sex act to frequent erotically-charged writing at this time. Also common in Restoration and eighteenth-century erotica are depictions of sexual initiation (in which sexually-innocent girls transform into sexual animals), sex scandals involving Catholic priests, sexual flagellation (usually towards men), homoeroticism and didactic exchanges (ranging from midwifery manuals to whore dialogues) – and much more.[23] Thus, the presence of rape in erotic texts during this period does not demonstrate that rape was a universally-arousing trope or even that rape was more arousing to audiences than other sexually-charged displays. Rather, the presence of rape in erotic and pornographic texts tells us that there was demand for pornographic descriptions of rape, that rape depictions were compatible with sexual arousal for most viewers and that rape was likely a direct source of titillation for many audience members. When taken together, the English public's association of rape with sexual pleasure and the highly-sexualized manner in which these scenes were staged, make it very probable that audiences would have interpreted tragic scenes of sexual violence, in no small part, as erotically-charged spectacles designed to elicit a sexual response.

Sexual Violence as a 'Natural' Impulse

How, one might ask, could audience members be expected to be erotically invested in a dramatic rape scene, if such investment requires the viewer to relate to the villainous rapist – especially at a time when so many dramatic villains were painted in melodramatically repugnant colours? Would not the abhorrence of such a detestable and barbarous act (one punishable by death at this time) be enough to deter audiences from deriving erotic pleasure from such scenes?

The answer to these questions lies in seventeenth- and eighteenth-century ideologies towards rape, ideologies that in no way associate the desire to rape a woman with villainy and perversity. While rape was viewed (at least in theory) as a devastating crime that should be punished with the utmost severity (when enacted on a chaste woman), the *desire* to rape was understood as a mainstream urge widely-felt by most men, rather than as a warped urge felt only by the perverse. This attitude can be seen in an overwhelming number of Restoration and eighteenth-century plays, wherein dramatists continually advance the notion that rape is a natural impulse shared by most men. As the Emperor in Dryden's *Aureng-Zebe* (1675) describes it, a woman's resistance is the catalyst for male arousal:

> 'tis resistance that inflames desire:
> Sharpens the Darts of Love, and blows his Fire.
> Love is disarm'd that meets with too much ease:
> He languishes, and does not care to please.[24]

Even when rapists are portrayed in unambiguously evil ways (a common practice especially during the height of heroic tragedy), their urges to rape are never chastised, and their capacities to rape are shown to be a product of other flaws (such as their cruelty, tyrannical policies, excessive lifestyle, unbridled passions, etc.). Never is a rapist's overall wickedness said to be caused by his desire to rape a woman.

Examples of this attitude abound. In Nathaniel Lee's *Mithridates* (1678), the blame for Semandra's rape is shared between the manipulative courtiers who convince their ruler to rape the innocent heroine and the rapist himself for being a weak ruler who could be swayed by his subjects and his passions. When Mithridates begins to regret his rape, his attention is firmly pointed at his scheming courtiers, and he blames them for not preventing the rape:

> When you had seen me going, to have stopt me:
> My struguling [*sic*] Virtue might, with some assistance,
> Have cast the Venom of my Passion up;
> But, with your poysonous breath, you made it rage,
> Till I was fit to ruine poor Semandra.[25]

Significantly, the fact that Mithridates had this 'passion' to rape Semandra in the first place is never called into question, lamented, nor seen as a matter for concern. Rather, it is Mithridates's inability to *control* this passion that is alarming. This pattern of portraying the desire to rape as acceptable is seen in an overwhelming number of plays from this era, including Thomas Shadwell's *The Libertine* (1675), Nahum Tate's *The Ingratitude of the Commonwealth; or The Fall of Caius Martius Coriolanus* (1681) and John Wilmot, the Earl of Rochester's *Valentinian* – to name only a few.

Even more remarkably, the heroes of these plays are often also aroused by fantasies of rape, and these desires are always treated as completely natural and unproblematic. For example, in Dryden's *The Conquest of Granada by the Spaniards, Part II* (1671), the heroic Almanzor comes very close to raping his great love-interest in the play, Almahide. After trying to convince Almahide that he deserves to have sex with her after saving her in battle, he threatens, 'I will not move me from this place: / I can take no denial from that face!'[26] Almanzor only yields his sexually-violent designs when Almahide threatens to stab herself. While a modern-day heroine might be apt to scold her near-rapist for considering raping her (and for coming so close to doing it), Almahide praises Almanzor for overcoming his lust:

> 'Tis gen'rous to have conquer'd your desire;
> You mount above your wish; and loose it higher.
> There's pride in vertue; and a kindly heat:
> Not feverish, like your love; but full as great.[27]

Almahide's reaction is fully in keeping with the attitude expressed again and again in these plays: to want to rape is natural, and to stifle the desire to rape (through reason, pity and restraint) is necessary and virtuous.

Plays from this period abound with virtuous and/or 'harmless' characters who, like Almanzor, express the desire to rape. For instance, in the comic sub-plot of Thomas Porter's *The Villain* (1662), Boutefeu, La'march and Delpeche sing of the force they will use with the town women:

> When the houses with flashes do glitter,
> We can sever our sweets from the bitter,
> And in that bright night
> We can take our delight,
> And no Dam'sel shall scape but we'l hit her.[28]

In another example, from Roger Boyle, the Earl of Orrery's *The Generall*, Filadin speaks jocularly of committing wartime rape:

> Good Man, he but for one wench fights, but when
> Wee take the place, each of Us will have tenn!
> When townes are conquer'd by the force of Warre,
> Walls first are storm'd and then the Women are.[29]

In yet another instance, this time from Nicholas Rowe's *Tamerlane*, the heroic titular character expresses his desire to rape the beautiful and virtuous Arpasia:

> I might have us'd a Victor's boundless Power,
> And sated every Wish my Soul could form.
> But to secure thy Fears, know, *Bajazet*,
> This is among the Things I dare not do.[30]

Rape, in these plays, is represented as a desire shared by all men, from heroes to foolish supporting characters to villains. What was thought perverse was when a man *acted upon* this desire (with a chaste women), not that he had the desire in the first place. The fact that rape was understood as a mainstream, normal desire gives us additional reason to believe that some (or even many) theatregoers would have felt the same way these characters did, viewing rape as a titillating activity.

The notion that rape was a widespread desire among all men has been overlooked in recent scholarship. For instance, Roy Porter argues that throughout Western history, rapists have generally been on the outskirts of social order, not condoned by mainstream patriarchy. He writes,

> rape has flourished mainly on the margins; at the frontiers, in colonies, in states at war and in states of nature; amongst marauding, invading armies (though sex among soldiers is generally institutionalized in the brothel). Rape has also erupted on the psycho-margins, amongst loners, outsiders, who fail to be encultured into normal patriarchal sex.[31]

Yet rape was understood during the seventeenth and eighteenth centuries as something entirely central to mainstream ideologies of masculinity – if fantasized about, rather than acted upon. When tragic rape depictions became prevalent in the Restoration and early eighteenth century, this attitude was well rooted in the English collective imagination. As Garthine Walker points out in her study of early modern rape, 'male force and female submission were culturally coded as erotically appealing ... sexual discourses imagined rape in terms of "normal" male desires'.[32] Richard Steele further reveals, in the prologue he wrote for Delarivière Manley's *Lucius, the First Christian King of Britain* (1717), that a tragic writer looking for success should 'Write for the Heroes in the Pit, a Rape', a telling indication that these sexually-violent displays were the particular favourites of the rowdiest, mostly male group of viewers sitting closest to the stage.[33]

In fact, even though tragic rape scenes of this era were figured as unambiguous violations that were enacted against the woman's will, we must remember that rape was often spoken of as something that women only pretended to abhor, but which they actually enjoyed. John Dennis betrays this attitude, for instance, when he asserts that,

> Rape is the peculiar Barbarity of our *English* Stage ... a Rape in Tragedy is a Panegyrick upon the Sex: For there the Woman has all the Advantage of the Man. For she is suppos'd to remain innocent, and to be pleas'd without her Consent; while the Man, who is accounted a damn'd Villain, proclaims the Power of Female Charms, which have the Force to drive him to so horrid a Violence.[34]

Rape, in this view, is understood as a favour to women. In fact, the sentiment that a partner's resistance is sexually enticing is one that is even shared, at times, by female characters, as in Manley's *The Royal Mishchief*. Manley's heroine, Homais, describes her desire as follows:

> No more expostulate a growing flame,
> More than Ambition bold, than anger fierce,
> Nor can but with possession be abas'd.
> My Life, my Soul, my All, is fixt upon Enjoyment,
> Resistance but augments desire:
> If thou wouldst live threaten no more despair,
> I've nam'd the Goal, lend me thy aid to reach it.[35]

Thus, viewers may have, at once, pitied a tragic heroine for enduring a horrid violation, and they may have enjoyed the thought of a sexual encounter that was not, in every scenario, thought to be so unwelcome.[36] When one couples the highly-sexualized content of tragic rape scenes with the mainstream belief that rape was in no way a perverse or deviant desire, one can see the erotic potential of these sexually-violent displays.

Evading Censorship

Even though tragic rape scenes clearly capitalized on the sexual interests of audience members, these scenes were rarely explicitly described, by viewers and critics of the era, as lewd or inappropriate erotic displays. In fact, contemporary writing reveals that dramatic rape was in no way thought to be an aesthetically or morally off-limits subject. While many viewers today interpret films containing rape scenes as visually-disturbing and even offensive, during the Restoration and early eighteenth century, such displays were not considered lewd or inappropriate. In fact, perhaps the most surprising reaction to these scenes from the perspective of modern-day readers, is that they were considered *beautiful* by their original audiences.

One indication of the 'beauty' associated with sexual violence in tragedy comes from *Thesaurus Dramaticus*, a 1724 collection of the most 'celebrated' and 'beauti[ful]' passages in English dramatic history. Remarkably, this collection devotes an entire thematic section to beautiful passages on 'rape'. The segment on 'rape' is significant for both its length and its content. This section is one of the largest of the entire collection: of the 474 themed categories in this text, only twenty-four of them garner longer entries than does 'rape'. In a text designed to 'delight' readers of taste and 'instruct' aspiring writers, it is significant that these brutal dramatic displays garnered such a prominent position.[37]

Yet, even more remarkable than the prevalence of passages on 'rape' in *Thesaurus Dramaticus* is the fact that most of the cited passages actually condone sexual violence, portraying rape in a pleasurable and/or praiseworthy light. Some of these quotations, such as one from Rochester's *Valentinian*, favourably associate sexual violence with masculinity and power:

> 'Tis nobler, like a Lion, to invade
> Where Appetite directs, and seize my Prey,
> Than to wait tamely, like a begging Dog,
> Till dull Consent throws out the Scraps of Love.[38]

Others, including a passage from Joseph Addison's *Cato* (1713), describe the pleasure a man derives from raping a woman:

> I Long to clasp that haughty Maid,
> And bend her stubborn Beauty to my Passion.
> How will my Bosom swell with anxious Joy,
> When I behold her struggling in my Arms.[39]

Still another, from Dryden's *The Rival Ladies* (1664), excuses rape as something that women secretly desire:

> AND Women pardon Force, because they find
> The Violence of Love is still most kind:
> Just like the Plots of well-built Comedies,
> Which then please most, when they do surprize.[40]

In fact, of the twelve quotations categorized under 'rape', an astonishing seven portray sexual violence in an unambiguously positive way.[41] The surprising presence of these pro-rape sentiments in this book of 'beautiful' passages indicates that rape scenes were viewed as part of a 'high' art form, and that they were not understood as offensive or meriting censorship.

Even Jeremy Collier, who lambasts the indecency of so many sexual expressions and displays on the stage, never once complains about rape scenes. In fact, Collier's only reference to dramatic rape at all, in his 288-page treatise, *A Short View of the Immorality and Profaneness of the English Stage* (1698), lies in a reference to Chærea's rape of a virgin (Pamphila) in Terence's *The Eunuch*. Instead of castigating this sexual and violent dramatic event, however, Collier discusses Chærea's rape as a praiseworthy example of how Terence kept his heroine properly silent, even after she had endured a great wrong. Collier writes,

> The Virgin injured by *Chærea* does nothing but weep, and won't so much as speak her misfortune to the Women. But Comedy is strangly [sic] improved since that time; for Dalinda [in *Love's Triumph*] has a great deal more Courage, tho' the loss of her Virtue was her own Fault.[42]

Nowhere does Collier explicitly disapprove of rape on the English stage, and he gives his contemporaries no reason to think that they should censor these depictions. Similarly, James Wright, in his complaints about the English stage in *Country Conversations* (1694), overlooks depictions of sexual violence altogether, claiming that even though lewd speech had taken over English drama, inappropriate *actions* had not yet been featured on the stage, 'They [English playwrights] have not been so Bold as yet (what it may come to in time, I know not) to Represent Obscene Actions on the Stage'.[43] By the time Wright published this comment in 1694, over twenty-five serious plays containing rape and/or attempted rape had been performed on the London stage since the theatres were reopened in 1660 – another indication that sexual violence was not understood as offensive and obscene at that time.

As puzzling as it may seem for Restoration and eighteenth-century writers and critics to overlook what appear to be erotically-charged displays of sexual violence, these reactions are compatible with contemporary ideologies towards female sexuality and censorship. We must remember that even though Collier and others complained about sexual displays on the stage, they were not offended by all forms of sexual content equally. What provoked these critics was when lost female virtue was shown and advocated: displays/discussions of nudity, violence and sex were almost entirely inoffensive in comparison with laudatory displays/discussions of 'whores'. And because tragic rape victims were, by definition, pristinely chaste and virtuous (any less-than-chaste heroine would be classified as 'seduced' rather than 'raped'), such rape scenes in no way displayed unchaste and loose heroines, nor did they advocate the loss of chastity. Tragic rape scenes were, under this view, the antithesis of the offensive content that bothered so many critics during the Restoration and eighteenth century.

Thus, even though rape scenes were almost certainly sexually exciting to many viewers, these scenes warranted neither complaint nor disapproval. In fact, one of the most successful qualities of rape scenes may have been their ability to proffer and conceal sexual content simultaneously. As Charles Bernheimer points out, sexually-titillating visual art that commodifies the female body 'is dependent on an ideological cover-up: the nude body is never overtly styled as a body for sale and imaginary possession'.[44] Rape scenes would have provided just this sort of complex arrangement, where enticingly sexual scenes were offered in a way that could never be accused of indecency.

Almost certainly, then, rape scenes did sexually excite many Restoration and early eighteenth-century viewers. First, we know that similar displays of sexual violence were depicted in pornographic texts from the period, indicating a market for erotically-charged displays of rape. Equally important, the staging of tragic rape scenes at this time capitalized on powerful sexual motifs from contemporary erotica and pornography. Secondly, we know that the desire to rape a woman was considered natural and commonplace, rather than perverse and disturbing. This ideology towards rape would have made viewers far more likely to indulge in fantasies of sexual violence, than they would have been if rape were solely associated with deviant desires and perverse brutality. Lastly, tragic depictions and descriptions of rape were considered beautiful and aesthetically-pleasing by their original audiences. Thus, even though these scenes probably titillated many viewers, they were not labelled licentious because they did not display culpably-sexual heroines. Ultimately, tragic depictions of rape during this era may have owed a great part of their success to the fact that they could sexually excite viewers without being blamed for doing so.

6 VIOLENTLY EROTIC: REPRESENTING RAPE IN RESTORATION DRAMA

Ann Marie Byrd

The Actress emerged on the English stage in 1660, much to the delight of Restoration audiences. Elizabeth Barry, Anne Bracegirdle and Nell Gwynn achieved great fame, and each specialized, for the most part, in playing a particular kind of role, either tragic or comedic. Dramatists began writing larger roles for women, because for the first time they were not played by boys, rather by seasoned actresses who could handle the complexity and difficulty of dramatic roles, poetic language and vast emotional range. In this sense, the actress shaped the drama of the period.

Restoration audiences were thrilled by seeing women on stage, and actresses were greatly admired for their beauty, charms and many talents. For the audience, she was the object of desire, both powerful and vulnerable – but ultimately irresistible. The audience paid to see them perform, so in a sense they became a public commodity. Even their seemingly private sexual lives were often public, such as the king's long-term affair with Nell Gwynn, as well as Elizabeth Barry's liaison with the second Earl of Rochester. Breeches roles dressed the women in tight trousers, which allowed (presumably) male audience members to admire (and desire) the lovely shape of the women's legs, which were normally otherwise concealed underneath skirts. But breeches roles also allowed a voyeuristic experience for the women in the audience: for a few hours on the stage, women watched actresses play men, which entailed gaining all his freedom, prowess and powers. Potential for actresses to improvise must have been endless. Both men and women in the audience revelled in the delight of sexual ambiguity, mistaken identity and erotic tensions.

The most important way in which playwrights brought visual focus to the actress and the display of her body was through scenes of seduction, ravishment and rape. During the English Restoration, representations of forced seduction were immensely popular with theatrical audiences, and became so prevalent that John Dennis, in his late seventeenth-century tract, refers to them as a 'peculiar barbarity of the English Stage'.[1] Of course, staging scenes of sexual violence was not a unique creation by Restoration playwrights. Scenes of this nature have historical grounding reaching back to the ancient Greeks and Shakespeare. However, the high instance of rape and/or attempted rape during the Restoration is remarkable, and in the course of my research, I have identified at least thirty-five works by male and female playwrights between 1660 and 1700 that include scenes of erotic assault. Each of the major forms of drama in the Restoration – namely comedy of manners, comedy of intrigue, tragedy and she-tragedy – treat ravishment and/or rape differently, with great variety in tone and style. However, they all share a similar characteristic, namely, the focus on the body of the actress.

Comedy of Manners

Restoration theatre comes in many genres, but the most popular and enduring in the history of theatre is the comedy of manners. Comedy of manners is centrally concerned with the social games played by the upper classes, emphasizing fashion, manners, reputation, appearances, repartee and seduction. The tone is sharply cynical and bitingly comic; the women are cruel in their actions towards other women, and the men brutal in their relentless sexual pursuit of other men's wives. The result is delightful, and the plays of dramatists such as William Wycherley and William Congreve are frequently produced by the finest of acting companies today. In comedy of manners, seldom do the games played by men against women result in harm, particularly in terms of violence against women. Rather, the tone is playful, like a game of sexual cat and mouse.

For example, John Vanbrugh's *The Relapse* (1698) stages a scene between Loveless and Berinthia in which they carefully plot to busy their partners, Amanda and Worthy, in a game of cards while they steal away for a secret interlude.[2] Berinthia is already in the chamber when Loveless enters, 'cautiously in the dark', making his way across a stage fully lit, but moving and gesturing in such a way to indicate the presumed darkness.[3] The result is delightfully comic and it sets the tone for the upcoming scene of seduction. Far from a rape, the scene is a hilarious mockery of sexuality and female resistance.

> LOVE. My dear, charming Angel, let us make good use of our time.
> BERIN. Heaven, what do you mean?
> LOVE. What do you think I mean?
> BERIN. I don't know.
> LOVE. I'll show you.
> BERIN. You may as well tell me.
> LOVE. No, that wou'd make you blush worse than t'other.
> BERIN. Why, do you intend to make me blush? ...
> LOVE. Come into the Closet, Madam, there Moon shine upon the Couch.
> BERIN. Nay, never pull for I will not go.
> LOVE. Then you must be carried.
>
> [Carrying her.]

BERIN.	Help, help, I'm ravished, ruin'd, undone. O Lord, I shall never be able to bear it.[4]

If any doubt remains of Berinthia's compliance, the scene concludes with the famous clincher 'Help, help, I'm ravished, ruin'd, undone ... I shall never be able to bear it' uttered 'very softly'.[5] In comedy of manners, women fain resistance and act the part of victim – and enjoy the seduction as much as the men seducing them.

This mockery prevails throughout the comedy of manners genre. For example, Congreve's *Love for Love* (1695) is centrally concerned with male and female role-playing and the absurdity of upper-class behaviours and rituals. In a scene between Miss Prue, a naïve country girl, and Mr Tattle, a 'half-witted' gentleman, Tattle educates Prue on the proper behaviour for a well-bred lady in matters of seduction. Most relevant to this study is Tattle's instruction that Prue should resist his advances, even if she desires him. He tells her 'All well-bred persons lie ... Your words must contradict your thoughts, but your actions may contradict your words'.[6] To test her, Tattle asks, 'And won't you show me, pretty Miss, where your bed-chamber is?' to which she replies, 'No, indeed won't I. But I'll run there, and hide myself from you behind the curtains'.[7] Thru this scene, Prue learns compliance to male violence in a sexual scenario. The physicality of the scene is very specific, and both of their actions are highly detailed through the dialogue. Tattle instructs that she should run away, hold the door closed to keep him out of the bed-chamber, be knocked down and be kept from crying out despite her inclination to do so. In a sense she is being trained to accept the reality of rape; i.e., that male force and female resistance are a necessary coupling and an integral part of upper-class seduction. Her eager acceptance to play the role in which she has been cast is both comic and disturbing.

Wycherley's *The Plain Dealer* (1676) includes an attempted rape scene which is comic in that the Lady Fidelia cross-dresses as a man when she first encounters Vernish. To prove she is a woman, the stage direction actually says that he 'feels her breasts', which would have shocked the audience with its inappropriate and somewhat graphic nature. He pulls her towards him and says,

VERNISH.	Come, there is a bed within, the proper rack for Lovers; and if you are a woman, there you can keep no secrets, you'll tell me there all unasked. [Thrusts her in a room, and locks the door.] Stay there my prisoner; you have a short reprieve. I'll fetch the gold and that she can't resist; For with a full hand 'tis we ravish best.[8]

The metaphor is significant, for the bed would be like a torture rack – and it is at this point that the tone of the scene changes from darkly comic to somewhat ominous. However, in the end no harm is committed, for Fidelia manages to escape out the window after his departure. Like similar scenes from the comedy of manners genre, the tone is mocking and the end result is more comic than tragic.

Tragicomedy of Intrigue

Aphra Behn, well known as the first female professional writer, and the most prolific female dramatist of the English Restoration, championed tragicomedy of intrigue. As the name implies, as a genre, tragicomedy of intrigue is an amalgam of dramatic forms, bringing together comic themes and complex plots which focus on romantic love or intrigue. Unlike comedy of manners, the subject matter can suddenly become quite serious, including life-threatening attacks upon the hero or heroine and acts of sexual violence – characteristics that could be attributed to the influence of Spanish Golden Age drama. In some of Behn's tragicomedies, heroines suffer rape and attempted rape; however, the genre still allows for happy endings, with the heroines' honour redeemed through marriage.

One of Behn's finest plays, *The City Heiress* (1682), is provocative and entertaining with fast-paced action, witty dialogue and beautifully written verse passages. The plot involves Lady Galliard, a rich widow, who is in love with the womanizing rake hero, Tom Wilding. Lady Galliard also suffers the unwanted advances of Sir Charles Meriwill, who pursues her relentlessly. Lady Galliard is in a unique position as a widow, for she has economic power and a privileged inheritance from her late husband, and therefore she is sought out by the men in the play for both her charms and her wealth – but her heart is set on Tom Wilding, and after much wooing, she surrenders to him. However, moments after they have consummated their love, a drunk and jealous Sir Charles Meriwill arrives at the door. Fearful that her indiscretion will be discovered, she sends away Wilding. With no one to protect her, Meriwill becomes a verifiable threat. In an effort to keep him at bay, Lady Galliard tries to get Meriwill out of her house by claiming that this is her evening time for prayer, to which Meriwill proclaims that she should instead get down on her knees in submission to him, an act that all at once becomes both sexual and holy in the context of the scene. He claims that he is the answer to her prayers, and insists that she swears she will marry him the very next morning. Lady Galliard consistently resists, but Meriwill is utterly determined to bed her and wed her:

> MERIWILL. Why I am obstinately bent to ravish thee, thou hypocritical Widow, Make thee mine by force ... Come, Widow, let's to bed ... No Frowning; for by this dear night, 'tis charity, care of your Reputation, Widow: and therefore I am resolv'd nobody shall lie with you but myself ... and swear me heartily as God shall judge your soul ... to marry me tomorrow.[9]

As the scene progresses, Meriwill's use of force intensifies, as indicated through the stage directions. He pulls her, she struggles against him, flings herself from his grasp, but ultimately he begins removing his clothing right in front of her eyes, insisting that she marry him. The audience would have been as shocked by his undressing as Lady Galliard. She is truly trapped like a fish in a net, and he says to her: 'You're caught, struggle and flounder as you please, Sweetheart, you'll but entangle more; let me alone to tickle your Gills'.[10] Lady Galliard, desperately wishing him gone and believing they are alone, swears she will marry him. Unfortunately, Sir Anthony has been leering at them and witnesses her promise, resulting in a binding verbal contract.

> MERIWILL. Gad, I'll not leave her now, till she is mine
> Then keep her so by constant consummation.
> Let Man a God do his, I'll do my part,
> In spight of all her fickleness and art;
> There's one sure way to fix a Widow's heart.[11]

The implication is that Meriwill intends to rape her not once, but repeatedly until she surrenders utterly, both physically and emotionally. The next day, when her true love, Tom Wilding, arrives at the door, he is greeted by Meriwill, who states her predicament most clearly:

> MERIWILL. Now for a Struggle betwixt your Love and Honour!
> Yes, here's the Bar to all my happiness, you would be left to the wide world and love, to infamy, to scandal and to Wilding; But I have too much Honour in my passion to let you loose to ruin: Consider and be wife.
> GALLIARD. Oh, he has toucht my Heart too sensibly.
> Love at last has vanquished me.
> Here, be as happy as a Wife can make ye.
> One last look more, and then – be gone, fond Love. [*Sighing and looking on Wilding and giving Sir Meriwill her hand.*][12]

In the end, Lady Galliard chooses to marry Meriwill, but she does so with regret and undying love for Wilding. For modern audiences, the ending is a hard sell, for by contemporary standards, she is marrying her rapist. However, for Restoration audiences, the reinstatement of her honour through her allegiance to Meriwill provides a (somewhat) happy ending and necessary closure.

Other writers from the period such as John Crowne and John Dryden also utilized the intrigue genre to stage attempted rape, but the tone is more light-hearted than the style exhibited by Behn. In Crowne's *City Politiques* (1688) the ladies are loose, worldly women, a status that makes them less likely to be perceived as victims in a scene of sexual assault; they are knowing opponents in a sport they have already mastered. For example, the scene between Artall and Lucinda is a spirited one in which he chases her round the stage, and she is secretly delighted to be pursued. Lucinda alternately squeals for help and declares her attraction to her 'attacker'.

LUCINDA.	I am betrayed! Drawn into a snare.
	But tis a sweet one (*Aside*). Help! Help! Help!
ARTALL.	I need no help my Dear.
LUCINDA.	But I do, help! Help! Help!
	Oh, tis a lovely gentlemen (*aside*). Help! Help!
	Tis a delicate gentleman (*aside*). Help! Help!
ARTALL.	Why do you call so loud? I can help you to what you Want.
LUCINDA.	Help! Help! Will you force me?
	I can't resist him (*aside*). Help! Help!
ARTALL.	All this is to no purpose.
LUCINDA.	Oh fie upon you, what a man you are?
	A handsome man I mean (*aside*). I am out of breath
	With striving. Help! Help! Oh my heart pants! Help! Help!
	[*Artall carries her off.*][13]

Unlike Behn, Crowne stages a pretend rape, and the heroine is only playing the part of victim. Similarly, in Dryden's *Sir Martin Marall* (1677), Lord Dartmouth and Mrs Christian are both sexually experienced, but are merely pretending to be a fair maiden and a persistent lover. Their scene, on paper, reads as if it is an attempted rape; however, Mrs Christian has been coached by Lady Dupe to feign resistance, so in performance, the final result is comedic.

The scene begins with Lord Dartmouth squeezing Mrs Christian's hand much too hard, presumably 'forcing' her to touch him:

CHRIST.	Why do you crush it so? Nay now you hurt me, nay – if you squeeze it ne're so hard – there's nothing to come out on't – fly – is this loving one – what makes you take your breath so short?
DART.	The devil take me if I can answer her a word, all my Senses are quite imploy'd another way.
CHRIST.	Ne'er stir my lord, I must cry out.
DART.	Then I must stop your mouth – this Ruby for a Kiss – That is but one Ruby for another.
CHRIST.	This is worse and worse ... Do you hear, my Aunt calls – let me go my Lord. [*Gets from him.*][14]

Both Crowne's and Dryden's scenes are extraordinarily physical: the first is staged as a chase scene and the second a physical struggle with the actress being squeezed, restrained and kissed (seemingly) against her will. The actress's body is the site of violation, but in these two intrigue comedies, the violation ultimately causes no harm. The genre is unique in that it allows for the staging of attempted rape in a variety of ways, but the ending remains a happy one.

Restoration Tragedy

Serious drama of the Restoration can be classified in a variety of categories, including heroic tragedy, which celebrates aggressively masculine heroes and their great deeds; Restoration tragedy, which is formal and serious with an elegant neoclassical style; pathetic tragedy, with subject matters of love and domestic concerns; and she-tragedy, which focuses on the sufferings of virtuous, innocent women in jeopardy.

Sexual violence exists in all forms of serious Restoration drama with the most dire of consequences, but she-tragedies often use the rape of an innocent virgin as the central focus of the drama. Thomas Otway's *Venice Preserved* (1682) is an early form of she-tragedy, and a forerunner of sentimental drama, and it includes a verbal retelling of attempted rape. Otway's description is remarkable in that both the victim, Belvidera, and her husband, Jaffeir, provide separate retellings of the assault in mirror scenes. Belvidera describes the attempted rape by Renault, her husband's friend, as a terrifying experience.

> BELVID. But that vile wretch approached me; loose, unbuttoned,
> Ready for violation. Then my heart
> Throbbed with its fears. Oh, how I wept and sighed,
> And shrunk and trembled; wished in vain for him
> That should protect me. Thou, alas were gone …
> He drew the hideous dagger forth thou gav'st him,
> And with upbraiding smile he said, 'Behold it;
> This is the pledge of a false husband's love'.
> And in my arms then pressed, and clasped me;
> But with my cries I scared his coward heart,
> Till he withdrew and muttered vows to hell.[15]

Belvidera's husband, Jaffeir, downplays the incident, for in the midst of political turmoil and public deceptions, he feels his life unravelling. Although he is concerned for his wife, he is preoccupied with matters of state. The attempted rape leads to a series of events that ultimately cause the death of his friend Pierre, Jaffeir's suicide and Belividera's madness and death, but the assault in this play is by no means the focus of the plot.

Otway's description of attempted rape is tame compared with those found in many of the she-tragedies of the period, for Belvidera manages to escape her attacker and go on to tell her tale. But this famous tragedy sets a standard that adheres to neoclassical rules and that refrains from showing violence on stage. As in ancient Greek theatre, Restoration plays described violence in detail, but refrained from showing such acts. That being said, it was acceptable for a woman to be dragged off-stage by her attacker and for the audience to hear her horrified, tortured screams from the wings of the theatre. Furthermore, the ravished virgin was usually displayed for the audience moments after the attack – the victimized female with her clothing undone to reveal her bare breasts, torn clothing and dishevelled hair, sometimes gagged and bound, sometimes bloody. The combination of violence, eroticism and suffering gave audiences a sexual jolt that they found both horrifying and irresistible.

Both John Wilmot, the Earl of Rochester's *Valentinian* (1685) and Mary Griffith Pix's *Ibrahim* (1696) revolve around plots of an evil emperor who rapes a beautiful woman as an abuse of his power. In tragedies such as these, rape can be interpreted as a metaphor for political tyranny in general, and audiences during the Restoration would have established associations between topical political turmoil and the corruption being played out on-stage. Unfortunately (or not) the political nuances and connections that may have been powerfully felt by Restoration audiences are mostly lost on contemporary audiences – but the general suffering of the female characters still resonates.

Rochester adapted *Valentinian or Lucinda's Rape* from an earlier Jacobean revenge tragedy by John Fletcher. True to the form of she-tragedy, Rochester highlights Lucinda's tragic demise. Valentinian, the emperor of Rome, is in love with Lucinda, wife of the Roman general, Maximus; but despite Valentinian's pressure on her to obey his wishes and become his lover, she remains steadfast in her loyalty to her husband. Throughout the play, the emperor manages to meet with her privately, trying to flatter her, but eventually his words fail. He employs her waiting women to try to convince her, but finally relies on force. He chooses to abduct her and rape her in his chamber while he stages a play within a play – *The Rape of Lucrece* – to be enacted simultaneously so 'if by chance odd noises should be heard, / As women's shrieks or so, say tis a play'.[16]

As the violation occurs, the servant Lycinius describes the sound that he hears coming from the bed-chamber. Despite the performance of *The Rape of Lucrece*, as well as the six dancing masters who attempt to distract the audience with their grotesque ballet, Lucinda's cries are still heard in the distance.

> LYCINIUS. Bless me! The Loud shrieks and horrid out cries
> Of the poor Lady! Ravishing d'ye call it?
> She roars as if she were upon the rack!
> Tis strange there shou'd be such a difference
> Betwixt half ravishing which most women Love
> And thorough force which takes away all Blame
> And should be therefore welcome to the virtuous.[17]

The screaming that Lycinius hears would have also been heard by the audience, allowing them to share in her suffering and terror. Following the rape, the scene opens with Lucinda 'newly unbound by the Emperor'.[18] His first words to her are to save her honour and tell no one what has happened, to which she replies, 'As long as there is Life in this Body, / And Breath to give me words, I'll cry for Justice'.[19] She pleads to him to kill her, for she is now 'Ceasar's whore', but her very pleading again arouses his desire and he tells her he would 'do it again ... I would attempt it. You are so excellent and made to ravish, there were no pleasure in you else'.[20] Lucinda's destruction is so complete that she even loses her faith in God:

> Why then I see there is no God – but Power,
> Nor Vertue now alive that cares for us,
> But what is either lame or sensual;
> How had I been thus wretched else.[21]

In the end, the emperor leaves her and she finds her husband, Maximus. She reveals what has happened, and he agrees that she has been 'made whore of' and that her resolve to die is 'well-considered'.[22] Her final words imply that her only victory is that the emperor will have to live without her, left only with 'robes to mourn in, and my sad ashes'.[23] After Lucinda dies, Maximus confronts Valentinian, only to find that he has no shame for his actions. He says: 'Would the Gods raise Lucinda from the grave / And fetter thee but while I might enjoy her / Before thy face I'd ravish her again'.[24] Valentinian is the embodiment of pure evil, which in turn amplifies Lucinda's victimization; in turn, the audience would have felt powerful feelings of both hatred and pity.

Pix's *Ibrahim, the Thirteenth Emperor of the Turks* shares a similar plot line to *Valentinian*, in that it demonstrates the abuse of political power leading to sexual violence. Pix (1666–1709) was one of the triumvirates of female playwrights including Catherine Trotter and Delarivière Manley who took the English theatrical world by storm. The plot concerns the rape of the virginal Morena by the emperor. Although he has sated himself with twenty virgins earlier in the night, he is encouraged by Sheker to seduce Morena. Once in his bedchamber, he threatens her at knifepoint and she is terrified at the prospect of being either murdered or raped. In a state of panic, she 'catches hold of the Sultan's naked scimitar and draws it through her hands'.[25] Suddenly, she feels the pain of the knife cutting her hands and screams, showing her bloody palms to the audience who share in her pain and fear. The playwright may not be able to show rape on the stage, but the knife serves as a phallic image. Morena holds up her hands to the emperor and says 'are these hands fit to clasp thee? Judge by this / my resolution – death has a / thousand doors'.[26] Although Morena thinks her actions will show her resistance to Ibrahim and set him off course, the result is precisely the opposite. Her resistance inflames his passion:

> I am all on fire!
> Drag her to yond Apartment
> I'll rifle her sweets, till sense is fully cloy'd;
> Then take my turn to scorn what I've enjoy'd.[27]

Unlike Valentinian, who promises to love Lucinda after he ravishes her, Ibrahim plans to rape Morena then scorn and reject her for her impurity.

The rape scene happens off-stage, and a description is provided by the Mufti, sparing no detail of blood and gore as the emperor tears out her hair and rapes her even after she loses consciousness.

> MUFTI   Her prayers, her tears, her cries,
> Her wounding supplication all in vain,
> Her dear hands in the conflict cut and mangled,
> Dying her white Arms in Crimson Gore,
> The savage Ravisher twisting his
> Hands in the lovely Tresses of her hair,
> Tearing it by the smarting Root,
> Fixing her, by that upon the ground:
> Then – (horror upon horror!)
> On her breathless body perpetrated the fact.[28]

When Morena emerges again later in the play, dressed in virgin white robes, she has lost her innocence and imagines that her body is contaminated and corrupt. The violation she has suffered has passed from her body into her spirit: 'My soul grows weary of its polluted cage, / And longs to wing the upper air'.[29] In her despair she drinks poison and kills herself as her 'dishonor rings through the universe', leaving behind her father and her fiancée weeping over her body draped in white.[30]

Women who suffer rape in Restoration tragedy die, either by the man who rapes them or by their own hand. More often than not, the heroine kills herself, taking poison (such as in Pix's *Ibrahim*, Otway's *The Orphan* and Crowne's *Caligula*), stabbing herself (Nicholas Brady's *The Rape* and Nicholas Rowe's *The Fair Penitent*), or even starving herself to death (John Dryden's *Amboyna*). Regardless of the method by which the heroine chooses to die, the excruciatingly painful expression of her self-loathing is uttered in a monologue before her death, a speech designed to move the audience to tears. This is particularly pronounced in Rowe's *The Fair Penitent* (1632) and Brady's *The Rape* (1692).

Brady's *The Rape* is an ideal example of how thrilling and exciting Restoration tragedy in the latter part of the Restoration could be. Although the story is titled *The Rape*, the complex plot includes other story lines beyond the assault, with a great deal of the action revolving around the concealed (and then revealed) identities of the prince and princess. The style of Brady's play is similar to Behn's tragicomedies of intrigue, with spirited, fast-paced action, romantic intrigues, threats to honour and a good deal of sword fighting. Also as in Behn's works, the play ends (somewhat) happily, for even though the pitiful Eurione commits suicide, the prince and princess get married and there is a general feeling of celebration and resolution. The title of the play states that it is a tragedy; however, like many late Restoration plays and tragic adaptations during this period, the ending has been shaped to provide a satisfying closure, presumably to please the audience. *The Rape*, overall, does not adhere to neoclassical unities, instead mixing genres, including multiple sub-plots and shocking the audience with the gender reversal of the prince and princess.

The play begins with a power struggle between the king and Genselarick, the king's nephew who seeks the throne. It is revealed that the (very effeminate) king's son, Agilmond, is to marry the captive princess Eurione; however, Genselarick wants her for himself and plans to rape her and blame the act on Agilmond. Unlike many other plays from the period, which seldom explore the psychological interiority of the rapist, Brady's play digs deeply into Genselarick's motivations. His friend Almeric asks him why raping women is appealing: 'My Lord, your joys have made you wanton, but methinks 'tis strange / That *pleasure forced* should give such vast delight', to which Genselarick replies: 'I hate a tedious Siege, but love to Storm'.[31] Genselarick has no interest in courtship and marriage; instead, taking by 'Storm' gives him the pleasure he desires. His monologues before and after the rape provide the audience with some of the most revealing lines from the Restoration period regarding rape and desire:

> GENSELARICK. I must enjoy Eurione, or die;
> This Night, the Eve of all my destined Sorrows,
> Shall make me blest, and revel in full Joys ...
> Shrouded from all eyes [I will]
> Expect her coming, seize the trembling Prey
> And rifle all the Treasure of her Beauty:
> Then if the Prince feasts on her Sweets tomorrow,
> He shall have but the leavings of my Riot ...
> Methink I see already
> Her dying Looks, her seeming faint Resistance,
> And feel the mighty Transport of hot Love![32]

Genselarick equates the value of his sexual desire with the value of his very life, and attempts to convince himself that his cruel, sinful actions are his blessed destiny. His description is an articulation of his rape fantasy as he imagines her trembling in fear, like a terrified animal. This image makes him feel powerful, and dehumanizes Eurione. The phrase 'rifle the treasures' or 'rifle her sweets' is used repeatedly throughout the play as a rape metaphor.[33] Since Genselarick is a warrior, a conqueror and a Pirate – his talk of seizure, rifling and treasure are his language of violence – she is his treasure chest. He also compares her to delicious food that he alone will be able to consume. His final revenge against the king is knowing that he has tasted Eurione's sweets before her wedding night; the prince will only have the leftovers that he has discarded on the metaphorical table. Finally, he again imagines that when he ravishes her, she will desire him in return, and that her resistance will be 'seeming faint', which again absolves him of blame. In his mind, she will pretend to resist, becoming like an actress on the stage, playing a sexual role just for him – not unlike a hired prostitute. The image is more than he can take, and he feels himself on the brink of orgasm, readying himself for the 'transport of hot love'.[34]

Only moments after Genselarick's monologue, the rape happens in the garden, unseen or heard by the audience. Eurione is discovered by her sister, bound to a tree and gagged, with her hair dishevelled. A dagger lies beside her. According to the acting and staging conventions of the period and the genre, it is likely that her clothing was torn, exposing her bare breasts and her legs, which would have been both shocking and titillating for the audience. She says:

> EURIONE. Alas! Here is she that was Eurione;
> Now she is nothing but a loathsome Leprosie,
> Which spread all over the Gothish Royal Blood,
> Infects the Noble race.
> Stand off, Valdaura,
> And come not near me; I am contagious sure,
> And all chaste hands will blister that but touch me.
> Were all the Gods that succor Innocence,
> Deaf to my Cries, and blind to all my Wrongs?
> That no relenting Power would send one Bolt
> To strike me dead, and save my Ravished honor?[35]

Eurione compares her ravished body to the diseased condition of a leper who has become disfigured, repellent and cast-out by society. Calling herself 'contagious', her metaphorical imagery reveals her fear of venereal disease that could tarnish all the royal blood and 'infect' the royal lineage; she believes her contaminated body would 'blister' even the most chaste of hands.[36] The only solution she imagines is death, which would save her honour. She discovers the knife lying next to her, but is prevented by Valdaura. Her sister (who is actually a young man disguised as a woman) swears revenge and takes up the dagger saying: 'My thoughts shall never know a moment's peace / Till I have drenched this Weapon in the Blood / That warms his lustful heart'.[37] Although at this point Valdaura is dressed as a woman, she speaks a man's act of bloody revenge, which foreshadows her change in gender. When Genselarick is finally discovered as the rapist at the end of the play, Valdaura (now Ambiomer) acts out his revenge and kills Genselarick. Eurione's honour is redeemed, and it seems that she might have her happy ending. Instead, she kills herself to end her suffering. Taking up the knife, covered in Genselarick's blood she says:

> I see the friendly means to end my Sorrow,
> And make my Fame Immortal;
> But shall I mix my Blood with such a Villain's?
> Stained and polluted as it is, tis fit
> To mingle with no other.[38]

All those around her mourn her death, but celebrate her suicidal act: 'Eurione has gained a Fame by dying, / Which the most happy life may envy'.[39] Not a moment later, the prince (Ambiomer, previously the lady Valdaura) is betrothed to Elismonda (previously Prince Agilmond), and the country is again united. In a truly peculiar ending, the tragedy ends happily – and perhaps signifies the churnings of the upcoming theatrical shift to the happy endings that were to become popular and prevalent in the bourgeois tragedy of the eighteenth century.

Rowe's *The Fair Penitent* also seems to be a bridge between high and mighty Restoration tragedy and more middle-class, domestic dramas, particularly in terms of characterization. *The Fair Penitent* was one of the most popular she-tragedies of the early eighteenth century, with tremendous longevity. *The Fair Penitent* is the story of a poor decision made by a beautiful young girl that results in widespread, disastrous consequences. However, although the subject matter and characters were perhaps more relatable and accessible to Restoration audiences, the language remains very elevated. The action involves a good deal of fighting and violence, ending in the suffering and death of the principal characters – precisely the kind of play that thrilled and engaged audiences in the early eighteenth century.

The plot concerns the lovely Calista and her unfortunate relationship with Lothario, a heartless libertine, who seduces her, then rejects her. Desperate to preserve her honour, she agrees to marry Altamont, who is Lothario's enemy. When her deception is revealed to Altamont, her fiancée must fight to defend her honour. As the two men engage each other, they agree to fight to the death to win Calista. Lothario is fatally wounded. Horror stricken, Calista cries out the wildly dramatic and emotional line: 'Distraction! Fury! Sorrow! Shame! And Death!', and then offers to kill herself.[40] Her father Sciolto, in despair over her defiance, then picks up a dagger and tries to kill her, shouting

> It is enough! But I am slow to execute,
> And Justice lingers in my lazy hand;
> thus let me wipe dishonor from my name
> And cut thee from the earth, thou stain to goodness.[41]

Altamont saves Calista, even as she begs her father to kill her, then resolves to commit suicide. The final act is staged at a funeral with Lothario's body laid out on a bier. A bell tolls in the distance and Calista describes what she sees and hears: 'These solemn sounds, this Pomp of Horror, are fit to feed the frenzy in my soul; here's room for meditation even to madness'.[42] She is then in turn visited and berated by her father, her fiancée and Horatio. Just before her death by her own hand, she declares herself utterly ruined, and her body taken over by the disease that was her lust:

> CALISTA. Hide your fair heads in clouds, or I shall blast you,
> For I am all contagion, death and ruin,
> And nature sickens at me; rest, thou World,
> This parricide shall be thy plague no more;
> Thus, thus, I set thee free. [*Stabs herself*][43]

Overcome by grief, Altamont tries to kill himself, but is stopped by Horatio. Her father enters, injured, and dies after absolving Calista of her sins. The stage is truly littered with bodies, with only Altamont and Horatio still alive. The last lines of the play state the theme with utter clarity: 'If you would have the Nuptial Union last, / Let Virtue be the Bond that ties it fast'.[44]

Unlike earlier she-tragedies of the Restoration such as *Venice Preserved*, *Valentinian* and *Ibrahim*, *The Fair Penitent* focuses less on the violation of a virgin, and more on the resulting disgrace and dishonour that comes from a woman who defies patriarchal authority. Her suffering is caused by the desires and the passions of her heart. This is perhaps what audiences found most appealing: the story of young love that unfortunately results in disaster. In the Prologue to the play, Rowe elegantly informs the audience of his intentions in choosing to write about the common man:

> Long has the Fate of Kings and Empires been
> The common Business of the Tragic Scene,
> As if Misfortune made the Throne her Seat,
> And none could be unhappy but the Great.
> Therefore an humbler Theme our Author Chose,
> A melancholy Tale of private Woes;
> No Prince here lost Royalty bemoan,
> But you shall meet with Sorrows like your own.[45]

Rowe's prologue informs the audience that the suffering they see onstage is not unlike their own, and that in turn made the drama more relevant and personal. It was the emotional journey, the immorality, the violence and the redemption that audiences at the turn of the eighteenth century enjoyed.

At the core of this theatrical experience is the body of the actress, which was desired, objectified and pitied. For audiences, watching sexual violence, understanding the motivation of a rapist and seeing the suffering of a victimized woman is a voyeuristic experience, which according to Aristotelian definition allowed for an emotional catharsis, a purification or purgation of potentially dangerous emotions to be released. By watching suffering, they felt pity; by seeing destruction and violence, they learned moral lessons. The theatrical experience raised powerful emotions, and those emotions gave the audience pleasure – and they could not help but come back for more.

7 'A MOST OBEDIENT WIFE': PASSIVE RESISTANCE AND TORY POLITICS IN ELIZA HAYWOOD'S *A WIFE TO BE LETT*

Loring Pfeiffer

In her only comedy, *A Wife to Be Lett* (1723), Eliza Haywood lionizes a virtuous wife, centring the play on an upstanding woman who evades her husband's attempt to rent her out to another man. A role originally acted by Haywood herself, Mrs Graspall is celebrated throughout; indeed, this character's reputation literally precedes her – before Mrs. Graspall enters the stage, Gaylove, a new arrival in town, declares that he has heard that she 'bears the Bell from all the rest'.[1] Mrs Graspall's greedy husband, on the other hand, serves as the play's antagonist: from the trustworthy Courtly's early description of him as 'the most covetous miserable Wretch that ever was' to his eventual proposal that his wife sleep with another man, Mr Graspall is avaricious and unfeeling, his cold-hearted miserliness set in contrast to his wife's generosity.[2] Despite *A Wife to Be Lett*'s negative characterization of Mr Graspall, the play does not conclude with his wife rejecting his authority. Late in the text, Mrs Graspall does expose her husband's attempt at pandering, but she does not ultimately gain the upper hand in their marriage. On the contrary, Mrs Graspall ends the play by reasserting her husband's power over her, telling him that 'I ... shall ever make it my Study to prove a most obedient Wife'.[3]

Previous critics of *A Wife to Be Lett* have read this play as an outgrowth of Haywood's proto-feminism, understanding it as a critique of the patriarchal structure of marriage.[4] The play does highlight some of the potential problems of the conjugal relationship; however, Mrs Graspall's ready submission in its concluding moments represents a challenge to feminist interpretations. If *A Wife to Be Lett* is designed to criticize husbandly authority, why does Mrs Graspall's closing speech emphasize this character's desire to be 'obedient', particularly to a man whom the play has shown to be unworthy of her compliance? In this essay, I forward a partisan-political reading of *A Wife to Be Lett*. Recent scholarship has emphasized the role that Haywood's Tory politics played in shaping her early work.[5] Building on such criticism, I argue that *A Wife to Be*

Lett stages one of the central political conundrums confronted by Tories of the period: how can an obedient person resist? As Toni Bowers has shown, resistance presented an ideological challenge for early eighteenth-century Tories.[6] The party had long been defined by its commitment to political obedience, but over the course of the early eighteenth century, as Whigs curried favour with monarchs and achieved a majority in Parliament, Tories began to recognize the necessity of dissent. Members of the party struggled to come up with a coherent set of principles that would reflect their ideological roots in loyalism while also allowing them to move forward in an environment of Whig hegemony. *A Wife to Be Lett* stages the conflict between obedience and dissent: Mrs Graspall is torn between her obligation to her husband and her dedication to morality. Ultimately, Haywood's heroine manages this tension by passively resisting her husband's commands. Refusing Mr Graspall's injunction to sleep with another man while simultaneously remaining subservient to her husband, Mrs Graspall strikes a balance between loyalism and defiance, and in so doing becomes an exemplar for early eighteenth-century Tories.

In eighteenth-century England, representations of sexuality had clear political valences. Political writers had long legitimized models of governance by drawing upon the purportedly natural hierarchies of heterosexual relationships; indeed, for much of the early-modern period, the popular imagination had licensed the king's authority through an analogy that framed his right to rule as an extension of man's power as head of the household.[7] As Julia Rudolph has shown, sexual violence was also a source of many of the period's political analogies: several late seventeenth- and early eighteenth-century political texts make their points by referring to acts of sexual violence.[8] In *Observations upon Aristotles Politics* (1679), for instance, the Tory Robert Filmer supports monarchical government by forwarding a defence of Tarquin, arguing that Tarquin's son did not deserve to be punished for his rape of Lucrece. On the opposite side of the political spectrum, Gilbert Burnet's *An Enquiry into the Measures of Submission* (1689) defends Whigs' actions against James II by making a metaphor of rape, asserting that if soldiers 'from single Rapes and Murders, proceed to a rape upon all our Liberties, and a Destruction of the Nation … then it is plain, that there is such a Dissolution of the Government made, that there is not any one part of it left Sound and Entire'.[9]

Like other crimes of sexual violence, so wife pandering stages issues of consent and resistance, authority and subjection; as such, this act has clear political implications. In *A Wife to Be Lett*, Haywood underscores wife pandering's political resonance from Mr and Mrs Graspall's first conversation about it. Over the course of the pair's initial exchange, Mr Graspall repeatedly emphasizes the importance of wifely obedience. At the beginning of the couple's conversation, Mr Graspall reminds his wife of the legal obligations of marriage: 'You know,

Spouse, the Duty of a Husband is to love and provide for his Wife; and, in return, the Wife is oblig'd to obey the Commands, and study the Interest of her Husband'.[10] Clearly more concerned with Mrs Graspall's marital responsibilities than his own conjugal duties, Mr Graspall goes on, in his next line, to clarify his reasons for bringing up the wifely obligation 'to obey': 'I mention Obedience to a Husband ... that it being fresh in thy Memory, thou might'st not boggle at any thing which tends to the enriching thy Husband'.[11] In a move that hints at Mr Graspall's awareness of the impropriety of the proposal he is about to forward, this character once again reminds Mrs Graspall of the deference she owes him before he reveals his plot to sell her, reiterating 'that Obedience to a Husband ought to be the *Primum Mobile* in a Woman' as he thrusts into her hand the letter that makes clear his intention to rent her to Sir Harry Beaumont.[12]

Mr Graspall's multiple references to obedience in this sequence are revealing. The term 'obedience' was, of course, linked to marriage in this period: the wifely vow 'to obey' had been a part of the *English Book of Common Prayer* since the text's initial publication in 1549.[13] At the moment Haywood was writing, though, the word had as clear a political significance as it did a marital one. The concept of political obedience had long shaped English subjects' expectations about appropriate behaviour towards their sovereign. Because the king ruled by divine right, the logic went, subjects owed him the same subservience that they owed God. As Richard L. Greaves has demonstrated, such a doctrine more or less held sway throughout the sixteenth century.[14] The notion of absolute obedience was challenged during Mary Tudor's reign, when certain oppositional figures contended that the Bible authorized rebellion and even tyrannicide, but this concept was again legitimized during the rule of Elizabeth I, when Anglican, Puritan and Catholic texts all condemned resistance as ungodly.

By the end of the seventeenth century, the concept of political obedience had come to occupy a more vexed position in English culture. Resistance theory, which licensed opposition to the monarch, reappeared in the early 1640s after having lain dormant for much of the late sixteenth and early seventeenth centuries, and it took on a powerful new form following Charles I's beheading, with certain English thinkers using religious rhetoric to defend the regicide.[15] As the seventeenth century progressed, more English people began to be persuaded by the philosophical justifications for disobedience. During the Exclusion Crisis of the early 1680s, radical Whigs drew on resistance theory to oppose the accession of James II; such arguments went on to prove influential to John Locke, the latter sections of whose *Second Treatise on Government* outline the situations in which subjects might justifiably overthrow their rulers.[16] More conservative than its predecessor from earlier in the century, the resistance theory of the 1680s and 1690s maintained political stability even while it legitimized the removal of a monarch.[17] Such an ideological mixture proved convincing to the English populace, and resistance theory came to trouble the vaunted place that political obedience had previously held, helping to set the stage for the Glorious Revolution.

In Mr and Mrs Graspall's opening conversation about wife pandering, the pair draw on different meanings of the term 'obedience'. When Mr Graspall describes the deference that he expects from his wife, he frames it as complete subservience, suggesting that Mrs Graspall is obliged to abide by his will no matter what he requests. Mrs Graspall, though, makes it clear that she understands herself to have license to defy her husband, at least in certain scenarios. In response to Mr Graspall's first two mentions of obedience, Mrs Graspall vows to 'answer [his demands] with a ready Compliance'; however, as the pair's conversation about wife pandering unfolds, Mrs Graspall adds qualifications to the obedience that she has pledged to provide.[18] When Mr Graspall attempts to confirm that Mrs Graspall 'would'st not scruple any thing for thy old Lovy', she replies by hinting at the limits of her compliance: 'I hope you can command me nothing I can make a Scruple of obeying you in'.[19] And when Mr Graspall becomes more forceful in his demands, advising Mrs Graspall that she 'had best consent quietly to what I desire, or I shall make you', Mrs Graspall refuses her husband definitively: 'No Husband's Power extends to force the Execution of unlawful Commands'.[20] Avowing her right to resist her husband if his demands of her are illicit, Mrs Graspall asserts a more bounded notion of wifely obedience than the absolutist conception championed by Mr Graspall.

A Wife to Be Lett's representation of Mrs Graspall, then, licenses a certain disobedience. Nevertheless, this play does not endorse Lockean resistance theory. In fact, what Haywood ultimately celebrates in *A Wife to Be Lett* is not Mrs Graspall's defiance but rather her compliance – her 'Resignation' to Mr Graspall's authority.[21] Nowhere is the emphasis on Mrs Graspall's obedience clearer than in *A Wife to Be Lett*'s final scene. At the start of that scene, Mrs Graspall asks her husband's permission to host a dinner party. Feeling flush with the £2,000 he has gained from Sir Harry Beaumont, the usually socially averse Mr Graspall acquiesces, allowing his wife to invite all of the play's characters into their home. Once she has assembled the group, Mrs Graspall stages the revelation of an alleged affair between herself and another of the play's characters. The partygoers are surprised by such an exposé, and in response to their outcry Mrs Graspall blames her husband for her purported indiscretion, explaining that having been sold to Beaumont provoked her to further affairs: 'Since you have now taught me, I'll now experience that Charm Mankind's so fond of, Variety – I'll give a Loose to each unbounded Appetite, range thro' all Degrees of Men, nor shall you dare to contradict my Pleasures'.[22] Such a line clearly evinces Mrs Graspall's resistance – after all, this sentence reveals Mr Graspall's efforts to pander her. Nevertheless, the scene ultimately frames Mrs Graspall as obedient rather than defiant. In the wake of Mrs Graspall's exposure of her husband's attempt to pander her,

Mr Graspall declares regret for his actions, vowing that 'were it again to do', he would not repeat his behaviour.[23] Following such a statement of regret, Mrs Graspall reveals that, in fact, she has remained as loyal as ever to her husband, engaging neither in the alleged affair with whose exposure the scene began nor in a dalliance with Beaumont. Declaring her intention to 'return to [Mr Graspall's] Embraces a true, a faithful, and a vertuous Wife', Mrs Graspall reveals her truly virtuous nature, and by the end of the scene, has shed the image of 'vicious Wife' that she had previously projected.[24]

Mrs Graspall works carefully to stage the events that culminate in her husband's expression of regret, coordinating with several of the play's characters in order to carry out the dinner party's dramatic revelations. Nonetheless, Haywood's heroine does not take credit for the scheme she has hatched. In *A Wife to Be Lett*'s concluding moments, it is not Mrs Graspall, but rather Sir Harry Beaumont who explains to Mr Graspall the goal of his wife's scheme: 'this Plot was laid on purpose to cure you, if 'twas possible, of that covetous, sordid Disposition, which has ever been the Blot of your Character'.[25] It is also Beaumont, and not Mrs Graspall, who instructs Mr Graspall as to how he should achieve his wife's forgiveness, directing the greedy husband to 'admire [Mrs Graspall's] Vertues, and entreat her Pardon'.[26] Mrs Graspall's actions in this sequence make clear that she is Mr. Graspall's ethical superior, but Haywood's heroine does not go on to lord such moral authority over her husband. In his final line in the play, Mr Graspall gets down on his knees and pleads with his wife, '*Pudsy*, dear *Pudsy*, can'st thou forgive me'.[27] Mrs Graspall, though, does not accept the position of power that such a plea affords her. Instead, this character commands her husband to get up and reassume his dominant place in their marriage: 'Rise, Sir, this is not a Posture for a Husband – I form'd this Design only to make you worthy of that Name, and shall ever make it my Study to prove myself a most obedient Wife'.[28] Despite having spent much of the play defying Mr Graspall's orders and working to expose his depravity, Mrs Graspall is not ultimately characterized as resistant. Refusing credit for the clever plot she has carried out and renouncing the power over her husband she has won, Mrs Graspall ends *A Wife to Be Lett* submitting to Mr Graspall's rule.

In its emphasis on obedience, *A Wife to Be Lett* differs significantly from its immediate predecessor in the wife-pandering comedy genre, Aphra Behn's *The Lucky Chance* (1686). As in Haywood's play, so in Behn's a greedy husband tries but fails to sell his wife to a man who is courting her. In *The Lucky Chance*, however, the pandered wife actively resists her husband's commands, and the play celebrates her defiance. Lady Fulbank's disobedient streak is clear from her first appearance in the play. In *The Lucky Chance*'s second scene, well before Lady Fulbank is sold, she steals money from a counting house belonging to her husband, Sir Cautious, and gives it to her erstwhile lover, Gayman, eager to help the young gallant resolve his financial woes. As the play unfolds, Lady Fulbank's acts of resistance only mount – she dances with Gayman at a wedding celebration as Sir Cautious watches on, and she schedules an assignation with her beau that her husband nearly discovers. Lady Fulbank's defiance reaches its apex when she discovers Sir Cautious's intent to pander her. After learning that Gayman has won a night with her by besting her husband at a dice game, Lady Fulbank lashes out at both men. Decrying Gayman's attempt to 'make me a base prostitute, a foul adulteress' and Sir Cautious's complicity in leaving 'my honour thus unguarded', Behn's heroine lambasts the two for the disregard that they have shown for her reputation, expressing her disgust with them in no uncertain terms.[29] Refusing both men's attempts to pacify her, Lady Fulbank swears to Gayman that she will 'never see you more' and, a few lines later, vows 'by all things just and sacred, / To separate for ever from [Sir Cautious's] bed'.[30] In a revealing parallel to the concluding moments of *A Wife to Be Lett*, Sir Cautious tries to atone for his attempt at pandering by falling to his knees and begging his wife for forgiveness; however, Lady Fulbank rejects such a ploy. When Sir Cautious implores his wife to 'Hold, oh hold, my dear', Lady Fulbank responds by instructing him to 'Stand off; I do abhor thee', and in her next line, she tells him to 'Rise, 'tis in vain you kneel'.[31] Unlike Mrs Graspall, who acquiesces to Mr Graspall's authority as soon as he apologizes, Lady Fulbank remains impassive to her husband's pleading. Appalled by the bargain that Sir Cautious and Gayman have struck, Lady Fulbank draws on the resistance she has demonstrated throughout the play to make plain her disappointment with both men. By the final scene of *The Lucky Chance*, Lady Fulbank has rejected both her lover and her husband, and she ends the play having renounced masculine authority entirely.

Behn and Haywood were both Tories. As such, they might be expected to take similarly favourable approaches to authority and submission. *The Lucky Chance* and *A Wife to Be Lett* were written at distinct moments in the party's history, however, and the two plays reflect the disparate attitudes towards obedience that were circulating among Tories in 1686 and 1723, respectively. For much of the late seventeenth century, Tories were committed to the principle of passive obedience. Grounded in Anglican interpretations of scripture, the doctrine of passive obedience held that the Bible mandated complete subservience to monarchical authority. Such a doctrine afforded its adherents little room to resist; indeed, the only act of defiance that passive obedience permitted was the option to suffer rather than obey leaders' illicit dictates.[32]

Espoused frequently in the years between Charles I's beheading and James II's accession, the doctrine of passive obedience was particularly important to Tories during the Exclusion Crisis. In response to Whig efforts to block James II from power, Anglican divines drew on the notion of passive obedience to contend that such efforts were tantamount to resisting God himself. Even while Tories used the doctrine of passive obedience to license the rule of James II, however, the idea fell out of favour almost as soon as he took the throne. As Mark Goldie has shown, James II's actions against the Church of England alienated members of the Anglican clergy, and these divines, many of whom were Tories, began to resist his rule as early as 1686.[33] By the time the events of 1688 came to pass, Tories had grown more accepting of resistant behaviour, and passive obedience no longer held the prominent position in party ideology that it had once occupied.

Behn's works of the 1680s reflect the Tory party's vexed relationship to the principle of passive obedience. Long an advocate of Stuart rule, Behn makes clear her support for Charles II and James II in texts such as *The Rover, Part II* (1681), *The Roundheads* (1682) and *The City Heiress* (1682).[34] Corrinne Harol argues that Behn's dedication to the Stuarts, as well as Behn's commitment to the doctrine of passive obedience, continued throughout her career, claiming that *Oroonoko* (1689) 'offers a unique theorization of the virtues of passivity'.[35] Other scholars, however, have argued that Behn's support for both the Stuarts and the concept of political obedience waned in the latter years of James II's reign.[36] Anita Pacheco, for instance, contends that in Behn's cit-cuckolding comedies of 1681 to 1686, she experiments with the genre as a way of critiquing Stuart rule.[37] In her reading of *The Lucky Chance*, Pacheco argues that the play presents a surprisingly flexible take on oaths, framing them 'not [as] absolute but mutual and conditional upon both parties' fulfilment of their respective duties'.[38] Such an approach to oaths is not in keeping with the doctrine of passive obedience, but rather suggests the possibility of resistance. Written in the lead-up to the Glorious Revolution, which many conservative Englishmen and -women came to support, *The Lucky Chance* reflects Tories' increasing disillusionment with both James II and passive obedience. Ultimately, Pacheco reads this play as implying 'that the Tories had a case against James'.[39]

The decline in the popularity of passive obedience that began in the late 1680s continued into the early eighteenth century. In the wake of the Glorious Revolution, the concept was anathema in many English political circles: Whigs particularly rejected passive obedience during the period surrounding the Assassination Plot of 1696, when party members began to speak out in favour of active resistance and defend the overthrow of James II as an act of popular sovereignty.[40] Some proponents of passive obedience remained, however, and the doctrine began to return to the mainstream during the early years of Anne's reign.[41] By 1710, when the concept featured heavily in the rhetoric surrounding the trial of Doctor Henry Sacheverell, passive obedience had once again come to occupy a central place in English politics. Doctor Sacheverell had espoused the principles of passive obedience and non-resistance in his 1709 sermon 'The Perils of False Brethren', and Parliament Whigs indicted him as a result, accusing him of undermining the Glorious Revolution. Popular support for Sacheverell was strong, though, and he ended up being given a shorter than expected sentence. By the end of the Sacheverell trial, passive obedience was no longer the bête noire it had once been; indeed in the latter years of Anne's rule, even moderate Tories such as George Berkeley came to advocate the doctrine publicly.[42]

As the Sacheverell scandal demonstrates, early eighteenth-century Tories valued obedience. Nevertheless, the political position in which party members found themselves required them to resist. The Tories briefly achieved political power in the years following the Sacheverell trial: in 1710, Anne stacked her ministry with Tories, and from 1710 to 1714, the party held a majority in Parliament.[43] Such political favour was short-lived, however. Several powerful Whigs wielded influence over George I's advisers, and when he acceded the throne, George proscribed the Tories from his ministry. Compounding the effects of such a proscription, the Tories were defeated at the polls in the 1715 election. In the wake of the Jacobite rebellion of the same year, English voters restored the Whig majority to Parliament, and Whig representatives passed a series of election bills that secured a Whig majority for the next thirty years.[44] Tories thus faced both an ideological and a practical dilemma: on the one hand, the party had long espoused doctrines that forbade resistance to authority; on the other hand, Tories needed to resist if they were going to regain their political capital.

The central tension at work in *A Wife to Be Lett* parallels the one faced by Tories of the period. Focused on a woman who is required to obey her husband (because of the authority vested in him by English law) and to resist him (because the wife pandering in which he has asked her to engage violates religious and moral codes), Haywood's heroine must negotiate the conflicting terrain of subservience and defiance. Ultimately, Mrs Graspall strikes a balance between these poles by reforming her husband passively, modelling virtuous behaviour for him rather than actively disobeying him.

The final moments of *A Wife to Be Lett* characterize Mrs Graspall as virtuous; however, the play's first three acts frame this character as a woman struggling to remain faithful to her husband. *A Wife to Be Lett*'s early portions portray Sir Harry Beaumont favourably – in the play's first scene, Courtly tells Gaylove that 'I know nothing of [Beaumont's] Character that a Man of the strictest Honour wou'd not be proud of' and describes him as a witty figure whom anyone would 'be infinitely charm'd with'.[45] Mrs Graspall has clearly been swayed by Beaumont's allure: she 'blushes' in response to her maid's first reference to Beaumont; in the same scene, she deems him a man 'most form'd to charm'; and later in the play, she is so distracted by thoughts of the gallant that she complains of being unable to read because she sees '*Beaumont* ... in ev'ry Line – *Beaumont* in all the Volume'.[46]

Just as Mrs Graspall struggles with her lust for Beaumont, so Mr Graspall battles his own desires. For much of *A Wife to Be Lett*, Mr Graspall's hunger for wealth is portrayed as overpowering, and he only begins to gain control of this weakness in the play's closing moments. Even before Mr Graspall appears on stage, the audience is aware of his greed. In Courtly's first description of the miser, he notes that Mr Graspall 'denies [Mrs Graspall] the Privilege of any Company ... for fear she sho'd be at any Expence in entertaining 'em'.[47] Later, the foppish Toywell attempts to court Mrs Graspall by drawing a contrast between his own willingness to spoil her and her husband's obsession with wealth, telling Mrs Graspall that he is 'ready with my Person and Fortune to make you happy in all those Enjoyments your Husband's Age and Avarice denies'.[48] When Mr Graspall finally appears on stage in the play's third act, his avarice is made manifest. Relaying the details of the wife-pandering bargain he has struck with Beaumont, Mr Graspall figures his wife as an object to be traded:

> Now, Sir *Harry*, says I, whoever has the use of my Sword, it's but reasonable he pay for the furbishing – and if you really have so violent a Passion for my Wife, as your Letter intimates, pay the Money down she has expended me in Clothes, and allow me some Consideration for the Pity I have of your Sufferings, and I here give you free Ingress, Egress and Regress[49]

Controlled by his avarice, Mr Graspall has come to see his wife not as a person to care for but rather as a thing to be exchanged. When Mrs Graspall protests her husband's commands, telling him that she cannot 'yield to such a detested Bargain', Mr Graspall asserts his view that the £2,000 he stands to earn is more important than her reputation: 'Dear, dear *Pudsy* – don't be too hasty in resolving – consider, will Fame ever get thee 2000*l*? Remember, Pudsy! two thousand Pounds! when I think what a Sum it is, I sweat at the Apprehension of Virtue'.[50] Driven only by his desire for wealth, Mr Graspall characterizes his wife as an object, and eagerly bargains away her virtue in exchange for Beaumont's cash.

Both Graspalls, then, struggle with illicit desire: Mrs Graspall yearns for a man other than her husband and Mr Graspall wants wealth that he does not possess. Mrs Graspall, however, triumphs over her lust in a way that her husband does not, defeating her affection for Sir Harry Beaumont despite Mr Graspall's encouragement to sleep with the gallant.[51] *A Wife to Be Lett*'s epilogue, delivered by the actress who played Mrs Graspall, underscores the hard-fought nature of this character's victory over passion:

> *But to be grave – the Heroine of our Play*
> *Gains Glory by a hard, and dangerous Way*:
> Belov'd, *her Lover pleads – she fears no Spy,*
> *Her Husband* favours *– and her* Pulse *beats high.*
> *Warm glows his Hope – her Wishes* catch *the Fire,*
> Mutual *their* Flame, *yet Virtue quells Desire.*[52]

Highlighting how '*hard, and dangerous*' it was for Mrs Graspall to resist her '*Wishes*', the epilogue characterizes Haywood's heroine as having won an exacting battle over desire, managing to vanquish her lust for Beaumont only by drawing on her reserve of '*Virtue*'. Such a victory of course, stands in clear contrast to her husband's battle with greed. Whereas Mr Graspall gives in to his avarice easily, offering up his wife's honour for the sum of £2,000, Mrs Graspall holds steady in her refusal of Beaumont, withstanding her attraction by drawing upon her moral rectitude. Such a display of virtue makes Mrs Graspall a model for her husband, who does not display the same strength in his own struggles with greed.

After spending much of the play overpowered by his avarice, Mr Graspall concludes *A Wife to Be Lett* vowing to change his ways. In the end, what effects such a transformation is not Mrs Graspall's active resistance to her husband, but rather her modelling of virtuous behaviour: after seeing his wife's virtue in action, Mr. Graspall cannot help but regret his greed and pleads for his wife's forgiveness. Mrs Graspall's approach to reform is in keeping with the Tory doctrine of passive obedience, and the play's epilogue emphasizes this fact. At the end of its first stanza, after having summarized *A Wife to Be Lett*'s 'new *and* rare' plot and having poked fun at Mr Graspall's 'Av'rice', the epilogue turns its attention to Mrs Graspall's actions, making a comment about insubordinate wives:

> Women, *however* stirring *in their Way*,
> Are ne'er too active, *when they move* t'obey;
> *They rather would* (*if I can* understand *'em*)
> *Not* do *at all* – than do *as* Spouse *commands 'em*.[53]

Acknowledging that women enjoy not doing what their husbands ask, the epilogue characterizes such not-doing not as an act of resistance, but rather as a gesture of passive obedience. Describing wives as responding to their husbands' '*commands*' by being '*ne'er too active*' and by '*Not* do[ing] at all' what has been requested of them, the epilogue distances these women from the practice of out-and-out defiance, instead framing their behaviours as passive. By making use of the tactics of inaction and not-doing, Mrs Graspall manages both to obey her husband and to transform him. Embodying a solution to the contradictory injunctions to obey and to resist, Haywood's heroine behaves in a way that suggests a resolution to the ideological tension faced by Tories of the period.

In the early eighteenth century, Tories confronted a dilemma: grounded in an ideological heritage that valorized obedience, how were they to resist? In *A Wife to Be Lett*, Mrs Graspall faces a similar conundrum. Confronting the conflicting social mandates to obey her husband and to maintain her chastity, Mrs Graspall negotiates a path that allows her both to be subservient and to assert her will. Ultimately, this character becomes an exemplar for Tory partisans, carrying out an act of resistance while simultaneously remaining obedient to her husband.

In late seventeenth- and early eighteenth-century England, husbands who rented out their wives were discussed with some frequency.[54] Blending anxieties about finance and gender, wife panderers appeared in court, in the periodicals of the day and on the stage. Existing discussions of the politics of sexual violence have overlooked wife pandering, perhaps because eighteenth-century representations of wife pandering are largely comedic, and as such have not been taken seriously by scholars. Nevertheless, this act has clear partisan implications. Uncovering the politics at work in *A Wife to Be Lett* reveals the partisan complexity of Haywood's only comedy and allows insight into the politics of wife pandering more broadly.

8 STAGING RAPE IN THE AGE OF WALPOLE: SEXUAL VIOLENCE AND THE POLITICS OF DRAMATIC ADAPTATION IN 1730s BRITAIN

Jennifer L. Airey

In *Protesilaus: or, The Character of an Evil Minister*, a 1730 propaganda tract, author Charles Forman describes in extended and visceral terms the dangers that a bad prime minster and disinterested king pose to a kingdom: 'What causes Murmurs, Revolts and Rebellions in a State? It is the Ambition, the Insolence, the Rapaciousness of a Minister, and the mercenary Grandees who prostitute their Honour, become the Tools of his Designs, when the Prince gives too great a Liberty to their Rapine and Oppression'.[1] Dedicated to Sir Robert Walpole, the tract purports to differentiate between good political leadership and bad, between the altruism of the effective prime minister and the harmful rapaciousness of the selfish politician. Forman praises Walpole for his 'personal Courage', 'Humility' and 'Justice and Impartiality', along with his 'Benevolence to Mankind in general'.[2] Of course, such fulsome praise is employed satirically, as the tract actually seeks to condemn Walpole's selfish plunder of the English nation. Walpole has, the author warns, 'prostituted' his honour and committed 'Rapine' against the English people, sexual terminology applied to an economic form of crime.

Integral to Forman's condemnation of Walpole's leadership is the use of sexually violent imagery to describe the minister's deleterious effects on the nation. Walpole, Forman complains, has engaged in acts of 'Rapine and Oppression',[3] while the king has effectively protected the 'Minister in all his Plunder and Rapine'.[4] Forman was not alone in using the language of rapine to describe acts of political and economic wrongdoing. Indeed, like *Protesilaus*, many opposition tracts of the period depict Walpole as the violator of English citizens, English liberties and English trade. *Claudian's Rufinus: or, The Court-Favourite's Overthrow* (1730), for instance, describes Walpole as a 'wild Beast of Rapine',[5] who violates the nation physically and politically, while the author of *Are These Things So?* (1740) complains that England has been

> Polluted by your all-corrupting Hand;
> With rank Infection [Walpole] deluges the Land;
> Parent at once of Want, and Luxury,
> Of open Rapine and dark Treachery.[6]

Taken together, such tracts reflect the prevalence of rape imagery in propaganda condemnations of Sir Robert Walpole. Because rape was viewed throughout the period as a form of property crime, the misappropriation of a female body that rightly belonged to her male relatives, it represented a convenient and emotionally-charged means to decry ministerial theft and popular economic distress.[7] Female bodies in such tracts function as stand-ins for male political sufferings, the violation of those bodies encoding loss of property and the political overreaching of a tyrannical regime. Despite the popularity of such imagery in the fight against Walpole, however, the use of rape imagery in political propaganda was not original to the culture of the 1730s. As we shall see, seventeenth-century propagandists created a series of stock rapist figures to protest perceived governmental tyranny, figures who were resurrected in the writings of the 1730s as partisan writers used the language of sexual violation to protest acts of political and economic violence. My purpose in this chapter is therefore threefold: to expose the centrality of sexually violent imagery in popular condemnations of Sir Robert Walpole; to trace the continuities between seventeenth-century and 1730s uses of rape rhetoric as a political trope; and to explore the co-option of that imagery by the 1730s British stage. The 1730s occasioned a spate of rape plays: Henry Fielding's *Rape Upon Rape* (1730), William Hatchett's *The Fall of Mortimer* (1731), John Breval's *The Rape of Helen* (1733) and Michael Clancy's *The Sharper* (1738), along with revivals of Aphra Behn's *The Rover, Part I* (1677), Thomas Otway's *Venice Preserv'd* (1682), Nathaniel Lee's *Lucius Junius Brutus* (1680), Nicholas Brady's *The Rape* (1692) and Thomas Shadwell's *The Libertine* (1675, now retitled *Don Jon; or, The Libertine Destroy'd*). In each of these plays, the author draws upon the once-common sexually violent rhetoric of seventeenth-century tracts to condemn the contemporary governmental regime. As Lance Bertelsen explains, 'older literary and dramatic material could be tailored to fit the needs of the political moment'.[8] The chapter concludes with readings of Fielding's *Rape Upon Rape* and Hatchett's *The Fall of Mortimer*, two representative examples of the political uses of dramatic rape, and two plays that reflect the continuing relevance of rape as political currency. Such an examination offers new insight into eighteenth-century political and theatrical cultures, and the ways in which propaganda authors frequently detached rape from a painful physical reality and transformed female bodily suffering into a symbol of male political or economic distress.

Throughout the *Craftsman*, one of the leading opposition journals of the 1720s and 1730s, anti-Walpole polemicists repeatedly resorted to the language of economic rapine and ravishment to condemn the prime minister's economic policy. According to a paper published on Saturday, 14 October 1732, when ministers gain power, they lose all sense of responsibility to their constituents: 'They have an Interest, which more nearly concerns Them. They are to repair a tatter'd Fortune; to redeem their mortgaged Farms in England; and to refit that Estate by Rapine'.[9] Such actions place the whole realm at risk, as 'ministerial Tyranny' has led to the fall of kings: 'the most unfortunate Reigns, since the Conquest, with Regard to the Prince, were Those of Edward II. Richard II. Henry VI. Charles I. and James II', and each of those reigns 'fell a Sacrifice to the Rapine, Treachery, or evil Counsel of their Ministers'.[10] George II, the paper implies, must beware lest he meet a similar fate; Walpole's economic rapine may occasion George II's destruction.

Not surprisingly, authors loyal to Walpole's regime challenged such accusations, but they did not protest the use of sexually violent language as a metaphor for political misdeeds. *A Letter from the People to Caleb D'Anvers Esq* (1729) demanded that the authors of the *Craftsman* 'prove upon them the Extortion, the Rapine, the Misapplication of publick Money, the Corruption, or any one of the innumerable Crimes you have so often charged them with'.[11] The language of rapine was thus adopted on both sides of the political divide as authors condemned or defended Walpole's economic policy. In coding Walpole as a rapist, however, propaganda authors drew upon a complex and often overlapping collection of tropes that developed in response to seventeenth-century political crises. As we shall see, Walpole-as-rapist is at once heir to the rhetoric of Roundhead anti-Cavalier tracts and Jacobite anti-Williamite writings. He is called both a physical rapist and an economic thief, simultaneously accused of the sorts of physical violence attributed to the royalist faction during the English Civil Wars, and the economic violence attributed by Jacobites to the Dutch faction. The language of economic ravishment had become particularly prevalent in the years surrounding the Glorious Revolution, as authors sought to justify popular revolt. As I explore in *The Politics of Rape: Sexual Atrocity, Propaganda Wars, and the Restoration Stage* (2012), early Jacobites turned to rape imagery to describe the economic and political takeover of the nation, implying that neither women's bodies nor men's property would be safe under William III's rule.[12] Propaganda authors complained that the Dutch had committed 'Rapines ... upon our trade', and participated in the 'Ravishment of Ancient Freeholds'.[13] As a result of the governmental upheaval, the English have opened themselves to political ravishment and invited the Dutch to 'commit Rapine upon our Liberties'.[14] Other Jacobite tracts rhetorically transformed William and Mary's act of usurpation into an act of sexual violence and depicted James II, by extension, as a rape victim. Charles Blount, for instance, complained that the king's 'Crown, as well as his Life' were 'most unjustly ravished from him',[15] while Robert Ferguson described the Glorious Revolution as 'an outragious Rape ... such an open deflouring of the Chastity, which their Church had hitherto preserved in point of Allegiance to Lawful and Rightful Monarchs'.[16] In such tracts, England itself is described as a rape victim; the nation was a 'Rose so virgin white before, / Now blusing [sic] with the stain of Gore'.[17] In using the rhetoric of rapine, then, anti-Walpole authors become the heir to Jacobite rhetoric, with Walpole serving as a political and economic monster who metaphorically defiles the financial 'chastity' of the nation.

At the same time, the use of sexually violent imagery to attack Walpole's regime was designed directly to attack the prime minister's perceived libertinism. In these tracts, Walpole becomes both a supporter of and a participant in acts of rape. Here rape is not only an economic crime, but a physical reality that proves the prime minister's unfitness to rule. In Eliza Haywood's 1738 *Adventures of Eovaai, Princess of Ijaveo*, for instance, the evil minister Ochihatou, Haywood's rendition of Walpole, tries first to seduce and later to violate the beautiful and innocent Princess Eovaai, rightful heir to the throne.[18] While he initially disguises himself as a handsome young man, Ochihatou is actually a disgusting and disfigured sorcerer whose physical ugliness reflects his internal corruption. Eovaai describes him as 'crooked, deformed, distorted in every Limb and Feature, but also encompassed with a thousand hideous Forms, which sat upon his Shoulders, clung round his Hands, his Legs, and seem'd to dictate all his Words and Gestures'.[19] Capitalizing 'upon Walpole's reputation for libertinism',[20] Haywood depicts Ochihatou as a rapist, a murderer and a devotee of the demonic Ypres, 'at whose Instigation' he commits 'Rapes, Murders, Massacres, Treasons, all Acts which tend to universal Ruin'.[21] Ochihatou is more than willing to violate Eovaai (and by extension, her kingdom), both to gratify his illicit passions and to gain control over the realm. The attempted rape of Eovaai is also the attempted violation of the nation as a whole.[22]

Authors were also able openly to attack Walpole's rumoured sexual profligacy by denouncing his friendship with Francis Charteris, an aristocrat convicted in 1730 for the rape of his servant, Anne Bond. Widely hated for being 'a swindler, South-Sea profiteer and political opportunist who had made too many enemies',[23] Charteris became the focus of intense media scrutiny, and his conviction was hailed as a triumph of impartial justice. When Walpole subsequently arranged his pardon, tempers ran hot, and opposition authors claimed that Walpole's own sexual deviance had obscured the cause of justice and rendered him unfit to rule.[24] Authors thus linked the behaviour of Charteris, England's 'Rapemaster General', with Walpole, a connection Alexander Pope exploited in his *Epistle to Bathurst*. According to one circulating ballad, 'On Colonel Francisco, Rape-Master General of Great Britain', Charteris 'would ravish, forswear, and pick Pockets, and cheat, / And by Men was oft beaten, and Women did beat: / A

Favourite worthy of B—Y the Great!'[25] The *Craftsman* likewise linked Walpole with Charteris, calling him the 'Friend, Confident, and Patron' of the convicted felon.[26] As Bertrand A. Goldgar explains,

> the parallels between Walpole and Charteris, both wealthy 'great men', proved irresistible; Pulteney, a year after the pardon was issued, pointed to the similarity of their 'characters and circumstances', and a government paper listed 'Col. Charteris' as one of the names the Prime Minister was most frequently called by the *Craftsman*.[27]

In depicting Walpole as an economic rapist, authors drew on Jacobite rhetoric developed in the wake of the Glorious Revolution. By accusing him of committing or condoning physical acts of rape, they reached back further still, drawing on the rhetoric of the English Civil Wars to condemn their enemy. Throughout English Civil War propaganda, Roundhead authors fixated on the supposed deviance of their Cavalier enemies, and particularly on their acts of sexually violent atrocity, accusing the Cavaliers of encouraging the rapes of Puritan women as proof of their loyalty to the king. According to a 1642 propaganda tract, *A Wicked Resolution of the Cavaliers*, one royalist soldier exclaimed, 'we desire nothing but to cut throats, take purses, ravish maids, plunder houses, murder Roundheads, defie the Parliament, and like Phaeton, set all the world on fire'.[28] Author William Cartwright concurs: the Cavaliers 'invade the Subjects Estates and Persons that continue firme in their Allegiance to the King ... plundering their Houses, and inforcing their wives and daughters to their lusts'.[29] Likewise, George Lawrence describes 'the many Rapes and Chamber-Adulteries' of the Cavaliers, along with their 'Spirituall Uncleanness, which is Idolatry, that cannot be free from their Campe, having so many Papists and prophane ones in their unhallowed and Pseudo-Catholique Army'.[30]

The spectre of the debauched Cavalier, that lascivious and evil royalist soldier, was invented to encourage loyalty to the parliamentary cause. Roundhead tracts begged the reader to 'stand up in defence of your Lives, your Liberties, your Estates, your Houses, your Wives, your Children, your Brethren', by opposing the royalist army.[31] After the Restoration, however, images of debauched Cavaliers did not disappear, but instead transformed into protests against the debauched libertines of Charles II's court, bored aristocrats who valued their own pleasure over the lives and liberty of the women around them. Representations of debauched libertines also show up regularly in the drama of the period, appearing in plays such as Behn's *The Rover, Part 1*, where Willmore's romantic Cavalier spirit is linked with a darker, sexually violent edge. Likewise, in Shadwell's *The Libertine*, aristocratic male excess leads to egregious acts of sexual violence, and later, onstage damnation. It is this heritage into which the anti-Walpole tracts tap. Francis Charteris represents a 1730s real-life embodiment of Shadwell's Don John, while Walpole, as Charteris's friend, condones his acts of violence. It is no wonder, then, that plays like *The Rover* (reprinted in 1716, 1724 and 1729), *The Libertine* (reprinted in 1724 and 1736), Brady's *The Rape* (reprinted in 1730) and Lee's *Lucius Junius Brutus* (reprinted in 1727 and 1736), all of which contain depictions of debauched libertines who rape innocent women, were republished and performed so frequently on the mid-eighteenth-century stage. Through these revivals, memories of the debauched Cavalier/libertine are resurrected and redeployed in the fight against Walpole.

Not surprisingly, such imagery also filtered into new drama of the period as authors co-opted the imagery of the propaganda tracts for their own political ends. Fielding's *Rape Upon Rape*, first performed in 1730, borrows both the trope of the debauched Cavalier and the language of economic ravishment to criticize Walpole's government. Several critics have argued that *Rape Upon Rape* is not one of Fielding's more cutting satires.[32] Unlike his later plays (and especially *The Historical Register*), *Rape Upon Rape* does not offer a full-scale condemnation of Walpole, and as such, it was never a target for government censorship. Still, it certainly sought to capitalize on the Charteris craze and it offers a definitive comment on Walpole's regime.[33] The play's main action begins when Ramble, a drunken young libertine, encounters Hilaret on the street at night. Although Hilaret is a chaste young lady, her presence on the streets belies her claim to respectability, and believing her body must be for sale, Ramble attempts to assault her. He exclaims, 'to encounter danger is my profession; so have at you, my little Venus – if you don't consent, I'll ravish you'.[34] The play is revealing of mid-eighteenth-century understandings of female sexuality and female sexual consent; the respectable woman is indistinguishable from the whore if she is in the wrong place at the wrong time.[35] Underlying the gender politics of the play, though, is a broader political commentary. The exchange between Ramble and Hilaret replays the encounter between Willmore and Florinda in Behn's *The Rover, Part 1*, linking Ramble with Interregnum-era Cavalier violence. Although Behn was herself a staunch royalist, *The Rover* evinces her discomfort with libertine behaviour and treatment of women. Willmore is both a romantic hero, a man who has sacrificed all for his king and a violent beast who attempts to rape an innocent woman. Like Willmore, Ramble explicitly refers to himself as a Cavalier. When Hilaret asks him, 'who are you, sir', Ramble responds, 'A cavalier, madam, a knight-errant rambling about the world in quest of adventure. To plunder widows and ravish virgins; to lessen the number of bullies, and increase that of cuckolds, are the obligations of my profession'.[36] Ramble's understanding of the Cavalier lifestyle, coupled with his violence towards Hilaret, represents a throwback to descriptions of the debauched Cavalier, invoking the older form of political propaganda as filtered through Charteris's crime.[37] His behaviour also calls into question both the actions of the aristocratic libertine set and by extension, a prime minister who would sanction such actions.

While Ramble begins the play an intended ravisher, he is later himself (ironically, metaphorically) ravished in the text. By forcing Hilaret to swear a rape against Ramble,[38] Squeezum becomes a ravisher in the economic sense, using rape threats to extort money. Upon his release, Ramble tells Constant, 'I hope when next we meet, we shall meet / In happier climes, and on a safer shore, / Where no vile justice shall invade us more'.[39] Ramble and Constant have been invaded non-consensually by the justice system, penetrated by false accusations and ravished of their funds. Linguistically, Ramble implies (however disingenuously) that he and Constant have fallen victims to judicial ravishment, 'raped' by a justice system that privileges legalized theft over impartial application of the law. Here, then, the trope of the debauched Cavalier merges with the trope of the economically ravished male, as the careless libertine of the play's beginning becomes Squeezum's intended prey. Given that Squeezum may be read as one of Walpole's corrupt appointees, or in Goldgar's words, 'a comedic version of the Prime Minister himself',[40] Walpole has, in effect, become a judicial ravisher as his friend Charteris was an actual rapist.

Rape Upon Rape was not the only play of the decade to feature sexual violence as political commentary, nor was it the only play to rely on earlier propaganda tropes to make its point. William Hatchett's *The Fall of Mortimer*, an adaptation of John Bancroft's 1690 *King Edward the Third, With the Fall of Mortimer*, was shut down by the government after only sixteen performances, and it occasioned a spate of pamphlets debating the author's perceived sedition. Hatchett, even more explicitly than Fielding, uses the process of dramatic adaptation to comment on contemporary politics; while Fielding merely alludes to Behn's *The Rover*, Hatchett actually takes scenes and passages from Bancroft's play wholesale, altering the play as necessary to increase its relevance to a contemporary audience.

Hatchett was not, of course, the only author of the period to invoke the memory of Edward II to comment on Walpole's government. Allusions to Gaveston and Mortimer, along with Cardinal Wolsey, Sejanus and Buckingham, were relatively common in critical discussions of the Great Man's court.[41] On Saturday, 27 May 1732, for instance, the *Craftsman* commented, 'The Reign of Edward II. was one continued Scene of ministerial Tyranny, under a Succession of insolent Favourites, who at last brought their Master to a most cruel and deplorable Death'.[42] Hatchett's alterations to Bancroft's play, however, reveal much about the changing political priorities of the 1730s. Although Mortimer and Isabella are the main villains in both Bancroft's and Hatchett's versions, Bancroft's original features an act of attempted sexual assault performed by Tarleton, Bishop of Hereford and Chancellor of England. Aroused by the beautiful and virtuous Maria, Tarleton purchases the girl from her uncle, who is all too willing to sell his niece in exchange for political and economic patronage. In the context of 1690s politics, Bancroft's depiction of Tarleton represents an example of customary anti-Catholic propaganda. Throughout the century, anti-Catholic polemicists accused Catholic priests of pride, lechery and a willingness to commit acts of violence, up to and including treason. An early seventeenth-century tract, *A Bloody Tragedie* (1607), succinctly summarizes these accusations:

> They say the Iesuites are bloody, and stirrers up [sic] sedition in Christian kingdomes, that they are lyars, that they are proude, that they delight in rich apparell ... that they are Epicures and make their belly their god, that they are lascivious, and love women, having Gentlewomen for their chamber-maides and young wenches for their bedfellowes.[43]

A Bloody Tragedie goes on to describe the horrible fate of sixteen young virgins who fell victim to imprisonment, rape, impregnation and murder at the hands of Jesuit priests. While Tarleton is not quite so murderous, he, too, is overly secular and sexually violent. Sounding much like the author of *A Bloody Tragedie*, Mortimer complains,

> You pamper your varatious [sic] Appetites,
> Indulge Praedominance to that degree,
> You exceed the very Sultan of the East ...
> Under the holy Covert of Confession:
> You shrowd the Priest and Sanctify the Whore,
> Did I not bolt upon your Rank Devotion:
> And caught you acting Tarquin on Lucretia.[44]

Tarleton cares not for his holy vocation, telling his intended victim, 'No matter for my Coat child'.[45] Since the act of rape 'agrees with my body, nay, I must plunder'.[46] In the context of 1690s politics, Tarleton's behaviour offers a justification of the Glorious Revolution; the popish presence in England (and especially in the highest echelons of the government) must be purged, lest innocent women fall prey to Catholic acts of violence.

According to Susan Staves,

> Bancroft chooses Edward as a hero because he cooperates in overthrowing the tyrannical Mortimer, because he summons a parliament immediately, and because he was a brave warrior king who fought valiantly against the French. All these traits, of course, he shared with William III.[47]

By excising Tarleton from the text and reassigning his act of attempted rape to Mortimer, Hatchett offers a much different message to 1730s viewers. Stripped of the anti-Catholic elements that defined Bancroft's *Edward the Third*, *The Fall of Mortimer* refocuses its criticisms on Mortimer/Walpole, who represents instead another combination of economic ravisher and debauched Cavalier. Mortimer, the common people explain, has 'bubbled' the nation and the king, a phrase that carried obvious contemporary resonance.[48] His economic degeneracy manifests in his willingness to embezzle public funds, a form of fiscal rapine. It also manifests in his libertine willingness to attack Maria, the act of rape once again functioning as a symbol of governmental overreach.[49] Through Mortimer, then, Hatchett demonizes the evil Protestant Walpole, not the nefarious popish faction.

Interestingly, both Bancroft's and Hatchett's versions of the play work to sanctify Edward II's behaviour, and to sanitize the story of his fall. With the exception of one reference to Ganymede – Bancroft's Mortimer calls Spencer 'A Ganemede'[50] – gone from both versions of the play are the stories of Edward II's illicit relationships with his male favourites. Instead, Edward II is celebrated as a martyr, one unfairly destroyed by an evil counsellor and a malicious wife. The dialogue in each version suggests that Gaveston and Spencer, far from leading Edward II astray, were actually attempting to save the king from his wife. Hatchett's Isabella commands Mortimer to kill her son's new counsellors, saying, 'Be thou as once, when Spencer, Gaveston, / The Minions of my Husband, did attempt / To curb my Will, and I defy'd them all.'[51] Indeed, Queen Isabella emerges from each play as an even bigger villain than Mortimer. Isabella is a poisonous traitor, an unnatural mother who turns on her own child – in Hatchett's play she calls Edward II a 'Rebel-Son' and 'a Disease' whose 'Venom' she must purge 'from my blood, / As if a Leprocy had compassed me'[52] – and in Bancroft's play, an adulterous wife. Here Hatchett draws on another long-standing trope of seventeenth-century political propaganda. Debauched Cavaliers in English Civil War tracts rarely act alone; their actions are encouraged and condoned by what I call the figure of the poisonous Catholic bride, the dangerous religious Other who glories in the destruction of Protestant society. Many of the attacks on poisonous Catholic brides were directed in the 1630s at Charles I's wife, Henrietta Maria, who was frequently accused of conspiring with evil priests to lead her husband astray. The author of *The Great Eclipse of the Sun, or, Charles His Waine* (1644) complains,

> The King being in full Conjunction with this Popish Plannet, the Queen, hee was totally eclipsed by her Counsell, who under the Royall Curtaines, perswaded him to advance the Plots of the Catholickes ... Ordinary women, can in the Night time perswade their husbands to give them new Gowns or Petticoates ... and could not Catholick Queen Mary ... by her night discourses, encline the King to Popery.[53]

As a foreigner and a Catholic, Henrietta Maria is doubly dangerous, and writers accuse her of seeking to destroy her husband's reign, to encourage the rapes of English women and to propel the slaughter of English men; she will spread 'murther, rapine' and 'lamentation' throughout the nation.[54] Bancroft, too, describes Isabella as eclipsing her husband – Delamore complains, 'The King should know how much he is Ecclip'st'[55] – tapping into the rhetoric of the anti-Henrietta

Maria tracts, which by 1690 would have been filtered through thirty years of similarly phrased attacks levelled first against Charles II's powerful Catholic mistresses and later against James II's wife, Mary of Modena.

Frequently, poisonous Catholic brides were also depicted as monstrous and unnatural mothers, in some cases giving birth to literally monstrous offspring. The mothers of *A Nest of Nunnes Egges* (1680) 'sit on Egges, with Diligence and Care' until fully formed priests and nuns finally hatch.[56] In other cases, they seek to destroy their own progeny. Catherine de Medici, mother of Charles IX of France, for instance, was accused of fostering the rapes and murders of French Protestants before murdering her own son to retain her throne. Of 'her own nature and proper desire enclined' to order 'the utter ruine of the Protestants by a total slaughter', Catherine forces her unwilling son to order the 'slaughters and rapines' of the St Bartholomew's Day massacre.[57] Afterwards, the king 'died in less than two years ... of a Bloudy-flux, proceeding, as was suspected, from poison given him by the procurement of his Mother and Brother'.[58] Similar figures also appeared on the Restoration stage, most notably in Edward Ravenscroft's adaptation of Shakespeare's *Titus Andronicus*. Ravenscroft's Tamora is violent, heartless and cruel, a religious and cultural outsider who uses her position of power in the kingdom to foster the rape of Lavinia and ensure the destruction of the Andronicus family.[59]

Hatchett's Isabella, like Tamora, is heartless and cruel. Although Hatchett removes all references to Isabella's affair with Mortimer, the Queen still condones Mortimer's acts of rape and exposes herself as a monstrous and unnatural mother. She forbids her son's education and assumption of his rightful position so that she can maintain her power, and when her son finally bucks her authority, she is all too willing to have him assassinated. 'My Gall boils up, and I am all on Fire', she exclaims.[60] 'Come, then, Revenge, thou Banquet of the Gods, / And let me gorge my rav'nous Appetite'.[61] Like Lady Macbeth, she asks the gods to 'Drive from my Soul the Weakness of my Sex',[62] so that she may destroy the hated 'Viper' to whom she gave life.[63] Read in the context of 1690 politics, Bancroft's depiction of Isabella offers a warning against French Catholic queens, and a celebration of William and Mary's successful rule. The play would have had a much different resonance in 1731. As Maynard Mack argues, 'Allusions to a woman who ruled her husband, loathed her heir, entertained too much affection for a royal favourite, or indulged herself in theological heterodoxies were almost certain to intend the Queen'.[64] The depiction of Isabella thus reflects on Queen Caroline of Ansbach, who served as regent during her husband's absences in Hanover, and who publicly despised Frederick, Prince of Wales, her oldest son and heir. Caroline famously called her son an 'avaricious, sordid monster' and 'the greatest ass and the greatest liar and the greatest *canaille* and the greatest beast in the whole world', and she wished that 'the ground would open this moment and sink the monster to the lowest hole in hell'.[65] Like Isabella, Caroline is an unnatural mother, a poisonous Protestant bride who would destroy husband and child in her quest for power. She is also willing to overlook the sexually violent acts of her favourite debauched minister, the evil of rape paling before her desire for more and greater power. The play thus represents not only a criticism of Walpole, but a striking condemnation of the Queen, which probably helps to explain why it was so quickly suppressed. In Mortimer and Isabella, the play stages the (nonsexual) union of debauched Cavalier, economic ravisher and poisonous Catholic bride, and it finally celebrates the banishment of such unwholesome influences from Edward III's court.

A full history of rape scenes on the eighteenth-century stage has yet to be written, but it is my hope that my research can offer new insight into the continuities between seventeenth- and eighteenth-century depictions of sexual violence and into the interplay between fictional acts of sexual violence and offstage political realities. Fielding's *Rape Upon Rape* and Hatchett's *The Fall of Mortimer*, along with the myriad other opposition works of the period, all rely on images of sexual violence to protest perceived forms of economic and political wrongdoing. They also draw upon seventeenth-century propaganda tropes as a form of emotional shorthand to provoke audience outrage and foment much-desired social change. To read political works of the 1730s in the context of the longer seventeenth-century tradition is to gain a new understanding of the continued cultural resonance of rape rhetoric. Such works also expose the ways in which the physical suffering of actual female bodies is finally subordinated to and subsumed in the use of rape to protest political and economic wrongs done to men.

9 'WHAT DO YOU TAKE ME FOR?': RAPE AND VIRTUE IN *THE FEMALE QUIXOTE*

Robin Runia

Near the beginning of Charlotte Lennox's *The Female Quixote* (1752), Arabella confronts Mr Hervey, a man she banishes from her presence after his attempts to court her. Upon his innocent approach on horseback, Arabella commands her servants to apprehend him. Hervey cries, 'what do you mean by using me in this manner? Do you suppose I had any Intention to hurt the Lady? – What do you take me for?'[1] This incident, in part, ridicules the anxieties and expectations Arabella has adopted as a result of her immersion in romance reading. Arabella's response illustrates this as she explains that she takes him, 'For a Ravisher ... an impious Ravisher, who, contrary to all Laws both human and divine, endeavor to possess yourself by Force of a Person whom you are not worthy to serve'.[2] While the novel repeatedly uses humour to critique romance reading and its potential to inculcate unrealistic expectations in women, the contrast between Mr Hervey's innocence in this incident and the genuine dangers found in the novel's subsequent dramatizations of Arabella's intense anxiety about rape, highlights the real danger of sexual violence against women. In dealing with the threat of sexual violence, the novel also fleshes out an alternative notion of female virtue, one that relies on piety instead of chastity. However, this revised notion of female virtue redirects some of the blame for sexual violence back at the female victim, rendering female intellect responsible for the success of male sexual predation.[3]

Ultimately, understanding the link between women's sexuality, intellect, piety and virtue in *The Female Quixote* means the novel's dissatisfying ending – Arabella's apparent rejection of romance values – must be reconsidered.[4] Arabella's reaction to Mr Hervey's perceived violation of 'all Laws both human and divine', quoted above, illustrates the first instance of the novel's commentary upon sexual violence. The apparent unreason of Arabella's insistence that, 'A little more Submission and Respect would become [him] better' and her claim that he is 'now wholly in [her] Power' has led many critics to read Arabella's expectations about the female agency and courtship as a general commentary on the ascendancy of realism over romance.[5] However, Arabella's changing assumptions about female sexuality throughout the text highlight the novel's redefinition of female virtue, one that qualifies, through piety, the synonymy of intellect and chastity perpetuated in both realism and romance.[6] Studying the threat of sexual violence in this novel, real and imagined, offers an original interpretation of the narrative's complicated representation of women's minds and bodies that goes beyond simple generic concerns.

In Arabella, Lennox presents her readers with an extremely sheltered woman whose world-view has been shaped by isolation and romance novels. Arabella's introduction into eighteenth-century society highlights the glaring contrast between heroic and polite society and the corresponding expectations for female behaviour.[7] The heroine's refusal simply to acquiesce to her father's choice of a husband launches Arabella on an unusual courtship trajectory. Thus, at one point early in the novel and in a parodic rewriting of Samuel Richardson's *Clarissa*, Arabella attempts to escape from this forced marriage through the garden gate for which she 'always keep[s] the Key of that private Door'.[8] In Lennox's comedic rendering of these events, Arabella, 'beg[s] Heaven to throw some generous Cavalier in her Way, whose Protection she might implore, and, taking every Tree at a Distance for a Horse and Knight, hastened her Steps to meet her approaching Succour'.[9] Unsurprisingly, these expectations are 'miserably balked'.[10] Clarissa's tragedy has set this precedent. When the disabled Arabella eventually encounters 'Succour' in the form of a gentleman upon the road, this 'Generous Stranger's' ogling strikes an off key, and while Arabella 'suffer[s] no Apprehensions from being alone with a Stranger', the reader's concern at the Stranger's delight 'at having so beautiful a Creature in his Power' grows.[11] While the reader replaces feelings of concern with relief upon the arrival of Arabella's friends and laughs at Arabella's ensuing misapprehension of the former gardener, Edward, as her 'Ravisher', her cousin Mr Glanville's worry in returning Arabella 'safe home' suggests the real threat of sexual violence she has nearly escaped.[12] Ultimately, this incident indicates the seriousness of rape and the culpability of those involved. Arabella cannot be both blameworthy and laughable within the serious context of rape.

While Arabella's assumptions about seduction and sexual predation definitely remain a source of humour in the novel, these assumptions reveal her privileging of women's intellect as a sufficient defence against sexual predators. Early in the novel, Arabella's beliefs in the superiority and centrality of women to heroic culture fuel her interests in the 'Adventures' of other women. Take, for example, the case of Miss Groves. The impropriety of Arabella's inquiry into Miss Groves's history, Mrs Morris's corresponding malicious gossip and the hypocritical indignation of Miss Groves all highlight the disconnect between the worlds of romance and realism. However, Arabella (representing romance) and Mrs Morris (representing realism) both see women's intellect as a necessary preservative of their virtue. Both women and both worlds seem to hold women responsible for the sexual predation to which they may fall victim. They both insist that good sense and a developed understanding should be adequate to preserve a woman from rape.

According to Mrs Morris's relation, Miss Groves's moral failings are linked directly to her intellectual deficiencies, and Mrs Morris highlights these failings by placing them in direct contrast to a superior model of femininity:

> for Miss Groves, who inherited her Mother's Pride, *tho' not her Understanding*, in all things affected an Equality with those young Ladies, who, conscious of the Superiority of their Birth, could but ill bear with her *Insolence and* Presumption. As they grew older, the Difference of their Inclinations caused perpetual Quarrels amongst them; for his Grace's Daughters were serious reserved and pious. Miss Groves *affected noisy Mirth, was a great Romp, and delighted in Masculine Exercises*.[13]

Mrs Morris goes on to explain how Miss Groves's lack of understanding, her predilection for affectation and her masculine capriciousness explain her train of inappropriate lovers. And despite Mrs Morris's acknowledgement that the 'unpardonable Neglect of [Miss Groves's] Mother' led directly to her ruin, Mrs Morris ultimately blames Miss Groves for her own fall.[14]

Despite Arabella's ostensible sympathy for Miss Groves, she too persists in holding women to an intellectual standard that she believes would allow them to ensure their chastity. She accordingly assumes that Miss Groves was only 'betrayed into an involuntary Hearing of' those 'Addresses' not worthy of her and that she must have been victim to the 'ingenious Artifices' of noble lovers.[15] According to Arabella, Miss Groves should be smart enough to avoid, whenever possible, conversation that threatens her chastity and, thus, her virtue.

The novel's further detailing of Miss Groves's 'Extravagance', pregnancies and mercenary marriage that make up her 'Ruin', puts the reader firmly in Mrs Morris's camp.[16] Unlike Arabella, 'Who seemed so little sensible of the Pleasure of Scandal, as to be wholly ignorant of its Nature; and not to know it when it was told her', the reader recognizes the truth of Miss Groves's failings as related by Mrs Morris.[17] Lennox implicates the reader as one of those 'sensible of the Pleasure of Scandal', as one of those who would blame Miss Groves for her fate. Despite this gap between scepticism of Miss Groves's intellectual and moral capabilities and Arabella's generosity, this incident reflects romance's and realism's shared standard for women's 'Understanding' as guarantor of chastity and, thus, female virtue.

Miss Glanville comes under similar fire from Arabella for the great liberties she has allowed her past lovers. At one point, in an attempt to defend herself against what she perceives as a malicious 'sneer', Miss Glanville rebuts: 'You have made no Scruple to own, Madam ... that you think me capable of granting

Favours to Lovers, when, Heaven knows, I never granted a Kiss without a great deal of Confusion'.[18] In response:

> And you had certainly much Reason for Confusion, said Arabella, excessively surprised at such a Confession: I assure you I never injured you so much in my Thoughts, as to suppose you ever granted a Favour of so criminal a Nature.[19]

Miss Glanville's subsequent violent weeping in response to what she perceives as an attack upon her virtue, however, does not prevent Arabella from continuing her judgement of her cousin's behaviour. In comparing Miss Glanville's behaviour to that of the 'inconsiderate Julia, who would receive a Declaration of Love without Anger from any one', with the caveat that Miss Glanville's granting of favours was much more 'considerable', Arabella blames Miss Glanville for the deficient intellectual development betrayed in her confession.[20] This culpability marks any subsequent behaviour (in this case allowing herself to be the victim of sexual advances) as equally blameworthy.

As the novel progresses, Arabella continues to believe that women require a developed intellect that would allow them to perceive and avoid all sexual threat, and her own misapplication of that awareness provides additional instances of humour within the novel that tend to obscure the real threat Arabella faces following her garden escape. The absurdity of Arabella's apparent failure to acknowledge the reality of rape veils its dangers. For example, when Mr Hervey happens across her path and she interprets his appearance as a 'renew[al of] his Attempts' 'to carry [her] away', Mr Glanville forces himself into a heroic defence of his lady's reputation against this 'Ravisher'.[21] The extreme irony of this scene emphasizes through repetition Arabella's utter absurdity, obscuring the implications of this logic, for, in this case, Arabella's intellect clearly fails to protect her from sexual assault.

These incidents with Miss Groves, Miss Glanville and Arabella assume that a woman's understanding can ensure her chastity, an assumption that allows the reader to blame victims of sexual predation. According to this logic, a woman must be smart enough to know and avoid cases where she might be, in a sense, 'asking for it'. This commentary on the nature of female virtue reflects a mid-century rejection of earlier eighteenth-century narratives that blamed fallen women for their own lascivious and avaricious inclinations. The opening of the Magdalen Hospital in London in 1758, just six short years after the novel was published, exemplifies the influence of this shift. Like *The Female Quixote*, the Hospital and the literature produced as part of the media-blitz promoting the Hospital's charitable efforts to provide asylum for women, including, for example, *The Histories of Some of the Penitents in the Magdalen House*, reconsiders the role of chastity in female virtue. Specifically, this literature asserts the ability of fallen women to, through acting as wives and mothers as well as contributing productively to Britain's economic interests of manufacture and local trade, regain their virtue. However, where these slightly later fallen-woman narratives reflect the period's evolution of sentimental discourse and its emphasis on the reforming power of manners, Lennox's redefinition of female virtue is grounded in women's abilities to make their own rational arguments.

However, the novel's next meditation upon the connection between rape and female virtue highlights the beginning of Arabella's revision of her tightly held assumptions. When Arabella again predicts her own rape, reasoning that the highwaymen upon the road to Bath were coming to carry her or Miss Glanville away, their quick retreat leaves her with questions that force her re-examination and she begins to reconsider her suppositions. Confronted by Mr Glanville, Arabella concludes, 'I have been strangely mistaken, it seems'.[22] But her insistence, 'However, I apprehend there is no Certainty, that your Suspicions are true; and it may still be as I say, that they either came to rescue or carry us away' maintains the drama, revealing a foundational shift in Arabella's fears of rape.[23] Unable to interpret accurately the situation, the foundations linking Arabella's faith in the ability of intellect to secure the autonomy of her person, her chastity and her virtue begin to crumble.

A subsequent episode with Mr Tinsel shows Arabella further revising her criteria for female virtue. Finding the boundaries of her own room violated, Arabella begins to acknowledge laws 'human and divine' contrary to those she had assumed in the novel's opening pages, and she 'g[i]ve[s] herself over for lost'.[24] Her subsequent speech begins a redefinition of female virtue dependent upon attitude and intention as opposed to a superior intellect's preservation of physical chastity:

> Inhuman Wretch, cry'd she, with a faint Voice, supposing herself in the Hands of her Ravisher, think not thy cruel Violence shall procure thee what thy Submissions could not obtain; and if when thou hadst only my Indifference to surmount, thou didst find it so difficult to overcome my Resolution, now that by this unjust Attempt, thou hast added Aversion to that Indifference, never hope for any Thing but the most bitter Reproaches from me.[25]

Here, Arabella acknowledges that she has no power to resist physical violence perpetrated against her and that, instead, her only agency lies in her subsequent censure of the situation and those involved. She also insists upon the inviolability of her virtue, implying its location in her resolution and not a body preserved from sexual predation.

The novel's ultimate crisis once again mocks Arabella's fear of sexual violence even as it acknowledges real danger, allowing for a final interrogation of the link between intellect, chastity and virtue in women. Arabella, searching for the 'melancholy Cynecia' quits her efforts as the fading daylight is replaced by suspicious shadows:

The young ladies finding it grew late, express'd their apprehensions at being without any Attendants; and desir'd Arabella to give over her Search for that Day. Arabella at this Hint of Danger, enquir'd very earnestly, If they apprehended any Attempts to carry them away? And without staying for an answer, urg'd them to walk Home as fast as possible, apologizing for the Danger into which she had so indiscreetly drawn both them and herself.[26]

Their 'apprehensions' in this moment are founded. The 'Danger' is real. The encroaching darkness and the cover it provides for sexual transgression threatens female virtue defined as chastity and even Arabella's celebrated sense cannot in this instance prevent it. Thus, the absurdity of this moment lies not in Arabella's fears of rape but, instead, in her insistence on the probability of their rescue by a 'generous Cavalier' and on the possibility of earning a celebrated 'immortal Fame' via Thames escape.[27]

Up to this point, Arabella has made significant steps towards disconnecting intellect and culpability in the victims of sexual predation. Confronted with the realities of eighteenth-century society, she not only conceives of her mistaken notions but sees also their consequences for herself. And when Arabella's near-death experience proves to her that there are things to be feared more than rape, she must admit her lack of control over her bodily circumstances. She becomes 'sensible of her Danger, [and] prepar'd for Death, with great Piety and Constancy of Mind'.[28] This revelation results in Arabella's immediate reformation. No matter how intelligent a woman is, she cannot always prevent her own victimization by sexual predators. She cannot anticipate and avoid all circumstances that endanger her chastity, and she cannot, therefore, protect a virtue so defined. Her corresponding reformation takes the form of an attitude adjustment and she 'solemnly assur'd Mr. Glanville of her Forgiveness' without demanding any of the trying explanations, arguments and proofs of the love and constancy previously required to exonerate him from suspicions of sexual predation.[29] At this point, suffering the deleterious effects of her Thames escape and having already commenced her reformation, Arabella desires 'Assistance' with her preparations for death, assistance that seems almost unnecessary in the face of her now clearly visible 'unfeign'd Piety' and 'uncommon Firmness of Mind'.[30] She has acknowledged her error. 'Rash and vain-glorious', she had located her virtue and honour in her intellectual power over her person.[31] Once she admits this vanity has 'prompted her to so rash an Undertaking', she also admits the impossibility of preserving her virtue through control of her body and situation, for her Thames escape proves she can guarantee neither.[32] She cannot always anticipate intellectually the circumstances that might jeopardize such a narrowly defined virtue. She reasons instead that her virtue must consist in an attitude or intention. She realizes the superlative importance of piety.[33] Arabella's gradual acknowledgement of her inability to secure intellectually her virtue defined according to chastity and her corresponding embrace of piety need not be read as a rejection of women's potential intellectual agency. Arabella uses her power of reasoning to come to this interpretation, but her final conversation with the Learned Divine also demonstrates the compatibility of women's intellect and piety.

The identity and role of the Learned Divine illustrate Arabella's agency in the novel's revision of female virtue. Many have simply read the Learned Divine as a direct representation of Samuel Johnson and the Learned Divine's argument as Johnson's denunciation of romance, but O. M. Brack and Susan Carlile's examination suggests otherwise. While Brack and Carlile do insist that the novel's end acts as Lennox's celebration of Johnson's didactic criticism of fiction, they also qualify such simple relations by faulting this celebration as a weak imitation, calling it 'Johnsonease' and 'a pastiche of [the] *Rambler* essays' and concluding that, 'This is an extremely pale shadow of Johnson, without his forcefulness or sentiment'.[34] In fact, their observation that the entire argument through which Arabella is 'cured' lacks structure and definition suggests that something else may be going on. Anna Udden takes such a notion to the extreme to argue that the novel's structural irony suggests the novel critiques Johnson and engages in 'mockery of the critical father figure of its day'.[35] Ruth Perry and Susan Carlile's emphasis on Lennox's often prickly relationship with Johnson could support Udden's rejection of the Learned Divine as a celebrated Johnson.[36] However, Norbert Shürer's edition of Lennox's correspondence provides a more complete and contrary view of a complex and close intellectual relationship with the ups and downs, misunderstandings and reconciliations common to figures such as these, suggesting that Lennox, who Johnson himself called 'a powerful mind' and 'a Great genius', unlikely would either so poorly mimic someone she so respected nor deliberately mock him by creating such a dissatisfying ending.[37] Instead, the Learned Divine's argument is an ironic parody and clear wresting of authority from the kind of bad male upper- and middle-class criticism that Ellen Gardiner sees in Sir George and not specifically in Johnson. Thus the ending organically concludes the novel in its entirety, which specifically emphasizes the progress Arabella has made in bringing about her own cure and revising female virtue.

Read as an ironic parody, Arabella's final conversation with the Learned Divine is purposefully dissatisfying: such a poorly crafted and executed argument could only have convinced someone who had already convinced herself.[38] Arabella's autonomous conversion begins with her explanation of her previous conduct and the romance values underlying it. She outlines for the Learned Divine the world view that a woman's intellectual superiority determines her ability to control her person and reputation and to protect herself from sexual predation. A woman who encounters danger must understand its implications and act accordingly. In response to the Learned Divine's further inquiry, Arabella subsequently provides a structured argument that acknowledges her previous confrontation with circumstances and authority beyond the power of her intellect, as well as her embrace of an alternative piety. This step acknowledges the insufficiency of a woman's intellect to insulate her against the real dangers and threats of the world and imagines a female virtue that can't be blamed for its own victimization.

Early and often in her conversation with the Learned Divine Arabella exerts her superior intellect in an attempt to define female virtue. She offers a solution; he struggles to reject it. For example, despite having been informed about the idiosyncrasies of Arabella's behaviour by Mr Glanville, the Learned Divine is stumped by her initial explanation of romance values:

> And tho' in the Performance of his Office he had been accustom'd to accommodate his Notions to every Understanding and had therefore accumulated a great Variety of Topicks and Illustrations; yet he found himself now engag'd in a Controversy for which he was not so well prepar'd as he imagined and was at a Loss for some leading Principle, by which he might introduce his Reasonings and begin his Confutation.[39]

Interestingly, while the Learned Divine admits to himself his ignorance upon the subject of 'Heroick Virtue', he nevertheless proceeds in his attack against it. When he finally does light upon a plan of attack, he tries to undermine the value of Arabella's advantages and question her happiness. Once the narrator relates the result of this tactic: 'The Doctor saw he had not introduc'd his Discourse in the most acceptable Manner; but it was too late to repent', the wisdom of a Learned Divine who would insist on arguing against that about which he appears to know little with an opponent that he has clearly misjudged falls under question.[40]

When he pushes forward with another failing line of reasoning, his further clarification consists of a backtracking flattery that Arabella refuses. Further, only upon Arabella's encouragement can the Learned Divine delineate the culpability of Arabella's 'Imaginations', claiming the very happiness and advantage he had previously denied her, but now grants her, would be better replaced with the 'Peace of Poverty or Ignorance'.[41] When Arabella maintains the link between 'Wealth and Knowledge' and 'Judgment', the Learned Divine simply insists on her error in reading the intentions of those around her. And in another disappointing move, he engages Arabella's rebuttal that 'Human Beings cannot penetrate into Intentions, nor regulate their Conduct by exterior Appearances' with only a desperate 'course Epithet' and the excuse of 'Rugged' scholasticism.[42] When he finally iterates only the most basic of empiricist arguments for knowledge based upon experience, he degenerates into invective. He denies the usefulness of experience 'gain'd by Books' even while he also admits his 'absolute' ignorance and only faint remembrance of them.[43] He concludes with accordingly unfounded categorical derision of them as 'contemptible Volumes' providing 'senseless' and 'Absurd' 'Fictions'.[44] Again the narrator alerts the reader to the weakness of this reasoning: 'The Doctor, whose Vehemence had hinder'd him from discovering all the Consequences of his Position, now found himself entangled'.[45] Finally, the generous Arabella acknowledges the Learned Divine's desperation and seizes control of his failed argument. Arabella then outlines the purpose and shape of the argument against her romances as 'Fictions', 'absurd' and 'Criminal'.[46] Thus far Arabella's superior intelligence has offered sober reason to the Learned Divine's impassioned ignorance. She has repeatedly reigned in his digressions and offered useful direction and repetition of the higher intellectual standard to which Arabella continues to hold herself.

The rest of Arabella's 'cure' follows a similar pattern. The Learned Divine offers less than compelling reasoning that Arabella clarifies and applies. First, he denies the value of romance according to their fictionality, a fictionality he 'proves' by denying the possibility of carefully researched 'Records, Monuments, Memoirs, and Histories' to provide modern writers insight into ancient history.[47] When he is unable to present 'any other Evidence' to support this claim, Arabella concedes for the sake of argument.[48] When he proposes to add circular reasoning to this lack of proof, Arabella allows him to continue in the hopes that his failures might be remedied. But Arabella does not grant the Learned Divine's bad reasoning. Instead, she simply overlooks his failures to follow what she views as the more important point. Upon her insistence that narrative must be true to have value, he goes on to undermine his own argument, allowing 'the most solid Instructions, the noblest Sentiments, and the most exalted Piety, in the pleasing Dress of a Novel'.[49] This, of course, requires Arabella's clarification of the terms of the argument once again. No longer proving only the absurdity of all fiction, he must instead only prove culpable those 'told with the solemn Air of historical Truth, and if false convey no Instruction'.[50]

At this point Arabella again concedes the Learned Divine's rationale for the sake of argument only to be offered his own 'authoritative' 'decision' about the correspondence of romance with the world based on his own experience.[51] Finally, speaking to the experience Arabella has gained throughout the novel, the Learned Divine insists that 'knowing the Ways of Mankind' 'cannot be learned but from Experience, and of which the highest Understanding, and the lowest, must enter the World in equal Ignorance'.[52] Arabella slowly and painfully realizes the disconnect between the world and her previous understanding of it. While she might have once judged herself and those around her for the accidents that befall them, holding them responsible based on the highest of intellectual standards, Arabella's multiple real and misperceived encounters with sexual violence have led her to revise this association. Then, for only the second time in this conversation, the Learned Divine speaks to Arabella's most recent experience, suggesting that the behaviours exemplified in romance 'must be suppressed if we hope to be approved in the Sight of the only Being where Approbation can make us Happy'.[53] When he subsequently apologizes for turning the conversation in a direction 'too serious' for a young woman, she replies, 'I have already learned too much from you ... to presume to instruct you, yet suffer me to caution you never to dishonor your sacred Office by the Lowliness of Apologies'.[54] Arabella here reveals her privileging of the piety implied by his 'sacred Office' above all other claims. No longer able to insist on linking intellect and virtue with chastity in the face of real powerlessness, Arabella rationally embraces attitude and intention as defining features of female virtue.

Initially, the Learned Divine sets out to prove that Arabella's Thames escape was without cause. In order to prove this, he needs to demonstrate that the precedent set by romance is fictional, absurd and criminal. Throughout the course of the argument, the Learned Divine fails to prove the fictionality of romance, nor does he prove the absurdity of fiction – offering instead an argument in support of fiction as a useful moral tool. Finally, Arabella stops short the Learned Divine's proof of romance's criminality, making clear her earlier privileging of piety as the definition of virtue. Ultimately, Arabella's willingness to outline and profitably redirect the Learned Divine's misguided failings only increases when he finally speaks to the hard won experience that each of her near-rapes and imagined near-rapes has given her. Thus, his mention of God's approbation as the only source of true happiness can garner her own approbation. Arabella's near-death experience has already taught her this truth, and she has already accepted the impropriety of holding a woman responsible for her own victimization. She reasons she must embrace a definition of female virtue defined instead by piety. She cures herself.[55]

The Learned Divine's conversation, however, does provide an opportunity for meaningful proof of Arabella's recent conversion. Upon his launch into a list of calumnies against the social values taught by romance, Arabella interrupts:

> It is not necessary, Sir, ... that you strengthen by any new Proof a Position which when calmly considered cannot be denied; my Heart yields to the force of Truth and I now wonder how the Blaze of Enthusiastic Bravery, could hinder me from remarking with Abhorrence the Crime of deliberate unnecessary Bloodshed.[56]

This result of her calm consideration follows immediately after the Learned Divine mentions 'Revenge' and her blushes at this clearly reveal her thoughts of Mr Glanville and Sir George. Her love for Mr Glanville prompts the conclusion: 'but whatever I suffer, I will never more demand or instigate Vengeance, nor consider my Punctilios as important enough to be balanced against Life'.[57] Significantly, Arabella's acceptance of her own suffering and the corresponding piety she has embraced paves the way for its manifestation in a Christian ethic.[58] Her 'Punctilios' cannot be the cause of their suffering.[59] Arabella's intellect allows her to confront, first, the injustice of holding women's intellect responsible for violence perpetrated against them; secondly, the impossibility of defending, as a woman, virtue defined as chastity; and, thirdly, to accept an alternative definition of virtue according to a Christian ethic. Reasoning upon her deathbed allows her to repudiate heroic virtue for herself, and only feeling the pricks of conscience upon the sufferings of her loved-ones allows her repudiation of heroic virtue as a standard for others. By the time she encounters the Learned Divine, she has already reformed her notions of female virtue; she has already replaced her previous notions of virtue as chastity preserved by superior understanding with virtue defined according to piety. Such a reading counters any direct correlation between the Learned Divine and Johnson, leaving his celebration as the author of the *Rambler* in parity with that of Richardson.[60] But such a reading also speaks to the commitment to women's hard won piety in the face of fragile reputation reflected throughout Lennox's work.[61]

Heretofore, the end of *The Female Quixote* and Arabella's conversation with the Learned Divine has been read as responsible for her 'cure', and her persuasion against romance has been seen as a negation of female values and voice. My reading of this novel considers the repetition of rape as the locus of a critique of female virtue that would use a woman's intellect to blame her for her own victimization at the hands of sexual predators. The novel's corresponding acknowledgement of women's frequent powerlessness explains more completely Arabella's marked alternative privileging of a pious heart and superior intellect in the 'laudable *Affection* of the Mind' of the novel's final words.[62]

10 'NOTHING BUT VIOLENT METHODS WILL DO': HETEROSEXUAL RAPE AND THE VIOLATION OF FEMALE FRIENDSHIP

Dawn A. Nawrot

The threat, the violent attempt or the actual rape of female characters is found in many eighteenth-century novels. Yet, in addition to depictions of male perpetrators of sexual violence, we also commonly find culpable women, who help to lure and trap the intended rape victims. Many female accomplices are minor characters who pose as virtuous and trustworthy friends. This is the case in Samuel Richardson's *Clarissa* (1748) and Eliza Haywood's *The History of Miss Betsy Thoughtless* (1751), as supposed female friends assist male perpetrators in luring and/or confining virtuous female protagonists. However, in Daniel Defoe's *Roxana* (1724) and Henry Fielding's *Tom Jones* (1749), the treacherous women are major characters responsible for instigating the rapes of women living in their own homes. These deceitful women are important participants in the rape narratives, yet they often get overlooked in analyses of patriarchal violence against women. These narratives of female betrayal and rape push readers beyond didactic messages that educate naïve, young women about the dangers of rakes and artful male seducers circulating within polite society. Rather, female perpetrators of rape presented in popular novels including *Tom Jones* complicate women's roles as continual victims of patriarchal aggression. These treacherous female characters force us to acknowledge women's acts of violence and betrayal against one another. Moreover, this repeated narrative leads readers to question why women's acts of betrayal are linked to rape, which is a violent violation of an individual's (and in these cases, a woman's) autonomy and consent.

I argue that these narratives of women's violated subjectivity through sexual violence and homosocial betrayal contribute to a broader political discussion about subjectivity, morality and the dangers of contractual relationships in a liberal and commercial society. Perhaps, as Nancy Armstrong suggests of Richardson's *Pamela* (1740) and similar eighteenth-century novels written about women's lives, even though the texts focus on personal narratives of women's virtues, selfhood and sexuality within the private domain, they promote Enlightenment political ideas concerning individual autonomy and political resistance against religious and aristocratic authorities.[1] She argues that the gendered shift onto women's personal experiences in domestic fiction reflects a shift in political power from the church and state to the individual, claiming that, 'Fiction began to deny the political basis for its meaning and referred to the private regions of the self'.[2] Yet, the lessons taught through domestic narratives of female experience must be 'at once highly personal ... and yet applicable to virtually everyone'.[3] As Armstrong theorizes, perhaps the depiction of personal relationships between women, the acts of deception and the violation of women's autonomy through rape also explore a broader social and political anxiety about liberal subjecthood and contractual relationships. Female friendships in rape narratives represent the liberal social contract that individuals hypothetically enter into, or that they literally enter into in the public sphere – in the market, civic government, etc. By entering into friendships, like other relationships, an individual sacrifices his/her self-interests for shared interests or denies his/her own interests for the best interests of others. Generosity and cooperation, ideally, can help to build a virtuous society, but reliance on others can also leave individuals open to betrayal and personal injury.

Novels that narrate women's treacherous friendships expose a pervasive social fear of deceptive relationships violated by self-interest. In these novels, one woman's corrupted self-interests trump her loyalty and benevolence to another woman and rupture their friendship. The ultimate betrayal is enacted through her facilitation of, or assistance in, a rape (or attempted rape) of the other often virtuous female character. The betrayal and rape depict a violent and profound violation of the female victim's body, her trust, her consent and, ultimately, her status as a subject. In these narratives, readers are led to sympathize with the female victim. Meanwhile, the female perpetrators who initiate the rapes are demonized for their extreme acts of deception. Thus, the deceptive female accomplice/rapist becomes a cautionary figure of excessive and corrupted selfhood in the novel, against which the virtuous female (and the reader by extension) must protect herself.

There are a number of eighteenth-century theorists and authors who wrestle directly with the belief in virtuous friendship against the frightening cultural reality of self-interest, deception and betrayal. After establishing how tenets of friendship compare to Locke's social contract theories, I highlight this eighteenth-century debate through the writings of Mary Astell, David Hume, Eliza Haywood and others. Then, I analyse how the narrative of female friendship and attempted rape in Fielding's *Tom Jones* participates in this debate. Fielding's novel provides an insightful literary case study of consensual relationships, trust and betrayal through its narrative of intimate female friendship and its subsequent violation through an attempted heterosexual rape.

Friendship as a Social Contract

In his *Second Treatise of Government*, Locke asserts that every man, 'being all equal and independent' under God, possesses the right to protect his 'life, health, liberty, or possessions'.[4] Yet, Locke believes that without social contract, the enjoyment of our rights and property 'is very uncertain and always exposed to the invasion of others'.[5] However, men can agree to join together in order to uphold their natural individual rights. In the social contract of civil government men agree 'together mutually to enter into one community and make one body politic' 'for their comfortable, safe, and peaceable living amongst one another, in a secure enjoyment of their properties'.[6] Locke envisions a commonwealth in which each independent individual rationally consents to a social contract in order mutually to protect personal liberties, interests and possessions.

In multiple ways friendship parallels Locke's vision of social contracts in which individuals agree 'together mutually to enter into one community'.[7] In Aristotle's classical theory as well as in eighteenth-century society, friendship ideally is regarded as a voluntary personal commitment in which participants loyally pursue mutual interests. Allan Silver, who examines British eighteenth-century theories of friendship and commerce, claims, 'As a private and unspecialized relation (*unlike the label of spouse or daughter, for example*), friendship is a continuous creation of will and choice', and 'friendship usefully serves as a prototype of the larger category of personal relations'.[8] Individuals freely consent to friendship much like in Locke's vision of social contracts. In addition, friends must be relatively equal and their participation mutual. Aristotle argues that to ensure a friendship is mutual, 'Each friend receives from the other in every way the same or nearly the same treatment as he gives'.[9] However the balance is created, ideal friendships should have a balance of strengths that creates an equal level of participation and respect. Otherwise, friendships, like social contracts, are corrupted through uneven assertions of power. As Marilyn Friedman clarifies in *What are Friends For?* 'Domination and subordination in a relationship are conditions that override the consent of one or both parties and, thereby, undermine the voluntariness of the relationship'.[10]

Friendship, like other social contracts, hinges on the shared trust that others will not violate one's best interests in pursuit of one's own. This is the premise of Locke's theory and also of private friendships. Like public contractual relationships, friendship values individualism and also creates a shared dependency and vulnerability between partners. However, unlike public relationships virtuous friendship depends on intimacy, or what Silver describes as 'the confident revelation of one's inner self to a trusted other'.[11] Trusting another individual with the intimate knowledge of one's needs, desires, history, etc., creates a great dependency on the confidant. Accordingly, the participants rely on 'the assurance that neither of the two friends will do injury to the other'.[12] Friendship may be a more private form of social contract. However, one's interdependence on others for personal protection is also the foundation of public social contracts.

The Virtues and Vices of Friendship

The social anxiety over excessive self-interests and betrayal are expressed by numerous eighteenth-century writers. In response, some authors promote moral ideals of classical friendship (i.e. trust and benevolence) as a safeguard against deceptive and injurious contractual relationships. Their writings often directly reflect Aristotelian models of virtuous friendship. Aristotle defines the 'perfect friendship' as the permanent relationship 'of people who are good and alike in virtue' who 'wish the good of their friends for their friend's sake' rather than for their own self-interests.[13] While ideal friends are to give and receive mutually, in times of trouble friends benevolently preserve the prosperity and safety of one another, lead each other from error, and take care of each other when aged and feeble.[14] He establishes such virtuous friendship above the impermanent friendships of pleasure and utility, which operate on the fulfilment of mutual self-interests rather than beneficence.[15] For Aristotle, virtuous friendship has significant civic implications as well. He claims that perfect or virtuous 'friendship is the bond that holds states together' because it does more than uphold justice. The mutual good will between friends ensures lasting social harmony within society.[16]

Jacqueline Broad has highlighted Mary Astell's reliance on Aristotle's theory of virtuous friendship in *A Serious Proposal to the Ladies* (1694). Astell suggests that in friendship, 'The truest effect of love' is 'to endeavor the bettering of the other person'.[17] Broad cites Astell's related claim that 'Virtuous friendship consists in mutual acts of un-self-interested benevolence between "two Persons of a sympathizing disposition, whose Souls bear an exact conformity to each other"'.[18] In Astell's view, mutual female friendships based on altruistic kindness, love and truth can ultimately promote moral growth for both participants. Moreover, like Aristotle, she believes that these relationships can improve the morality of society. She suggests that women who are 'Refined' and 'purified' through virtuous female relationships can 'become Antidotes to expel Poyson in others and spread a salutary Air on ev'ry Side'.[19]

Like Astell, authors and theorists promoted virtuous and altruistic friendship well into the eighteenth century. Samuel Johnson's first definition for 'friend' in his 1755 dictionary is 'One joined to another in mutual benevolence and intimacy'.[20] This definition focuses on the private or personal relationship friends share. It also claims that individuals 'joined' together in friendship are reliant on the virtues of benevolence, or mutual kindness and generosity, not self-interest.

In another mid-century text, 'Of the Remedy of Affliction for the Loss of our Friends', Henry Fielding notes that we experience significant grief due to the 'tender affection' we feel for our friends.[21] The separation of friends results in 'tearing the heart, the soul from the body'.[22] This intimate, emotional and spiritual connection is similar to the enduring bonds of affection and love both Aristotle and Astell describe. Moreover, Fielding assures his readers that a friend's heavenly 'virtues and good qualities', which are the cause of our tender 'affection on earth', are also 'the foundation of his happiness and reward in a better world'.[23] In Fielding's opinion, it is individuals' virtuous qualities that strengthen their affection for one another and ultimately lead to their spiritual salvation.

Finally, Adam Smith praises our human capacity for selfless benevolence in *The Theory of Moral Sentiments* (1759), claiming, 'that to feel much for others, and little for ourselves, that to restrain our selfish, and to indulge our benevolent, affections, constitutes the perfection of human nature'.[24] Smith expands virtue and generosity to relationships beyond friendship. Like Aristotle, he suggests that such moral qualities found in friendship can also produce a 'harmony' 'among mankind'.[25]

Despite the promotion of virtuous relationships during the long eighteenth century, there is a recurring fear of deception and personal violation. Mary Astell, David Hume and Eliza Haywood express the fear of fraudulent self-interest in their writing. In *A Serious Proposal to the Ladies*, Astell advocates for a protected space to foster women's virtuous friendships and their moral development away from the pervasive social corruption to which women often fell victim. She blatantly reproaches her contemporaries, arguing that the world is too full of selfishness to promote virtuous and charitable friendships. Astell decries, 'the love of many is not only waxen and cold, but quite benumb'd and perish'd.[26] She further questions, 'If our hearts be so full of mistaken Self-love, so unreasonably fond of ourselves, that we cannot spare the hearty Good-will to one or two choice Persons, how can it ever be thought, that we should well acquit ourselves of that Charity which is due to all Mankind?'.[27] In her opinion, personal vanity and greed inhibit individuals' ability to befriend one another and, ultimately, promote a benevolent society. Astell believes that the social implications of corrupted friendships are as far-reaching as the potential social benefits of virtuous friendships. Unfortunately, in these passages she presents a rather dark depiction of the current moral state of late seventeenth-century British society.

Similar to Astell, in the mid-eighteenth century, David Hume takes up the social issues of self-love and deception in 'An Enquiry Concerning the Principles of Morals' (1751). He acknowledges the prevailing social anxiety 'that all benevolence is mere hypocrisy, friendship a cheat, public spirit a farce, fidelity a snare to procure trust and confidence, in order to ... expose them the more to our wiles and machinations'.[28] This theory configures a variety of ways that pretences of virtuous friendship and faithfulness are used to manipulate others for ulterior self-interests. Yet, Hume immediately rejects this harsh generalization, fearing that 'Superficial reasoners, indeed, observing many false pretenses among mankind ... may draw a general and a hasty conclusion that all is equally corrupted'.[29] Hume does not deny that there are copious examples from which social sceptics may draw. However, he optimistically believes there are 'a thousand other instances' of 'benevolence in human nature' in which individuals do not merely serve their own interests.[30] In Hume's view, these instances disprove popular assumptions and theories of human selfishness that deny virtuous friendship and beneficence.

Like Astell and Hume, in the mid-1740s Eliza Haywood also warns her female readers against the pervasiveness of deception throughout society within personal relationships, community gossip, news publications and the government. In book eighteen of *The Female Spectator*, Haywood outlines the many ways reputations and relationships are broken by lies and deception. She argues that virtue and respectability rest on truth. However, when an individual lies, 'he forfeits all his pretensions to honour, courage, good-nature, and every other valuable distinction'.[31] She claims that widespread deception is corrupting eighteenth-century society. Haywood asserts that 'Lying is now become in a manner contagious', threatening moral societal bonds.[32] She writes, 'Confidence is the life of society, and the bond of friendship; without it, both must fall to the ground, and mankind regard each other as beasts of prey'.[33] All personal and public trust and security is lost when we have to suspect the promises and actions of everyone around us. The pervasive deception Haywood describes creates a very pessimistic notion of individualism based on fear and isolation. She questions:

> How is it possible, that people of any family, community, or even nation, can live together in that brotherly affection, so recommended by holy writ, and so necessary for the common good, when every individual must suspect all the rest, guard against all the rest, and live in continual fear, that everyone he converses with, is aiming to impose upon him![34]

The fear of deception that Haywood describes seems to resemble directly the dysfunctional state of war against which Locke's vision of liberal civil society aims to guard.

Tom Jones

Like the eighteenth-century theorists and conduct writers discussed above, Henry Fielding explores the personal implications of deceptive relationships throughout *Tom Jones*. There are many types and networks of relationships represented in the novel: between family members, neighbours, employers and servants, housekeepers and tenants and friends. However, these relationships often prove to be dangerous as the participants deceive and/or betray one another's best interests. Bridget Allworthy deceives her brother by withholding the information that Tom is her biological son. Blifil selfishly lies to Mr Allworthy throughout the narrative to incriminate others or promote his own interests. The gamekeeper, Black George, whom Tom befriends, steals all of his money and belongings. Tom, although often charitable, betrays Sophia by continuously having sexual affairs behind her back. Mr Partridge, Tom's voluntary although garrulous servant, betrays Tom's private secrets with his big mouth. However, of all these deceptions and betrayals, the most violent and profound is Lady Bellaston's plot to have the virtuous Sophia raped. Because this is such a violent attack on Sophia's trust and subjectivity, Fielding calls the rape attempt 'the most tragical matter in our whole history'.[35]

This act of betrayal is the most tragic because Sophia is characterized as the most virtuous, rational and vulnerable character of the novel. From the beginning she is described as a loving girl, possessing the virtues of 'innocence, modesty, and tenderness'.[36] Fielding's readers repeatedly witness her dutiful obedience to her father until he orders her to marry Blifil, disregarding her own best interests. Sophia evaluates her daughterly duty to marry Blifil as an imprudent and irrational self-sacrifice, and accordingly she rejects the coerced marriage. Eileen Jacques has argued that Sophia is 'Fielding's embodiment of Aristotle's concept of full virtue' because Sophia not only possesses knowledge and virtue, but she acts on her principles.[37] While she is not always honest or obedient, Sophia is motivated by goodness, prudence and reason. Thus, her character becomes the standard of virtue against which the other characters are measured.[38]

It is significant that Sophia's virtue is connected to her reason as a consenting young woman. In the eighteenth century, compared to married women, single women held legal autonomy over their sexual consent as well as greater economic control over their property. Perhaps this greater level of agency is why eighteenth-century novelists like Fielding choose unmarried women as the subjects/victims in these rape narratives that depict profound violations of individual autonomy. Also, in *Consensual Fictions* (2005) Wendy Jones suggests that women in the eighteenth century did begin to benefit from the liberal political model that Locke helped to articulate. Just as 'civil society originated in a social contract', 'legitimate relationships of various kinds, including marriage, began to be seen as based on consent rather than force'.[39] She argues that women's individual statuses as subjects gained credence as society began to favour women's rights to marital consent. If a woman was able to choose a spouse whom she loved and esteemed, 'she was presumably capable of other important choices and of taking responsibility for her own life'.[40] In addition, she argues that courtship narratives in the novel depicting women's marital consent for love rather than familial duty participated in 'determining the proper place of women in society'.[41]

Accordingly, in *Tom Jones*, Sophia's non-consent to Blifil's marriage proposal motivates her to establish or reject a number of other relationships. Although Sophia is an otherwise dutiful daughter, she acts on the premise that she possesses the right to grant or decline marital consent. She rationally disagrees with her aunt's and father's demands to marry Blifil, and then chooses to seek asylum away from their control by re-establishing her friendship with Lady Bellaston, a distant relative and long-time friend of her aunt. Sophia claims that she plans to stay with Lady Bellaston in London 'till my father, finding me out of his power, can be brought to some reason'.[42] In this passage, Sophia rightly asserts that she is a more rational agent than her father. The autonomy Sophia exerts in both resisting her father's control and reinitiating her friendship with Lady Bellaston demonstrates the subjectivity she possesses as a chaste, single woman.

Sophia's experience of betrayal and attempted rape is most troubling to readers because she has been shown to be a virtuous, prudent and rational agent. Yet, as an innocent young woman who recently left the patriarchal control and protection of her family, she is unfamiliar with modes of deceit and societal corruption. Her innocence and her embodied virtue – her chastity – make her vulnerable to violation. Unfortunately, Sophia trusts her superficial knowledge of Lady Bellaston and her (empty) professions of friendship. Without really knowing Lady Bellaston's character, she misinterprets their relationship as a virtuous friendship. Sophia remembers how Lady Bellaston treated her once with great kindness and how she earnestly requested that she visit her in London. Sophia is confident in the sincerity of Lady Bellaston's past expressions of friendship and generosity. When Sophia arrives at Lady Bellaston's London home, she confirms Sophia's belief in her honesty and benevolence as a virtuous friend. Sophia finds a 'most hearty, as well as most polite welcome'.[43] The Lady applauds Sophia's reason, her 'sense and resolution' in removing herself from the forced marriage and her father's power. Moreover, 'she promised her all of the protection which it was in her power to give'.[44] In this conversation there is a verbal confirmation of their mutual affection, of Lady Bellaston's respect for Sophia's virtue and her life choices, as well as an explicit promise of loyalty and generous protection over Sophia. This scene depicts a voluntary contract of virtuous friendship between the two women.

Lady Bellaston declares to Sophia's cousin that 'I shall be very glad to have my share in the preservation of a young lady of so much merit, and for whom I have so much esteem'.[45] Yet, regardless of the mutual respect and affection they seem to share and profess at the outset, this relationship is not an ideal friendship. First, their relationship is neither equal nor mutual. Lady Bellaston is independently wealthy and mobile. Yet, Sophia has little money or other means of assistance while she is separated from her family. Sophia also does not intimately know Lady Bellaston's character, or 'inner self' (to use Aristotle's term).

She only assumes that her virtue is similar to her own because of their brief past acquaintance and Lady Bellaston's relationship with her aunt (which, the reader learns, was most likely at court). There is also a disparity between their knowledge of the world: Sophia's protected, relative seclusion in her country estate causes her naiveté about Lady Bellaston's sexual promiscuity and moral corruption. Aristotle suggests that one friend's (Sophia's) superior goodness could balance another's superior wealth or rank (Lady Bellaston's), thus creating equality among friends.[46] However, in *Tom Jones* this balance between Sophia and Lady Bellaston is not achieved because Lady Bellaston does not really value Sophia's moral integrity or her chastity. In the end, Lady Bellaston's sexual self-interests violently supersede any moral desires to protect Sophia's best interests.

After meeting Tom for the first time, Lady Bellaston immediately plots to lure Tom into an amour, while she is fully aware that Sophia is still in love with him. Her plan quickly succeeds as Tom is a willing sexual partner and a content recipient of her financial support. This affair leads to a mutual deception between the two women. Because Tom is an unfaithful and penniless suitor, Sophia has told Lady Bellaston that she is no longer interested in him. Yet, when Tom arrives for a rendezvous with Lady Bellaston, he unexpectedly finds Sophia, whom he still loves, alone at her house. When Lady Bellaston walks in on their conversation, both women pretend they do not know Tom. After this awkward conversation of lies, the reader observes the great difference in virtue between the women. Lady Bellaston enjoys torturing Sophia, whom she regards as a personal threat to her own interests. Fielding states that she 'would willingly have tormented her rival a little longer' if other business had not prevented her.[47] From this point, Sophia is no longer a friend, but a rival to eliminate. Alternately, Sophia feels quite guilty for protecting her secret personal interests. This is her 'first practice of deceit' towards her friend and guardian, which she regards 'with the highest uneasiness and conscious shame'.[48] After a sleepless night, Sophia still cannot 'reconcile her mind to her conduct; for her frame of mind was too delicate to bear the thought of having been guilty of a falsehood, however qualified by the circumstances'.[49] Although she also protects her private interests in deceiving Lady Bellaston, her remorse exemplifies her virtuous character and her continued concern for their relationship.

Unlike Sophia, all of Lady Bellaston's friendly affection and benevolence turn to feelings of jealousy, rage and competition. Fielding writes, 'As she plainly saw that this young lady stood between her and the full indulgence of her desires, she resolved to get rid of her by some means or other'.[50] The means by which Lady Bellaston plans to dispose of Sophia is found through her friend, Lord Fellamar, who is smitten with Sophia. Lady Bellaston lies to Lord Fellamar, suggesting that Sophia is about to ruin herself by running away with Tom. She repeatedly and falsely insists that 'Nothing but violent methods will do' to 'preserve so inestimable a jewel'.[51] She ironically convinces Lord Fellamar that if he secretly rapes and coerces Sophia to marry him, Sophia's public reputation will be preserved. In this narrative, the male would-be rapist is demonized less than the deceptive female 'friend'. Lady Bellaston is depicted as the most base and treacherous perpetrator in initiating the rape plan and organizing the event. Meanwhile, Lord Fellamar wavers in his resolution to rape Sophia even though 'it appeared in no very heinous light to his lordship' because he faithfully planned to marry Sophia and thus, make amends for this crime.[52] When Fellamar is convinced that Sophia does not love him, he tries to back out. Yet, Lady Bellaston attempts to re-encourage him with false notions that Sophia actually admires him. Lady Bellaston also bribes him with the prospect of Sophia's wealth, which he would inherit as her husband. Yet, Fellamar refuses to consider the money, declaring that Sophia needs no money to recommend her, as 'No woman ever had half her charms'.[53] It would have seemed strange to contemporary readers that the would-be rapist holds more esteem for Sophia than Lady Bellaston. While both are culpable for attempting to violate traumatically Sophia's bodily and psychological autonomy, Lady Bellaston is presented as more culpable for the near rape because she cold-heartedly betrays Sophia's trust as an avowed friend who relies on her for protection.

Ultimately, Lady Bellaston facilitates the rape attempt in order to eliminate the agency Sophia possesses as a consenting, chaste, unmarried woman. A number of feminist rape theorists have established that victims' subjectivity is subordinated or disregarded in the act of rape. For example, Ann Cahill convincingly argues that the rapist's intention is 'to overwhelm the subjectivity' of the victim 'in a particularly sexualized way'.[54] In her discussion of heterosexual rape, she argues that 'He imposes his will upon her, imposes his body on her, imposes his sexuality on her ... prohibiting her from living her bodily, ontological autonomy'.[55] The perpetrator's purpose is to subject sexually, and thus to violate, the subjectivity of the individual. Constance Mui similarly suggests that rape 'cripples the victim's will to assert herself as an autonomous subject after the attack'.[56] Hence, the victim's impaired subjectivity can stretch far beyond the moment of the rape and affect her agency within future relationships. Mui attributes the victim's impaired autonomy to the fact that rape 'invokes a fear of the other's freedom, of what the other can willfully perpetrate upon us'.[57] If, in reaction to rape, victims/survivors continue to fear another individual's power to injure them, this would perpetuate their potential subordination in future relationships. Through the act of rape, Lady Bellaston and Fellamar violently intend to assert their will over Sophia's autonomy in order to prevent Sophia's consensual agency in the future. Lady Bellaston believes that violating Sophia's chastity would eliminate Sophia as her rival for Tom Jones's affection. She states that after the rape, 'the ravished Sophia would easily be brought to consent' to a quick marriage with Lord Fellamar.[58] As a 'ruined' woman, Bellaston assumes Sophia would lack the subjectivity to withhold her marital consent from her attacker.

Fielding draws an important parallel between the sexual relationships and friendships in *Tom Jones*. First, both are intimate relations between individuals through which participants expose aspects of themselves (their wants, desires, bodies, etc.) to the other. Such self-exposure creates a certain vulnerability for participants. Secondly, both friendship and sexual intercourse require an individual's unforced consent, if not also their active participation. The narrative of broken friendship and attempted rape in *Tom Jones* highlights these parallels between sexual relationships and friendships. While Lady Bellaston is not literally the rapist, she wishes to coerce Sophia into sex against her will. She attempts to violate Sophia's consent and her trust. In the rape plot she disregards Sophia's virtue, her love for Tom and her agency as a friend and a sexually embodied subject.

Thankfully, the rape is prevented. Sophia's chastity and her subjectivity are ultimately preserved as her father, Squire Western, storms into Lady Bellaston's home to reclaim his daughter. Yet, the narrative of attempted rape remains the most frightening depiction of deception and violated autonomy in the novel. Sophia, a character of virtue, reason and agency, proves to be profoundly vulnerable to deception and betrayal even within networks of extended family and friends. The women's broken friendship reflects a social fear of liberal relationships based on, or perverted by, self-interest. Eighteenth-century readers of both genders could perceive the personal dangers in trusting relationships through this disturbing narrative of violated female friendship and attempted rape. While virtuous and benevolent contractual relationships can protect people and improve society, Sophia's dangerous experience suggests that individuals need to be extremely cautious about entering into seemingly virtuous relationships. In an emerging individualist and capitalist society that increasingly valued privacy, readers needed to become savvy interpreters of others' private moral characters before entering into relationships based on interdependence and personal confidence. Otherwise, readers may also face a profound violation of their own subjectivities.

11 BRINGING SENTIMENTAL FICTION TO ITS (ANTI-)CLIMAX: LAURENCE STERNE'S *A SENTIMENTAL JOURNEY*

Nichol Weizenbeck

In the eighteenth century, a major cultural shift occurred in Britain with the rise of sensibility, referred to rather famously by G. J. Barker-Benfield as 'the cult of sensibility'. Due to this social shift, the word 'sentiment' itself underwent a transition: where it once meant moral judgement, during its evolution it would come to be understood as the connection or combination of head and heart, and eventually it became a melding of the two faculties.[1] While not limited to the literature of the period, Janet Todd nevertheless believes that this 'cult' was largely defined by the fiction written between the 1740s and 1770s. With this in mind, the tracing of this cultural turn may be accomplished by examining the literature of the period. And, arguably, Laurence Sterne's *A Sentimental Journey* (1768) provides the zenith of sentimental fiction and supplies some of the richest material to plumb; as Jean Hagstrum claims, 'In one sense [Sterne] can be said to have brought a great eighteenth-century movement, the cult of feeling, to its climax'.[2] Morality permeates sentimental fiction to varying degrees, yet any assurance that there is an underlying moral message in Sterne's novel is complicated by the text itself. On the one hand, Sterne offers a theory of moral behaviour that privileges the powerful and elevating properties of sentiment. Yet on the other, he subverts this theory with rampant sexual allusions and bawdy double entendre. Melvyn New asserts that the bawdy in *A Sentimental Journey* holds the sentiment of the novel in check; however, one may conclude that the inverse is equally true.[3] While Sterne portrays, through his protagonist, Yorick, the ideally sensible man and traveller as one who experiences the connectivity of heart and mind, he also privileges stasis and inaction – qualities that complicate, and are even antithetical to, his conception of sentiment. Additionally and importantly, Sterne reveals Yorick and his sexual impotence as an alternative model to the brutal treatment of women frequently found in other eighteenth-century novels.

The Sentimental

Establishing a connection between mind and body proved a complex and elusive concept for contemporary thinkers, and the crux of the controversy lay in the meeting point of these two faculties.[4] The physical manifestations of this intersection were often thought to be evinced by heightened corporeal reactions – blushing, crying, fainting and an elevated pulse – and such bodily responses were thought particularly common when one experienced sympathy for a fellow being. Sterne plays with this theory of the body and its extreme emotional reactions throughout *A Sentimental Journey*, at times seeming to mock sensibility while elsewhere appearing to embrace it. For instance, in his first entry at Calais, Yorick drinks to the king's health and acknowledges the 'mildness' of Bourbon blood, and after his effusion – which he teasingly admits wine alone could not have manufactured – he describes his own bodily sensations with amused irony: 'I felt a suffusion of a finer kind upon my cheek – more warm and friendly to man, than what Burgundy ... could have produced'.[5] Yet, in the paragraph following this light-hearted description of wine-warmed sentiment, he goes on to write earnestly of how performing charitable acts affect him: 'I felt every vessel in my frame dilate – the arteries beat all cheerily together'.[6] Such transitions and inversions occur repeatedly, and, therefore, *A Sentimental Journey* rests atop constantly shifting ground, where jest abuts earnestness, or perhaps more accurately, where sarcasm frames sincerity. Through Yorick's eyes, if not Sterne's, sentiment *should* effectively prevent immorality, and he is disgusted to discover that it is not always capable of doing so. Sterne's familiarity with theories of sensibility is obvious as he alludes to this concept throughout the novel, but he is also clearly aware of the cultural stigma attached to sentiment – its degrading feminization of men.[7]

Yorick, as well, recognizes that his sentimental response makes him 'weak as a woman'.[8] 'Weakness' is another term that appears consistently throughout *A Sentimental Journey*.[9] Yet, Sterne challenges the traditional notion of weakness in the novel. It is precisely the reportedly 'weak' traits that link the body and the mind, which therefore link individuals to one another socially – in bonds of sympathy and empathy – and allow for an appreciation of human suffering and joy. Describing his own experience with the bonds sympathy creates, in his considerations of employing La Fleur, Yorick confesses:

> I am too apt to be taken with all kinds of people at first sight; but never more so than when a poor devil comes to offer his service to so poor a devil as myself; and as I know this weakness, I always suffer my judgment to draw back something on that very account.[10]

In fact, Yorick defends sensibility as the:

source inexhausted of all that's precious in our joys, or costly in our sorrows! thou chainest thy martyr down upon his bed of straw – and 'tis thou who lifts him up to HEAVEN – eternal fountain of our feelings! – 'tis here that I trace thee – and this is thy divinity which stirs within me.[11]

The affect of sentiment is so powerful that it not only allows one to become more humane by the distance it erases between humans differentiated by sex, class and social condition, it also offers the possibility of transcendence – through sympathy and fellow feeling – of the mortal coil and the ability to experience the divine within.

Sterne often demonstrates the intensity of these manifestations of emotional connections through material exchanges as evinced by Yorick's dealings with the Monk. Conflating weakness, sentiment and good nature, Yorick describes his trade of snuff boxes to the Monk, causing the Monk to weep and clutch 'the box to his bosom'.[12] After discovering the Monk's death, Yorick sits at his grave and the situation 'struck together so forcibly upon my affections, that I burst into a flood of tears – but I am as weak as a woman; and I beg the world not to smile, but pity me'.[13] For all of his double entendre and manoeuvring, Sterne presents Yorick as appealing, sincere and capable of (if not driven by) concern and distress at another's suffering.[14] The relationship between the two men is sentimental in the sense that it arouses a physical response through emotion and moreover a united compassion and shared understanding.[15]

As many critics have noted, sentiment in *A Sentimental Journey* has little to do with amorous feelings, yet Sterne makes clear that sentiment has much to do with love.[16] Sterne places great value on filial love, and therefore he shows that the height of impropriety is to imagine making love or wooing with sentiments as that would defeat and defile the loftier ends of sensibility; Yorick would as soon 'think of making a genteel suit of cloaths [sic] out of remnants'.[17] In a letter Yorick copies from La Fleur, he writes that, 'Love is *nothing* without sentiment / and sentiment is even *less* without love'.[18] Here again Sterne asserts his wit: a thing cannot be valued as less than nothing, yet it remains possible that he alludes to the absolute interrelation between love and sentiment – one cannot be without the other. He holds that all springs from the fountain of sentiment; the connection of heart and mind radiates to connect one to society, not only through emotional sympathy, but with visible sympathy (a physical response like weeping). Through such a bond to one's fellow beings, one connects to the divine. While some may perceive abstinence and the embracing of 'the softer side' as a diminishment of a man, Yorick affirms that they are necessary to the discovery of sensible pathways, which allow for a far more meaningful human existence. Yet in order to link oneself to other human beings, one must place oneself in their paths, and the stationary act of waiting for such intersections comprises Yorick's journey.

The Journey

The titular journey of this novel necessarily implies that there is a traveller, and Sterne carefully defines the traveller 'model' to which Yorick adheres. Yorick begins by declaring that all travellers are 'idle people' and then subdivides that general pool of travellers by their various motivations, ending with the category to which he belongs – the 'sentimental' traveller, who travels 'out of *Necessity*'.[19] While he does not elaborate on what this 'necessity' is, Yorick contrasts the sentimental traveller to a 'Mundungus', who travels by blindly following the grand tour, who has no 'connections' and no pleasurable anecdotes, all because he does not look to the left or the right, 'lest Love or Pity should seduce him out of his road'.[20] According to Sterne, the sentimental traveller does not traverse much ground precisely because he allows himself to be affected by empathy and emotion, and he explores the panorama of experience rather than keeping to the straight and narrow. As Todd explains, 'because sensibility is reactive and unstable, the sentimental work of prose or poetry meanders rather than moves logically to its destination'.[21] The objective is not an outward and fixed physical point but an inward one, and the geography traversed follows the map of the heart rather than a prescribed series of cities. Due to Yorick's openness to human experience, his tour becomes an internal one, a journey of sentiment.

As a flight of sentiment, Yorick's is also an expedition towards self-improvement. *A Sentimental Journey* comprises Yorick's record of his inner exploration, and in his conscious retreat from sexuality, Yorick's voyage, as New avers, 'suggests a masculine victory, a triumph over desire by firm governance – a conquest over himself. *A Sentimental Journey*, however, contains a search not for moral triumph, but for the far more difficult victory of self-understanding and human love'.[22] Yet with this self-understanding comes the difficult selection of virtue over bodily pleasure, of which Yorick is well aware as he exclaims,

> I know as well as anyone, [the devil] is an adversary, whom if we resist, he will fly from us – but I seldom resist him at all; from a terror, that though I may conquer, I may still get hurt in the combat – so I give up triumph, for security, and instead of thinking to make him fly, I generally fly myself.[23]

Although he does not engage dynamically with his adversary, Yorick still comes down on the side of morality yet does not close himself off to the thorny experience of strong sexual temptations that cause his 'tremors' and therefore his connections to others.[24] Given his 'terror', his is paradoxically not a journey for the weak of heart; Yorick affirms that 'the man who either disdains or fears to walk up a dark entry may be an excellent good man, and fit for a hundred things; but he will not do to make a good sentimental traveler'.[25] The dark entries he speaks of are not those of the outer world full of urban life, but the interiors of the human heart, and Yorick battles this 'darkness' throughout his travels with almost every woman he meets. While his path meanders, Yorick's inner journey proves one of profound movement, evinced by his desire for a progress that reaches towards 'self-understanding and human love' over the temporary ecstasy of sexual gratification.[26] Yet this charity is not reserved only for the women of the novel; after meeting and refusing charity to the Monk at Calais, Yorick admits, 'I have behaved very ill ... but I have only just set out upon my travels; and shall learn better manners as I get along'.[27] Manners were of supreme importance in the eighteenth century and following; they provided not only a code of conduct but indicated a level of moral worth. Yorick's journey consists of navigating the manners of a foreign culture while simultaneously finding a path that will allow him to remain true to his beliefs, which is illustrated starkly in Yorick's conversation with the Marquis concerning sexual tourism. And when he faces the severe trial of temptation through his encounter with the *fille de chambre* – who, on an errand for her employer, remains trapped and helpless in Yorick's hotel room – and has conquered his demons, he realizes that temptation does not equate to trespass but proves that his is not a 'luke-warm heart', and it remains his own conduct for which a man is answerable. The voyage Yorick must undertake, then, is not one without passion but rather one that reflects his ability to deal with his passion virtuously.

Combating his lascivious demons results in Yorick's bodily impotence. Notably, for a 'journey' there is remarkably little travelling in *A Sentimental Journey*. In total, Yorick's tour includes six cities; in fact, the first sixteen entries encompass only one hour in Calais, and thirty-two entries, which comprise one day, complete the hero's stay in Paris (with a quick jaunt to Versailles). The effect this has on the reader and on Yorick is one of almost complete stasis, a comprehensive inaction; Yorick recognizes this himself writing, 'I think there is a fatality in it – I seldom go to the place I set out for'.[28] Although the text is riddled with sexual innuendos, according to New, sentimentality was a popular trope of the eighteenth century employed as a denunciation of sexuality, yet in Yorick the two become muddled and indistinguishable.[29] Yorick's continual striving to penetrate the feminine in covertly sexual ways complicates the text with its apparent denial of and simultaneous exploitation of physical arousal. However, the innuendos result in no ultimate development, no climax – they, too, are inactive.[30] The overall effect is one of impotence; even though a plethora of opportunity for licentious behaviour presents itself, Yorick's sensibility snuffs the flames.

The Stasis of a Sentimental Journey

The anti-climactic moments of the novel are intensified by Sterne's act of infusing the journey with the sentimental, which leads to an overarching static quality in the novel. Paradoxically, it is the lack of movement that allows Yorick to commence his internal sentimental travels. Yorick initiates his voyage of physical quietude in front of a locked door at Calais. In his encounter with a fellow female traveller, the Lady from Brussels, the first and most drawn out exchange with a woman, Yorick's utter incapability of securing her as a traveling companion is carefully constructed. Indeed, Yorick is not the sole character frustrated by impotence; Monsieur Dessin cannot breach his own *remise*, but nevertheless tries 'above fifty times' before he realizes he has brought the wrong key. His failure proves infectious as Yorick the passive bystander transforms to Yorick the incapable seducer. Waiting for Dessin to return, Yorick holds the Lady from Brussels's hand and launches an apostrophe to Fortune for joining their hands, when she interrupts, noting that his very attention to the situation belies his embarrassment and disengages her hand.[31] Mortified by the loss of her hand, he admits that the manner by which he lost it gives him a 'pain of sheepish inferiority'.[32] The Lady, recognizing his discomfort and with a 'triumph of a true feminine heart', allows Yorick to regain his position.[33] The pulsations of his arteries alert her to what passes within (i.e. physical arousal), which nearly makes her withdraw again, when his instinct directs Yorick to hold her hand in a limp posture and thereby keep the contact. He holds her hand until, finally pressing it to his lips, she draws back. As if this were not disappointment enough for one afternoon, Yorick is inspired to offer the 'distressed' Lady a ride when 'every dirty passion and bad propensity' of his nature is aroused by the thought.[34] After battling his doubts and deciding to act on his impulse, he turns to find the Lady had 'glided off unperceived'.[35] He longs to know her name and situation, but there was 'no such thing as a man's directly asking her – the thing was impossible', yet that is precisely what a French man does, which possibly alludes to the first line of the novel, 'They order ... this matter better in France'.[36] Finally gaining entry to the garage, Dessin puts Yorick and the Lady in a chaise (a chaise without horses, and therefore also immobile), and Yorick describes love as 'small', 'quiet' and 'silent', at which point the Lady declares blushing, 'then ... you have been making love to me all this while'.[37] This exchange proves the model for all of his other encounters with the women of France with one exception, which are constant scenes of withdrawals and frequent foiled reattempts, all cementing the episodes as stationary, all resulting without a climax.[38]

Playing on this ongoing paradigm of impotence, when trying to write to Madame de L—, Yorick proves incapable of authoring his own text and must substitute a drummer's words for his own from a letter La Fleur produces. Later, he can only purchase ill-fitting gloves from the *Grisset*, as *all* of the gloves in her shop are too large for Yorick.[39] Yet the most extreme example of his almost torturous impotence comes during his encounter with the *fille de chambre*. When he first meets her outside the bookshop, he does not see her as a possible conquest, which would have been a common assumption for an eighteenth-century reader – chamber maid as a sexual victim/partner.[40] He instead sees in her a family likeness and would have signed their parting with a 'kiss of charity, as warm and holy as any apostle'.[41] Later, Yorick takes her into his hotel room, and they even land on his bed, but instead of undressing one another, they literally seal off each other – she sews his collar down, and he buckles her shoe. As stagnant as the scene appears on the outside, Yorick must war with temptation; he is unable to write the card for which the *fille de chambre* came, he trembles, and realizes the 'devil' was in him, yet bears his expectation 'quietly'.[42] Finally, his leading her out of his room, locking the door and delivering her safe to the gate provides the denouement of the inert event.[43] When La Fleur returns and excuses Yorick's assumed amorous behaviour and ventures that Yorick may later wish to amuse himself, he interrupts La Fleur by avowing that he finds 'no amusement in it'.[44]

Other than the significantly repeating pattern of immobility and resulting impotence, of key importance in these meetings remains that Yorick and the women always share intimate moments of sensibility – the vibrations of the connectivity of head and heart.[45] As hands provide the gateway to touch, they present the danger of sensuality yet alternately may also allow for a deeper, more meaningful type of touch – that of spiritual epiphany – by creating a union between two bodies and therefore two souls. The Lady from Brussels feels the pulsations of his arteries, he measures the *Grisset's* pulse, and the *fille de chambre* blushes, which causes him in turn to blush.[46] Yorick continuously mentions how he must battle and deny his senses and inclinations during these encounters: his dirty passions inflamed by physical contact with the Lady, the impropriety of touching the (married) *Grisset* in public, the 'delicious sensation of the nerves' excited by his encounters with the women in the novel. Yet it is precisely these *frissons* of physical arousal that confirm the 'transfer between mind and body has been made'.[47] Consistently, Yorick overcomes his sexual demons with sentiment, his knowledge that virtue and morality are of the highest importance. Yorick valorizes a 'right' path of action through inaction.[48] Critically, these points of intersection between Yorick and the women most often transpire through their hands and wrists, the part of the body that is acceptable to view and to touch. As a result, Sterne conflates the emotive physical responses with coarse imagery. His interest lies not solely in the hand itself but also in the barriers that envelope them. He accepts the Lady from Brussels's hand 'without reserve' because she wears gloves 'open only at the thumb and two forefingers' and the *Grisset* with whom he interacts is surrounded by – and even earns her living by – the material objects that obstruct the hand from coming into contact with human flesh.[49] When faced with the possibility of touching hands, a fairly innocuous body part, Yorick desires a barrier, something to limit his access to bodily sensations.[50] The *fille de chambre*, too, gives him her hand 'as is usual in little bargains of honor', and in his ultimate conquest over vice, he places his hand in her lap for ten minutes alternately looking at her 'purse, sometimes on the side of it'.[51] Yorick denies himself the power and dominance of sexual force, and significantly, he renounces such sexual aggression by choice as there is no indication that Yorick is literally physically incapable of a sexual act. As is obvious from the Marquis's allusions to Yorick being a sexual tourist, Sterne anticipates the reader's assumption of and expectation for such carnal activities during a tour, yet he also refuses to fulfil those expectations by constantly and obviously denying their actuality.[52] Yorick responds to the Marquis's insinuations by renouncing such predatory behaviour:

> as for the nakedness of your land, if I saw it, I should cast my eyes over it with tears in them – and for that of your women (blushing at the idea he had excited in me) I am so evangelical in this, and have such a fellow feeling for whatever is *weak* about them, that I would cover it with a garment, if I knew how to throw it on – But I could wish ... to spy the *nakedness* of their hearts, and through the different disguises and customs, climates and religion, find out what is good in them, to fashion my own by – and therefore am I come.[53]

This passage explicitly describes the tension between the sensations of physical arousal (he blushes excitement at the idea of naked French women) and the sentiments that attend them (he would also weep over the sight of their victimized bodies), thus indicating the passageway of head to body while also demonstrating the moral connection between mind and heart. Robert Markley argues that such gestures from Yorick call attention to the hero's generosity but also to the inequalities of a fallen world and therefore, 'Sterne's theatrics of bourgeois virtue, then, are devoted paradoxically to demonstrating the sensitivity of a culture that shies away from acknowledging its responsibility for inflicting upon its victims the very injuries that it mourns and pities but does little to alleviate'.[54] Renouncing the impulse of sexual predation, Yorick declares his intentions for travel are not to participate in the sexual tour but to become a better man by overcoming such temptations. He is not a Lovelace or a Mr B. who views 'weakness' in women as opportunity for carnal satisfaction; he wants to have an understanding of their 'weakness' in order to elevate himself to a higher order of being.[55] Arguably, Yorick does not save the world through the crowns he bestows upon the women he encounters nor are the women remarkably different as a result of his actions, yet by actively choosing sensibility and its necessary impotence, he leaves in his wake no injured parties – women are as virtuous after he leaves as they were before he arrived.[56] Sterne's awareness of, and I would argue criticism surrounding, the industry of exploiting young women by powerful men surfaces most directly in the text when after meeting with the Hotelier's own *Grisset* and purchasing ruffles, Yorick sadly comments, 'The master of the hotel will share the profit with her – no matter – then I have only paid as many a poor soul has *paid* before me for an act he *could* not do or think of'.[57] By refusing to act on this opportunity, or any of the other opportunities of the novel, Yorick demonstrates the belief New describes where 'the aggressive act of possession is simultaneously an act of loss'.[58] After all, the ideology behind sensibility is one of conversion through sympathy and pity. The triumph of Yorick's sentimentalism is an affirmation that Christian piety *does* impact society (albeit in a passive manner) in his refusal to ruin and destroy, and in his rejection of the active and aggressive.

Do No Harm

Given that Sterne chose to wear a mask of abstinence if not impotence, it would appear that he wove himself into the very fabric of the novel and attempted to impart some kind of wisdom with a ubiquitous dose of humour.[59] With this combination of insight and comedy, he subverts traditional assumptions of a man travelling alone in Europe. He openly depicts the roles society constructs for men as lascivious predators and women as helpless targets and suggests that they remain unquestioned – even when brutality and victimization is involved. By incorporating these cultural assumptions in the novel – namely that men travelling must therefore be sexual tourists and poor young women are naturally prey to such men – Sterne is careful to present the women of the novel as conduits of opportunity for testing and proving a man's internal worth. While New asserts that Sterne sees the sentimental as an evasion of desire and also, therefore, of sexual violence, I would counter-conjecture that Sterne believes the sentimental offers men an avenue for mastery over the carnal. In addition to the myriad theories and writings concerning the sentimental, one must also look to the contemporary events that surrounded the culture of sensibility. Speaking specifically of eighteenth-century women writers, Barker-Benfield maintains as sentimentalists they concerned themselves most predominantly with the brutalization of women.[60] Sterne shared their concern, even if he chose to express it with tongue firmly planted in cheek.

12 'VIOLENCE THAT'S WICKED FOR A MAN TO USE': SEX, GENDER AND VIOLENCE IN THE EIGHTEENTH CENTURY

Lena Olsson

Sexual violence, and rape in particular, was a locus of conflicting ideas in the eighteenth century. These conflicting ideas concerned everything from the minutiae of individual acts of sexual violence – for example, how a particular act should be evaluated in a court setting – to foundational questions regarding the definition of rape, how seriously society should view this crime, or even if rape was possible at all. For instance, there was a clear discrepancy between how the crime of rape was viewed in theory by legal writers and how it was dealt with in practice in a courtroom setting.[1] According to English law at the time, rape was a felony, punishable by death and without the benefit of clergy, and it is often described in legal texts as a 'heinous', 'atrocious' and 'detestable' crime.[2] Simultaneously, however, the same texts tend to undermine the seriousness of rape by emphasizing its rare occurrence and the difficulties of securing reliable proof, as well as advancing a view on sexual assault as a venial offence, an understandable failure to control 'what nature on all sides promotes'.[3] In addition, juries tended to remain unconvinced by women's testimonies, even when the crime resulted in bad injuries, making rape the crime that had by far the lowest conviction rate of all prosecuted crimes in the eighteenth century.[4] In part, the legal inconsistency was due to the perception of rape as a crime 'secret in its kind, and generally confined to the knowledge of the party injured', so that 'the proof is extremely nice and difficult, and the law therefore, in some measure, useless'.[5] However, as Laura Gowing has pointed out, there was also 'a substantial gulf between legal and popular understandings of rape', both of which affected how rape was presented in testimonies given in a courtroom setting.[6] Apart from their presence in court reports, such popular ideas about rape can be found in a wide variety of fictional sources, testifying to a complex nexus of ideas surrounding rape and sexual violence, of which many serve to naturalize, normalize or obscure a crime that, at least in theory, was viewed as one of the most serious offences that could be committed.

Against this background, I would like to discuss one widespread popular belief: that it was physically impossible for a single man to rape a conscious, 'genuinely' resisting woman, because she always had the power to avoid being penetrated as long as she remained resolute in her defence.[7] This rape myth – what in this chapter is referred to as 'the myth of the "unrapeable" woman' – is interesting because it involves several contradictions and paradoxes that set it at odds both with the law and with other cultural beliefs about gender and sexuality: for instance, it flies in the face of conventional understandings of men's greater strength and aggressiveness, and it directly contradicts the letter of the law, according to which rape was defined as the 'unlawful and carnal Knowledge of a Woman, by Force and against her Will'.[8] That is to say, what the law defined as rape – forcible penile penetration of the vagina – was an impossibility according to the myth. The myth is of interest also because its foundation did not lie in popular culture alone; it was, in addition, promulgated in medical and medico-legal texts of the day, giving it the respectability and authority that comes from being supported and promoted by the medical profession. The existence of this myth could be a serious problem for rape victims attempting to prosecute their attackers: if it was impossible to rape a 'genuinely' resisting woman, the defence could always claim that the victim had not 'genuinely' resisted because she secretly desired sexual contact, and that consequently there had been no rape. Such reasoning allowed the possibility for rape as a concept and as a crime to be completely effaced. The emphasis on this line of questioning in many rape trials from the time testifies to the perceived effectiveness of such a defence.[9]

The cultural influence of the myth of the 'unrapeable' woman can be inferred not least from the literary and biographical material of the day. Indeed, one of the most striking things about rape scenes in eighteenth-century fiction is how rarely they depict or describe a single man forcing a sexual act on a conscious woman against her will. Instead, rapists are shown to need the assistance of an accomplice in order to overpower their victims, or to make use of narcotics to render the victim incapable of resisting at all. Moreover, rapists in eighteenth-century literature in general seem unwilling to risk a physical struggle with their intended victims. In some instances, the use of violence is avoided altogether, in that the rapist is presented as an opportunist who takes advantage of a woman who has fainted or fallen asleep in an isolated location, as does the young huntsman who finds Harriet 'in a deep swoon' in John Cleland's *Memoirs of a Woman of Pleasure* (1748–9).[10] In other cases, the use of force is shown to be a desperate measure that the rapist resorts to only after he has spent a good deal of time and effort trying to persuade the woman in question to consent to a sexual relationship. For instance, in Alexander Smith's *The School of Venus* (1716), the Earl of Rochester courts Madam Clarke for a whole year before losing patience and deciding to use violence – and then only at the suggestion of Clarke's grandmother, who is eager to have her granddaughter become the mistress of a nobleman.[11] Similarly, Mr C—d—t in *The Impetuous Lover* of 1757 attempts to convince Iris over a period of nine months to accept his advances before his sexual frustration becomes too acute and he conspires to rape her.[12] The preference for persuasion can even be found in libertine works that otherwise treat rape as a joke: 'The Taking of the St Maries', a poem full of sexual innuendo and bawdy puns that 'celebrates' the rape of the nuns of Puerto de Santa Maria in Cadiz by English soldiers during the War of the Spanish Succession, focuses not on the men's use of force to attain their ends but on

> How some kind Heroes gain'd upon 'em [the nuns],
> And by soft Elocution won 'em.
> Who scorning Force laid by their Swords,
> And try'd the pleasing Pow'r of Words.[13]

While the men make it clear that there is no alternative to having sex, they seem oddly concerned with forcing the nuns to voice their agreement and to not 'struggle but lie still', apparently being reluctant to perpetrate 'Violence ... / That's wicked for a Man to use, / Which you so eas'ly may prevent, / By kindly giving your Consent'.[14] There is a good deal of interest in removing any possibility of the victims fighting back, in this case by securing their reluctant consent by means of 'Elocution'.

Also, when men in eighteenth-century texts do decide to use force they seem to have very little confidence in their own ability to perpetrate a rape, and they rarely manage to do so unaided. Mr C—d—t is not unique in 'doubt[ing] his ability to overcome [Iris] by violence' and taking steps to increase his chances of success: 'unwilling to be frustrated in his purposes' he 'applied himself to an old *Scotchman*, who had served him many years in almost every capacity, and upon whom, he doubted not but he might depend, for his aid, at the critical juncture'.[15] Similarly, Rochester has little success in his attempt on Clarke, either with his '*Rhetorick*' or in the 'Tryal of Skill' that follows, until Clarke's grandmother loses patience and 'piously gave an helping Hand, by holding her [granddaughter's] Legs 'til his Lordship had robb'd her of that Jewel which never could be retriev'd again'.[16] Samuel Richardson's Mr B. is assisted by Mrs Jewkes, who holds one of Pamela's arms and tells Mr B. not to 'stand dilly-dallying' when Pamela's screams and fainting fits prove successful in warding off the attack.[17] In *Shamela*, Henry Fielding casts doubt on Squire Booby's (and, by implication, Mr B.'s) masculinity by having Mrs Jewkes announce to Squire Booby that 'I have one Arm secure, if you can't deal with the rest I am sorry for you', but at the same time he reinforces the myth of the 'unrapeable' woman by having Shamela refer to the 'Instructions' her mother gave her 'to avoid being ravished, and I followed them, which soon brought him to Terms'.[18] Whether the myth is used to reinforce women's claims to virtue or to satirize them, the rapist is in either case depicted as needing assistance to overcome a woman's resistance when she is resolute about not yielding to force.[19]

Another circumstance that makes it possible for the rapist to accomplish his aim is when the victim loses consciousness. For example, in Eliza Haywood's *The Lucky Rape* (1727) Florella/Emilia is gripped by such terror and agitation on finding that she has been conveyed to an inn instead of her home that she faints, whereafter Alonzo throws her on a bed and, 'all impatient of further Delays, while she was in that Condition, he perpetrated his vile Intent, ravag'd each sweet Charm about her, and left her only the Ruins of a Virgin'.[20] The rapist may also deliberately drug his victim. In *Genuine Memoirs of the Celebrated Miss Maria Brown* (1766) Mr Fitzherbert 'treacherously impose[s]' upon Maria 'soporific draughts' by putting laudanum in her wine, after which he proceeds to 'rob [her] of woman's most precious jewel'.[21] C[olone]l L[uttrel]l in *The Memoirs of Miss Arabella Bolton* 'prevail[s] on [Arabella] to drink a few glasses', after which she becomes 'entirely intoxicated with the noxious drugs that were mixed with the wine'.[22] When she is 'senseless', Luttrell 'perpetrated such an act of barbarity and villainy, as must shock not only the virtuous, but even the most profligate part of mankind'.[23] The best-known rapist in eighteenth-century literature, Richardson's Lovelace, resorts to '*somnivolences* (I hate the word *opiates* on this occasion)' when raping Clarissa, although he claims to have been motivated by '*mercy*; nor could it be anything else. For rape ... to us rakes is far from being an undesirable thing'.[24] Clarissa herself confirms the use of narcotics, and adds that because she was 'senseless' she 'dare not aver that the horrid creatures of the house were personally aiding and abetting: but some visionary remembrances I have of female figures flitting, as I may say, before my sight'.[25] The text thus leaves open the possibility that Lovelace was assisted also by his female accomplices, making doubly sure of avoiding the prospect of Clarissa resisting his attack. Viewed against the background of the belief that a woman could not be raped if she kept her resolution steadfast, Lovelace's talk of mercy becomes very suspect indeed.

In these texts, the rapist's elimination of all possible resistance is presented as a necessity, because while the woman remains conscious and at liberty she often proves more than capable of defending herself. In Smith's *The School of Venus* General Foulkes is unable to overpower Mrs Howard, appearing very passive and hesitant in contrast to the active and determined Mrs Howard:

> She made a very vigorous Defence; for though she could not hinder him from often kissing, not only her Face, but several other Parts of her Body, as by her struggling [*sic*] they came to be bare, yet by her Nimbleness in shifting her Posture, and employing his Hands so well with her own, they could never attain to the Liberty they chiefly strove for: She neither made great Noise, bit or scratch'd, but appear'd so resolute, and her Resistance was made with so much Eagerness, and in such good Earnest, that the

amorous Spark seeing that there was nothing to be done without breaking her Hands, and coming to downright brutish Force, and being pretty well tir'd let go his hold, and came to Persuasions.[26]

When Mrs Howard flings herself across the bed and onto the floor, the General, 'either not willing to come to greater Extremity, or perhaps not finding himself in a Condition of going through the Fatigues of a Rape, offer'd no farther Violence at present'.[27] The contrast between the two is significant: the General, although described as an 'amorous Spark', is 'tir'd', unwilling to 'come to greater Extremity', unable to go through 'the Fatigues of a Rape' and forced to resort to 'Persuasions', while Mrs Howard is 'vigorous', nimble, 'resolute' and eager in her defence. It is true that the author leaves the possibility of using greater violence open – the General could, if he wanted to, break Mrs Howard's hands – but the adjectives used to describe him are suggestive of nothing so much as his inability to perpetrate the rape on his own, and his status as a top military officer makes his lack of aggression and unwillingness to use violence even more noteworthy. Nor can the phrase 'not finding himself in a condition of going through with ... a rape' imply that the General is impotent, or that his libido is too low, as he is elsewhere in the text described as a man 'noted for Lewdness and Inconstancy', and his disinclination cannot proceed from an objection to rape as such, because he is perfectly capable of committing the crime when his victim is safely incapacitated.[28] However, the General fails in his attempts until he is assisted by Mr Howard, who first threatens his wife with his sword and swears that 'he would cut her in a thousand Pieces if she would not surrender her Virtue to his Friend' and then 'ty'd her Hands and held her Legs, whilst the General made him a Cuckold before his Face'.[29] Again the rapist is represented as unable to overpower a woman singlehandedly unless she has been rendered defenceless, in this case by having a sword held to her throat, being tied up and held down by an accomplice so that she is incapable of using her hands and posture to prevent the rapist from penetrating her body.

As noted above, the 'unrapeable' woman myth was also current in medical and legal texts of the time. The author of the report of the trial of John Drummond for raping Elizabeth Gallway stated that 'the perpetration of [rape] on Adult Persons [is] so very difficult, that it requires something of an implicit Belief to be credited'.[30] A little later in the century, the surgeon and obstetrician Guillaume Mauquest de la Motte, as translated by Thomas Tomkyns, looked upon rape as 'impossible to be done by one or even several men, without a girl's consent'.[31] Similarly, Johann Friedrich Faselius, as translated by Samuel Farr, asserted in the forensic manual *Elements of Medical Jurisprudence* that

> the consummation of a rape, by which is meant a compleat, full, and entire coition, which is made without any consent or permission of the woman, seems to be

> impossible, unless some very extraordinary circumstances occur: for a woman always possesses sufficient power, by drawing back her limbs, and by the force of her hands, to prevent the insertion of the penis into her body, whilst she can keep her resolution entire.[32]

The French obstetrician Jean Louis Baudelocque, by way of his translator John Heath, agreed:

> it seems almost impossible that a single man should be able to commit a rape, at least if there be not a great disproportion of age; or unless he make use of some artifice, as to give narcotics, or other things of that kind.[33]

Barrister Manasseh Dawes stated as a point of fact that 'force ... cannot be employed successfully by a man alone, on any single woman'.[34] The idea continued to be repeated in the following century, when 'almost without exception, jurists and physicians assumed not only that women would resist any attack on their honour, but ... that they were physically strong and thus sure to succeed'.[35]

Against this background it is hardly surprising to find that defendants in court cases sometimes claimed to have insufficient strength to overpower their victims. In 1715, Hugh Leeson claimed he could not possibly have raped Mary May, asking the jury

> whether one of his Stature and inconsiderate [sic] appearance, was fit for such an Act of Violence and Strength, as the Ravishment of so Robust and Sanguine a Woman as she was ... whom it was a very great Question, if one of twice the Strength as he was endued with, could Master, after the way she made mention of?[36]

In spite of this, Leeson was convicted, but in 1768 Frederick Calvert, Lord Baltimore successfully used a similar defence when on trial for raping Sarah Woodcock, claiming that he was 'totally against all force; and for me to have forced this woman, considering my weak state of health and my strength, is not only a moral but a physical impossibility. She is, as to bodily health, stronger than I am'.[37] Both in theory and in practice, reference was thus made to a man's inability to force a woman to have sex, whether the ultimate cause was identified as male physical weakness or the inherent capacity of the 'honourable' female body to resist sexual attack.

This persistent emphasis on male insufficiency and female activity and power of self-defence is especially noteworthy considering the conventional representation of sex and gender roles in eighteenth-century England. Physical strength, vigour and energy were distinctly male traits, and the language of active, assertive self-defence was also inherently male.[38] Karen Harvey has claimed that 'women in court were unable to claim that they had resisted *and* retain their reputation as modest', but considering the emphasis many writers put on the capacity of truly honourable women to defend themselves successfully against sexual attack, not to speak of the fact that the law required that the rape victim put up a vigorous struggle as a testimony of her sexual probity, this would seem to be a questionable statement.[39] It is, however, fair to say that women's methods of defending themselves are clearly gendered as female in representations of rape and constructed as different from male self-defence: Women scream, attempt to put up barriers between themselves and the attacker, deflect or take hold of his hands and try to avoid physical contact, but they are not, as a rule, described as assertive, forceful or aggressive, and they do not use physical violence.[40] Female self-defence is passive and defensive, not active and offensive.[41] In court as well as in literature, this made the representation of the kind of defence demanded by law a tricky proposition to combine successfully with a narrative of rape, and it was made all the more difficult by the existence of the myth of the 'unrapeable' woman: if the defence was too feeble, suspicions of collusion were evoked, if too active, the spectre of mannishness was raised, or the rape claim was invalidated by making it seem unbelievable that such a vigorous defence could have been overcome without complicity on the part of the victim.

The myth of the 'unrapeable' woman also testifies to cultural ambivalence about the use of male violence and the role it played in the relations between men and women. In early modern England, the ability to overpower a woman sexually may have been integral to masculine gender identity. From the Restoration through the eighteenth century, the adoption of libertine ideals of manhood, and the dissemination of these ideals throughout English society, created a masculine identity that was heavily dependent on sexual aggression and a forceful assertion of sexual privilege.[42] Many scholars have commented on the high degree of 'acceptable' violence in courtship situations and the conflation of rape and consensual sex.[43] The texts quoted above suggest that in the culture in which they were written, it was not only deemed reasonable to use force when words failed, but also to use words when force failed, and expect the woman in question to accept either one as a method of persuasion as though they were mutually interchangeable. Also, whereas it may be true that rape was not a rite of passage for young men in England, some men clearly found sexual violence against women titillating, and/or believed that coercing any woman to have sex was part of their male prerogative.[44] The extant court records testify to the heavy-handed violence used by some men to force women into submitting to sexual acts, but they also show the scant attention paid by juries to the resulting injuries and what these actually signified. The definition of what was *not* rape clearly included behaviour that the victims experienced as rape, and that met the criteria for rape as the law defined it, but the androcentric bias in the all-male court system and the cultural prejudices relating to gender and sexuality occasioned the occlusion or effacement of the violent aspect of the act in favour of the sexual one, in spite of the best efforts of victims to do the opposite: to foreground the violence and downplay the sex.[45] The myth of the 'unrapeable' woman was part of this effacement of the act of rape, which had serious repercussions for the ability of actual victims to obtain legal restitution in a courtroom setting. The repeated reference to marriage as a 'solution' to accusations of rape indicates that even for representatives of the legal system there was an interest in constructing rape as an (extreme) courtship practice in order to deal with a problem which they found difficult to distinguish from 'natural' sexuality.[46]

At the same time, rape was never completely effaced, nor the possibility of it totally denied. After all, the crime continued to be on the books throughout the long eighteenth century, and although it was a rare occurrence, men continued to be convicted of it. Jennine Hurl-Eamon has suggested that despite the abysmal conviction figures, the threat of arrest and conviction played some small role in curbing male behaviour. As she points out, 'in a world where "normal" heterosexual sex demanded male aggression ... it is significant that any men were even accused of rape'.[47] Certainly there was a pervasive fear among men of being prosecuted for rape, primarily in the guise of a perceived high risk of being falsely accused by a vindictive woman – what A. E. Simpson calls the blackmail myth – which was in no way related to the very small danger a rapist ran of actually being arrested and convicted.[48] Indeed, it is not impossible that the myth of the 'unrapeable' woman was, in some measure, a response to the blackmail myth, and that it functioned as a way to alleviate masculine anxiety regarding the possibility of being accused of a capital crime. If so, it may also have acted as a limitation on the behavioural curbs that Hurl-Eamon suggests followed from fears of being accused and arrested. Whatever its effect on male behaviour, it can be said that the myth of the 'unrapeable' woman, while ostensibly offering some room for female agency and even allowing for a degree of female physical strength, simultaneously appropriated this power and agency to undermine female sexual self-determination and reinforce the sexual status quo of eighteenth-century society.

13 THE RHETORIC OF RAPE: WILLIAM BLAKE'S *VISIONS OF THE DAUGHTERS OF ALBION* AS EIGHTEENTH-CENTURY RAPE TRIAL

Misty Krueger

While scholars have examined sexual violence in William Blake's 1793 *Visions of the Daughters of Albion* (*VDA*),[1] they have not explored the poem in light of legal discourse and the judicial culture of rape in eighteenth-century England. In the context of eighteenth-century laws on rape and testimonies from rape trials, this chapter examines Blake's characters in a metaphorical courtroom. The chapter examines not only how Blake's literary figures, like their real-life counterparts, put female sexuality and virtue on trial, but also how Blake criticizes – through his female protagonist-as-witness – a patriarchal culture that condemns any form of female sexual liberation, even when it results from assault. Rather than reprimanding a rapist or seducer, the poem shows a victim publicly pleading for her life and questioning the system of male authority and social scrutiny that forced her into a post-rape, downtrodden position. In reading *VDA* as an appropriation of eighteenth-century rhetoric on rape, I argue that Blake creates an imaginative text that turns 'the courtroom' on its end and envisions a redemptive space in which a seemingly disempowered rape victim – a ruined woman – vocalizes society's rather than a rapist's crimes against her person.

Rape Laws and Trials in Eighteenth-Century England

Eighteenth-century guides and commentaries written by judges and lawyers show that the legal system emphasized definition, diction, history, physical evidence, reputation and punishment when broaching the subject of rape. Sir Matthew Hale in *Historia Placitorum Coronae* (1736) defines rape as 'the carnal knowledge of any woman above the age of ten years against her will, and of a woman-child under the age of ten years with or without her will'.[2] Richard and John Burn's *A New Law Dictionary* (1792) expands the definition:

> It is not a sufficient excuse in the ravisher, to prove that the woman is a common strumpet; for she is still under the protection of the law, and may not be forced. Nor is it any excuse, that she consented after the fact.[3]

These definitions reveal that evidence from the *male* body substantiates the act of rape. Hale states that proof of rape relies on penetration and ejaculation;[4] likewise, Jacob Giles's *Every Man His Own Lawyer* (1736) states that 'there must be Penetration and Emission, to make this Crime; otherwise an Attempt to ravish a Woman, though it be never so outrageous, will be an Assault only'.[5] Hale's guide suggests the importance of diction. An indictment's phraseology needed to include 'essential words' addressing rape and not 'any other circumlocution', which were 'not sufficient in a legal sense to express rape'.[6] These writings identify the problematic nature of categorizing the crime legally, and the difficulty with which both a prosecutrix could appeal a rape and a court would prosecute a defendant.

Although English law in William the Conqueror's time endorsed castration or loss of eyes as a penalty for rape, when an eighteenth-century jury rendered a guilty verdict, it sentenced a man to death. Like Hale's guide, Sir William Blackstone's *Commentaries on the Laws of England* (1791) illustrates Englishmen's uneasiness with this punishment while at the same time condemning lenience that would classify rape as a mere 'trespass' – the penalty according to law from the Middle Ages.[7] Hale famously explains the problem:

> It is true rape is a most detestable crime, and therefore ought severely and impartially to be punished with death; but it must be remembered, that it is an accusation easy to be made, hard to be proved, but harder to be defended by the party accused, though never so innocent.[8]

Eighteenth-century juries valued legal advice that explained how victims should report and appeal charges of rape. As Hale explains, 'the party ravished' is instructed to,

> give evidence upon oath, and is in law a competent witness, but the credibility of her testimony, and how far forth she is to be believed, must be left to the jury, and is more or less credible according to the circumstances of fact, that concur in that testimony.[9]

As the most important witness to the crime, the prosecutrix must provide 'probability to her testimony' by having 'good fame'; by pursuing the offender; by showing signs of injury; by verifying whether or not the location of the attack was 'remote from people, inhabitants or passengers' and by demonstrating 'if the offender fled' the scene.[10] However great the probability of her testimony, it must be 'proved by others as well as herself'.[11] According to Giles, 'A Woman's positive Oath of a Rape, without concurring Circumstances, is seldom credited'.[12] Women's reticence to report rapes quickly, alongside public perceptions of women's false natures, often garnered not-guilty verdicts, regardless of evidence or witnesses. Even though explicit time limitations did not exist in reporting rapes as they did in the Middle Ages, time mattered. Blackstone comments that a 'jury will rarely give credit to a stale complaint'.[13] Giles argues that there would be made 'a strong Presumption against a Woman, that she made no complaint in a reasonable Time after the Fact'.[14] Hale confirms:

> If [the prosecutrix] concealed the injury for any considerable time after she had opportunity to complain, if the place, where the fact was supposed to be committed, were near to inhabitants or common recourse or passage of passengers, and she made no outcry ... these and the like circumstances carry a strong presumption, that her testimony is false or feigned.[15]

Rather than seeking justice for a crime against an innocent, some women were thought to feign an assault and take part in what Michael Durey labels 'ritualised rape', a phrase that describes a false accusation of rape brought about by a prosecutrix with the help of 'witnesses' in the hope of gaining money from the defendant and/or forcing him to marry the girl in question to avoid execution.[16] Ancient Jewish law, wherein a rapist would marry his victim (considered damaged goods) to excuse the crime against a family, established this model.

Owing to concerns about the authenticity of rape accusations, juries evaluated prosecutrices' reputations and evidence (the manifestation of sexually transmitted diseases, items of bloody clothing and the testimony of doctors, authority figures and family). Even with overwhelming evidence most juries acquitted defendants. As Anna Clark explains in her research on late eighteenth-century rape trials, English juries convicted only 7 to 13 per cent of accused rapists. Between 1770 and 1800 at the Old Bailey, three out of every forty-three men accused were found guilty of raping girls over twelve years of age.[17] Hale clarifies why many juries acquitted the accused: juries were warned to 'be the more cautious upon trials of offences of this nature' because 'the heinousness of the offense many times transport[ed] the judge and jury with so much indignation, that they [were] overhastily carried to the conviction of the person accused thereof by the confident testimony, of sometimes malicious and false witnesses'.[18] Judges and juries entered courtrooms with these warnings in mind; alleged victims took the stand not only to narrate the events of a rape, but also to defend themselves against accusations of naïveté, looseness and mendacity. Durey explains:

> Bringing a case of rape to trial ... required the victim to demonstrate considerable courage and fortitude. The process could be expensive; the prosecutor would have to face her alleged attacker in court; she was likely to be minutely examined on oath (owing to the possibility of malicious prosecution and the capital nature of the crime); and she knew that her reputation would be ruined, whatever the outcome of the trial.[19]

Old Bailey transcripts and popular published accounts show the eighteenth-century courtroom as a place of 'second assault' where alleged rape victims were 'violated first by the actual, physical act of rape and then by a legal system that does not take them at their word but demands further proof'.[20]

Late eighteenth-century rape trial transcripts demonstrate that most cases open with remarks from legal officials followed by grueling interrogations of prosecutrices – many of whom were adolescents, some as young as eight years old – and brief testimonies from witnesses.[21] These interrogations included repetitive questions meant to challenge the prosecutrix's authenticity. The 1780 case, *Christopher Morris* v. *Martha Linnett*, documents this rapid-fire rhetoric as fifteen-year-old Linnett is asked questions about the definition of rape, her sexual experience and details of the sexual encounter, how she reported the crime, the credibility of her sources/witnesses and her evidence.[22] The lawyer in *James Lavender* v. *Mary Lewis* (1793) forced Lewis to explain whether she had menstruated before the alleged crime and to describe how the accused rapist inserted a 'sharp instrument' into her vagina and 'tore [her] private parts'.[23] The Old Bailey trials illustrate that a prosecutrix was expected to corroborate rape by attesting that ejaculation followed penetration. To do this, young women were asked to provide credible sources to authenticate not only that they showed signs of violent vaginal penetration, but also venereal illness. In *John Foy* v. *Mary Powell* (1782) and *John Curtis* v. *Sarah Tipple* (1793) both girls were asked to verify ejaculation. The court asked Powell, 'Did you perceive any thing come from him?' and eighteen-year-old Tipple was required to explain that her master 'forced his private parts into [hers], and [that] something warm came from him'.[24] While early eighteenth-century folk beliefs equated ejaculation with orgasm and consent with conception, implying that rape could not produce pregnancy,[25] late eighteenth-century law relied on claims of ejaculation to validate the *charge* – not the *crime* – of rape. Consent was another issue entirely.

A prosecutrix was responsible for both swearing that she did not consent to sexual intercourse, and explaining why she had placed herself in a vulnerable situation in which she could be attacked. Linnett's case exposes this problem. She was accused of recklessly wandering in the night and asked to defend why she placed herself in a situation to be assaulted. The court suggested that Linnett either endangered herself by leaving the country and venturing to the city, or that she was familiar with the London streets and had sexual experience – a claim later reinforced by the defendant, who argued that Linnett instigated the sexual encounter and engaged in consensual intercourse. The establishment of consent was an important rhetorical tool in rape trials. Lawyers repeatedly made Powell and Tipple explain how they 'resisted' rather than consented to the defendants' sexual advances. As Toni Bowers points out, the trials show a 'paradox' that points to an 'either/or response' of consent or resistance.[26] Answers to questions about resistance either indicate defendants' ignorance of sexual activity, or imply their consent. Although Powell states, 'I did not know what resistance was', the lawyer's response of 'You know what resistance is now' represents a common tactic used to debunk alleged victims' testimonies.[27] Tipple is asked questions including, 'How did he manage to keep you down on the bed, did you resist?' and 'Did you make all the resistance in your power?' In addition to responding to numerous inquiries of resistance, Tipple was asked to account for her struggle by answering questions such as: 'Did you slap his face?', 'Did you pull his hair?' and 'Did you kick him at all?'[28] The court doubts Tipple's lack of agency, and it forces her to reveal explicit details of the alleged rape, including how the defendant held her down and inserted his penis into her vagina, whether or not her 'parts' hurt afterwards and how she treated the venereal disease she claims to have contracted. Tipple's and Powell's cases reveal how lawyers manipulated a rhetoric of resistance to evince prosecutrices' sexual blameworthiness.

According to religious and social mores, women should not make themselves available to sexual danger or lie about sharing in illicit sexual activity.[29] Young women were deemed culpable for the consequences of any sexual truancy, including seduction. Some men admitted to seducing women, and the court was at pains to distinguish seduction from rape if only to acquit a prisoner facing execution. In *William Hodge* v. *Elizabeth Smith* (1786), the court ruled that Hodge should be punished for 'taking any method to persuade a girl, his servant, of this age, in his house, under his protection [to have sex]; but as to a rape, there is no pretence'.[30] In another 'bad case of seduction', the jury ruled in *Barton Dorrington* v. *Eleanor Masters* (1788) that the 'seduction' was not a 'rape'; although the jury deemed Dorrington 'a very bad man', it could not 'convict without evidence'.[31] These men lured adolescents to sacrifice their virtue, but they committed no crimes under the law. Perhaps the most popular example of a 'seduction' story is found in *John Motherhill* v. *Catharine Wade* (1786). Twenty-one-year-old Wade accused Motherhill of offering to walk her home, accosting her on a street and repeatedly raping her in a churchyard, for which she received several bruises and incurred injuries to her genitalia.[32] *The Trial of John Motherhill* (a popular publication) characterizes Wade as a careless woman for being 'all of the sudden go[ing] out in a tempestuous night', 'leav[ing] her father's house' and naively trusting a stranger to walk her home.[33] The case included witnesses and evidence that corroborated Wade's assertions, but Motherhill was cleared of all charges because Wade's inconsistent testimony cast doubt on the veracity of her claims. The case was publicized as a milestone trial, even a celebration of a falsely-accused 'heroic rapist'.[34] The 1793 *Cuckold's Chronicle* published a lengthy account of the trial along with a sexually graphic image of Motherhill attacking Wade.[35] Motherhill published his version of the story as a defence of his innocence; he claimed to have misunderstood Wade to be a loose woman.[36]

Motherhill's explanation reveals attitudes about propriety and women's sexuality, the ways in which men were tempted by female sexuality and how men often regarded sexually-forward women as 'fair prey'.[37] Motherhill's trial speaks to Clark's suggestion that a conception of rape was 'publicly constructed by men and for men. For men, rape was a crime only if the victim could be seen as chaste, i.e., the property of another man; if not, the rapist felt he was exercising his right to "take" any woman'.[38] Frances Ferguson identifies 'taking' as a central component of discourse on rape, and as Beth Swan's and Deborah Burks's research on rape indicate, the theft of the woman's will, body and her father's or husband's property rights are crucial to an understanding of the destructive personal, social and economic ramifications of rape.[39] The growing number of rape trials and narratives printed in popular publications in the latter half of the century further complicated the 'moral' conversations that resulted from such public disclosure of private sexual details.[40]

Charges of rape, however, seemed to play a secondary role to the social indictments against women's virtue. In publications and trial transcripts, alleged rape victims were accused of harlotry. Although the law stated otherwise, Giles reminds us that socially 'it [was] said by some to be evidence of a Woman's Consent, that she was a common Whore'.[41] *Henry Vaughn* v. *Mary Hunt* (1787) offers a case-in-point when the court suggests that a man mistook Hunt for 'a common street walker'.[42] The prosecutor in *James Lavender* v. *Mary Lewis* (1793) likened fourteen-year-old Lewis to a whore because she worked as a servant at a 'house of ill fame, that receives all sorts of men and women', specifically 'loose women'.[43] Tipple fell prey to this accusation after a witness testified that previously she engaged in sexual activities with the defendant. Testimony compelled the counsel to call Powell's charge a 'cooked up story, calculated to extort money from the prisoner, who is represented to be a man in circumstances of ability'.[44] The court exonerated Foy and labelled Powell a sexually experienced schemer and a 'free agent' looking to profit – the same claim levelled against Tipple. Judges seemed to convict women – instead of men – of crimes as they argued that prosecutrices were condemned for consenting to the sex act out of ignorance, or trying to embezzle money from honest men. Occasionally women were accused of being both types. Powell, for instance, was labelled a 'young and unexperienced' girl who needed to 'be particular' in her language in order to prove to the jury that Foy raped her; however, she was accused of 'play[ing] these tricks' before by having charged another man with rape in the past.[45] The opening of *Matthew Costillo* v. *Elizabeth Tarrier* (1784) makes a similar claim of trickery:

> if the crime has not been committed, if this is a mere trick, a mere conspiracy, to bring an innocent man to this bar, you will then acquit the prisoner, and I am sure he is extremely fortunate, in having such respectable gentlemen as you, to decide on his life.[46]

In the end, rape trials and publications from the latter half of the century show that most cases ended in acquittal as juries refrained from executing defendants based on testimonies of young women whose reputations had been put on trial.

The Rhetoric of Rape in William Blake's *Visions of the Daughters of Albion*

Similar issues surrounding legal and social understandings of rape in the period, as well as the patriarchal systems that required female chastity but embraced male sexual prowess, underlie *VDA*. In a contextual reading of *VDA* alongside accounts of rape laws and trials we find that the visionary work corresponds to narratives of alleged rape victims in England: the real-life Daughters of Albion. Although Blake does not strictly structure *VDA* as a legal proceeding, the poem reflects some of its techniques. A trial's major figures are present in a fictive courtroom – the cave. We hear from a prosecutrix, Oothoon; a defendant, Bromion; and a representative of the family/patriarchy, Theotormon, who has had his property-to-be/lover pilfered. We are introduced to a judge, Urizen (bearing a phonetic likeness to *your reason*), who functions doubly as a regulator of crime and punishment for perpetrators and victims. In the Daughters of Albion a group of peers/courtroom audience hears Oothoon's tale. We might interpret the Daughters as rape victims who echo Oothoon's sighs because they identify with her. We can even recognize our own presence in the readership of the text as filling the role of jury.

As in a trial's opening statements, Blake's first two plates contextualize the narrative. The poem begins with an enigmatic proclamation: 'The Eye sees more than the Heart knows'.[47] This motto should remind us of Hale's and Blackstone's writings and of rhetoric from court cases that advise evaluating a case fairly and weighing physical evidence and witnesses' testimonies over emotions regarding rape. Interestingly, the motto syntactically resembles the warning to the jury in the Motherhill/Wade case: 'If he dies, he suffers less than her who lives.'[48] From legal guides and trial transcripts we know that a central conflict in any legal proceeding occurs between the presentation of physical evidence and the belief in testimony. The eye of the court relied heavily upon physical evidence to validate a rape charge. Victims were asked to show signs of rape – bruises, scars or deformities resulting from the act – and often such physical evidence was not available for the court to *see*, although victims might physically re-enact how they were attacked. In combining verbal descriptions with physical demonstrations, women were taunted during their testimonies and paraded as objects of spectacle for the courtroom's gaze. Such is the situation in *VDA* when Oothoon laments her case, and Blake displays her body as imprisoned (shown in chains on the frontispiece and plate 7) and as an object of prey, even 'fair prey' (demonstrated in plate 6 where Oothoon is devoured by an eagle).[49] Visually, Blake portrays the aftermath of the attack, as can be seen in plate 4. If 'the eye sees more than the heart knows', we might read the statement as a critique of the legal system – and of the social structure of morality and popular opinion in England – for invalidating what the heart *knows* and giving precedent to what the eye *sees* or does not see. After all, a prosecutrix's testimony alone would not supply enough proof for a court to convict an accused rapist, as evidenced by the dearth of alleged rapists convicted in England in the latter half of the eighteenth century.

In addition to the motto, the poem's prologue ('The Argument') resembles a rape trial's opening argument, which provides the background for a case of rape and functions as Oothoon's preliminary testimony. In reading this argument, we can imagine both the 'off-plate' voice of a prosecutor or a judge asking Oothoon what she was doing wandering alone at night, and her answer, which is the textual information we receive. Her argument begins the case as she defends her position. In two versions of the same line of reasoning – one officially called 'The Argument', the other explained by a narrator in plate 4 (possibly another version of the story to which Oothoon would testify) – readers receive an account of the incidents preceding the sexual encounter. 'The Argument' reads as Oothoon's defence for leaving home at night, much like Mary Powell and Catharine Wade did, and making herself available to an attack. Oothoon's abandonment of the vale signifies something more than openness to new sexual experience, however; it indicates that she willingly left the confines of safety to seek out love. Here we are reminded of Linnett and Wade, whom counsel accused of searching on a 'tempestuous' night for lovers.

In the context of a rape trial, it is possible to imagine the cross-examination of Oothoon's wandering in the night and then the receipt of her answer: she was going to see her love-interest, Theotormon. As *VDA* continues, or begins – depending upon one's interpretation of the tale – with plate 4 entitled, 'Visions', Blake retells what readers have learned in Oothoon's opening testimony, perhaps in the role of judge himself or in another version of Oothoon's testimony. This circuitous narrative style speaks to the repetitive nature of late eighteenth-century interrogations of prosecutrices. In Blake's tale, Oothoon was wandering, soul-searching, trying to find the answers to her questions about love and sex. As in 'The Argument', readers get a sense of Oothoon's reflections on her actions before the encounter with Bromion; her metaphorical conversation with the marigold serves to facilitate her own and readers' understandings of the tension she felt in pursuing a course that might lead to sexual blossoming. Oothoon's ability to 'pluck' the flower from its bed (which connotes female sexuality), put it between her breasts and seek out Theotormon illustrates her agency.[50] Unfortunately, this openness to romantic, if not sexual, experience puts Oothoon's virtue and body in jeopardy, possibly making room for an argument that she is a whore – an accusation levelled widely against alleged rape victims, including Mary Hunt and Mary Lewis.

The agent of intent in these lines is crucial to Blake's situating of Oothoon's mental state prior to the attack. As readers who witness Oothoon psychologically processing her concerns, we understand that she supposes that sexual activity (with Theotormon, presumably) will renew 'sweet delight', rather than stunt her growth.[51] In the courtroom, a rhetoric of sexual freedom would have been used against prosecutrices, for if women admitted awareness of sexual satisfaction, the court likely suggested that they were making themselves available to assault. It is the danger of intent – recognized by a jury as consent – on the victim's part that comes into play here as in typical rhetoric against rape victims. A critique of careless actions, such as those of Martha Linnett, is reflected in plate 4 when Blake describes Oothoon's action as an 'impetuous course', writing: 'Over the waves she went in wing'd exulting swift delight; / And over Theotormons [*sic*] reign, took her impetuous course'.[52] Women were instructed constantly to guard their bodies and sexuality, and any slippage in conscientiousness of this self-protection was used against them in the court and by society at large. In building a vision of Oothoon as errant, first wandering, then flying hastily to see her lover, Blake's words echo the sentiment of society: Oothoon was not aware of her surroundings, and thus she is culpable for the attack.

Blake ascribes only two lines to Oothoon's sexual encounter with Bromion, which is not labelled as a 'rape' but as a 'ren[ding]' of Oothoon's 'virgin mantle'.[53] The lines in plate 4 read: 'Bromion rent her with his thunders, on his stormy bed / Lay the faint maid, and soon her woes appalld his thunders hoarse'.[54] Anne Mellor might consider such a textual issue typical of Blake's 'evasion of violence',[55] but if we compare Blake's language with that of legal discourse we reach another conclusion. Legal guides address the problematic nature of diction, and if Oothoon and the narrator do not state 'particularly' (a word habitually used in rape rhetoric) that the young woman was raped, then perhaps Bromion did not force her to have sex with him. In rape trials alleged victims did not always articulate the word 'rape' to describe sexual assault. Euphemistic language such as 'ill-use' or 'lay with', or in Blake's case 'rent' was commonly used. Blake's avoidance of the word 'rape' could mean that he is suggesting that Oothoon was not raped, or that he is calling attention to the complicated linguistic labelling of consensual or forced sexual activity. It is worth noting that Blake's use of 'rent' carries a double message, as 'to rend' can mean both 'to tear, to pull violently or by main force, *off, out of,* or *from* a thing or place; to tear *off* or *away*' and 'to take forcibly away *from* a person'.[56] The first of these two definitions should remind us of Mary Lewis who claimed that the prisoner violently 'tore [her] private parts' in an act of forced sexual intercourse. The second definition literally signifies a substitution for 'rape' and certainly recalls the importance placed by scholars on the act of 'taking'. This 'taking away' becomes a critical point of inquiry if we think of it as an act of taking away a female's virginity from her 'self' and from her patriarch – the future husband who will be responsible for managing this valuable commodity. Likewise, Blake applies 'rent' to Theotormon in plate 5 as he notes, 'Then storms rent Theotormons [sic] limbs'.[57] In such usage, Blake might indicate that Bromion has raped Oothoon and Theotormon; thus, Bromion has taken something precious from both characters.

What Blake omits from his plates is as important as what he includes: the space between the lines, so to speak, clouds sexual intention in two ways. Namely Blake's depiction of the sexual encounter reads ambiguously as consensual sex or as rape. Blake does not narrate resistance, as a proceeding might in its questioning. Between the narrator's description of the moments preceding the attack and Bromion's subsequent monologue, readers must infer the meaning of the act. We must interpret Blake's linguistic clues in plate 4 – 'stormy', 'her woes', 'appalld' and 'thunders hoarse' – to interpret the event as ravishment.[58] Blake does not allow Oothoon to display the physical evidence of a rape. Instead, his enigmatic lines in plate 4 – 'on his stormy bed / Lay the faint maid' – point to general sexual activity rather than specifically defined forced or consensual sex.[59]

Following these brief but vital lines, the poem diverges in form and resembles rape trial depositions as three central characters utter testimonies in the form of monologues. Although Mary Lynn Johnson and John E. Grant argue that the characters speak past each other,[60] Bromion's speech might be directed at Theotormon and Oothoon in a defence of his actions and as a testimony of masculinity. Bromion's words smack of a 'heroic' rapist's rhetoric. Through libertine discourse, Bromion boasts of his conquest by demeaning Oothoon's morality and negating her humanity. He labels her a 'harlot', a term connected to sexually experienced women (often of a lower class), and he identifies Theotormon as jealous. Bromion speaks to Oothoon, saying to her in plate 4, 'thy soft American plains are mine and mine' and suggesting that her body is 'stampt with [his] signet'.[61] This imprint lays hold of her first sexual experience and forever brands her with rape, a mark that society will associate with sexual ruin and dishonour.

Because Bromion's defence identifies him as a master/enslaver, the poem's master–servant relationship can be read as a colonial narrative, but *VDA*'s projection of mastery also speaks to sexual subjugation. In a sense, *VDA* suggests that women serve as sexual objects; they are made to bow down to masters, and as sexual victims they are unable to resist their attackers. As Bromion says in plate 4, 'resist not, they obey'.[62] After all, as the trials of Mary Powell and Sarah Tipple suggest, servants did sometimes engage in consensual sex with the hopes of recompense. Blake's poem evinces multi-level readings of the master–slave paradigm, including one in which Bromion is a master charged with raping his servant. Another interpretation of the master–slave narrative might place Oothoon in the role of wife and Bromion as master–husband. As such, we might tie the two images depicting Oothoon chained to Bromion and then hovering over Theotormon in chains to ancient Jewish law, which ordered rapists to marry (and therein purchase) a victim rather than face criminal punishment. As such, Bromion would exonerate himself of rape if he were to 'chain' himself to Oothoon. Whether or not Bromion is a slave-master or boss-master, or if he figuratively masters Oothoon, he certainly uses a 'Rape-Master General'[63] rhetoric to flaunt his flagrant power. Bromion brags that his slaves – or victims – are obedient and non-resistant, and his diction implies that he is a seducer, if not a repeat sexual offender. His claim that his victims – the daughters of England and America – worship terror and obey violence recalls a rhetoric that argues that victims of rape desire the attack or deserve what they received because of their impetuousness. Bromion's testimony also suggests that Oothoon enjoyed having sex with him and that she will become pregnant with his child. After he gives Theotormon the right to marry 'Bromions [*sic*] harlot', a term that stamps Oothoon as his property in plate 5, he implies that she will bear the 'child of Bromion's rage, that Oothoon shall put forth in nine moons time'.[64] These statements correspond with folk beliefs from the century, which might indicate that Bromion's words raise suspicion about whether or not a *rape* took place. His testimony defends his actions as much as it suggests that Oothoon openly received his sexual advances.

As prosecutrix, Oothoon takes a stand (and *the* stand) in the poem, but Blake's appropriation of a rhetoric of rape provides her with a voice that uses the language of the court to plead, or as Blake puts it in plate 5, to 'howl', her case with more power than any real-life prosecutrix.[65] In Blake's first mention of Oothoon's behaviour since sexual contact with Bromion, he indicates in plate 5 that Oothoon 'weeps not, she cannot weep! her tears are locked up' – a similar case was made for Catharine Wade.[66] Perhaps Blake implies that Oothoon has not yet spoken of the crime, thereby not reporting it in a timely fashion. However, eventually Blake gives Oothoon a voice: in plate 5 he shows her actively beseeching the 'kings of the sounding air',[67] the Urizenic judge of a courtroom and society, to cleanse her body and clear her name of the crime against her. Here Oothoon appropriates the word 'rend' to describe the symbolic process of salvation that she wishes to receive from the court and society. In plate 5, she asks the 'kings' to 'rend away this defiled bosom' – an image of her body and virtue in society's eyes.[68] Oothoon asks everyone in this fictive courtroom, including Theotormon, to remove *by force* the stigma against sexual experience, and she envisions the elimination of all violations of women.

In reading Oothoon's defence, we might consider how, in Clark's words, 'rape was engraved on [women's] minds by lack of consent, and on their bodies by physical pain which no amount of cultural conditioning could soothe'.[69] Oothoon experiences trauma; initially shame and guilt function as psychological vehicles of self-destruction, but eventually they facilitate self-repair. Oothoon wishes to purge *her* punishment, and the Daughters of Albion sigh like a chorus with every detail of her testimony. As Oothoon's character develops, she does not mirror a weak victim; instead, she becomes a powerful rhetor trapped in a dangerous stance. Ironically, her ability to voice her concerns and attempt to right the wrong done to her by Bromion only isolates her more. Although Ferguson argues that in rape trials women must remain weak to strengthen their testimonies, Oothoon's testimonies show her verbalizing her pain and questioning the rationale that consigns to her the status of pariah. Repeatedly Oothoon questions in plate 6 the 'thoughts of man' and queries 'with what sense' man constructs his evaluations.[70] She attacks the social system that allows both her attacker and her lover to abuse her physically and mentally. Through logical inquiry she addresses how reason ascribes sense to some things but responds senselessly to the heart of a woman. Oothoon's lamentation rejects the obligatory rhetoric of rape victims when she questions, 'How can I be defiled when I reflect thy image pure?' in addition to the defilement of the mind that might accompany the ravishment of the body.[71] Unfortunately, Blake shows that the Urizenic society in which Theotormon has been indoctrinated does not listen.

Through the act of verbalizing as mental processing, Oothoon sees herself as a 'new wash'd lamb' in plate 6,[72] but in the words of Bromion's testimony and in the eyes of society, she remains a harlot robbed of purity. Theotormon cannot accept her because he will not accept tainted goods, and he appears torn between Oothoon's pleas for reconciliation and the heavy social decrees that relegate 'impure' women to the status of fallen objects. Instead of testifying for his love, Theotormon bears witness to his own misery. He is trapped in a mental state of jealousy, as his name implies, which will not allow him to feel sympathy for Oothoon. In the few words that he utters, Theotormon fails to criticize Bromion's 'taking' of Oothoon; rather, he laments the destruction of his vision of treasured chastity and the depreciation of his prospective property. Theotormon's testimony only bears witness to his selfish patriarchal sense of honour. Blake's visual images reinforce Theotormon's refusal to face Oothoon in the frontispiece and in plate 7 as she hovers over him while he buries his face in his robe.

VDA provides a complicated picture of sexuality in its critique of Bromion's senseless passion, Oothoon's impulsive flight, her subsequent deflowering and Theotormon's rigid reasoning that upholds society's stigma against sexualized women. With these issues in mind, Blake gives Oothoon a second testimony that narrates the systemic problem of the subjugation of women. In Blake's first mention of Urizen as the creator of humankind, Oothoon calls him the 'Demon of heaven' in plate 8.[73] In her series of questions about the nature of things, this time directed at society, we could read her harangue on Urizen as reprimanding a late eighteenth-century culture that cannot rectify its social injustices.

The Rhetoric of Rape 161

Oothoon questions a society that alienates and oppresses women; her role as a rape victim doubly embitters her stance on this topic. Not only has she lost her value through the act of rape, but also she has been assigned the role of harlot. When Oothoon asks, 'Does not the eagle scorn the earth & despise the treasures beneath?' metaphorically she implies that man scorns woman and despises her sexuality.[74] The eagle, synonymous with Theotormon and analogous to the act of men preying upon women, resurfaces as a symbol of a society that picks women apart virtue by virtue. When Oothoon invokes a Urizenic motto 'Take thy bliss O Man! / And sweet shall be thy taste & sweet thy infant joys renew!' in plate 9, she criticizes a world where men continually 'take' from women (often in acts of violence) their sweetest rewards – their sexuality, their freedom – to quench their masculine desires.[75] Oothoon lashes out at the night and all that it hides from the light of day, and she accuses it of branding and selling women. Night, a dissembler, has taken her innocence and turned it into something ugly; it has changed her 'virgin joy' into the 'name of whore' in plate 9.[76] Using the rhetoric of the attacker against Theotormon, her present oppressor, she sarcastically calls him a hypocrite and a sick man, and she mockingly labels herself a whore, a harlot and a 'crafty slave of selfish holiness' in plate 9.[77] As the poem develops, the notion of attacker and oppressor diverge as the attacker appears less dangerous than the oppressor, as represented by Urizen, his followers and Theotormon. Perhaps Bromion and Theotormon represent two aspects of Urizenic society, the former as the initial agent and the latter as the sustainer of a corrupted reason.

Blake's poem radically departs from contemporary rhetoric on sexuality by having Oothoon put the men in *VDA* on trial. Rather than cowering under Theotormon's questions, she fires some of her own. Instead of withering away, she builds a second defence that appropriates the stigmatized words 'whore', 'harlot', 'slave' and 'holiness' to vouch in plate 9 for a newly educated woman who is no longer 'a virgin fill'd with virgin fancies'.[78] She cross-examines religion itself, and the rewards of self-restraint and self-denial. She calls Urizen the 'Father of Jealousy', equating him with Theotormon, and she questions why men are jealous of one another and of women.[79] She queries why sex, consensual or not, defiled love, and why her newfound sexuality, even if born out of a situation of rape, threatens Theotormon. This questioning exposes how, as Terry Eagleton puts it, 'those most sensitive to cultural difference ... project the ideologies of their own piece of the world on humanity at large'.[80] As Bromion falls out of the picture, literally absent from Blake's plates now, Oothoon's second appeal puts Theotormon and English patriarchal society on trial. Instead of making Bromion the recipient of a discursive attack, Oothoon judges the patriarchal system that destroys her character. By the end of the poem, Blake has exonerated Bromion of his crime because his initial role as agent of rape is now a moot point. In fact, not a single character directly condemns Bromion, as in real trials. Theotormon and Urizen are blamed for the aftermath of the rape, and this transference gives credence to Ferguson's claim that in the eighteenth century the story of a rape and its effects became more important that the physical violence.

If Blake evades violence in *VDA* by devoting little space to the sexual act, he certainly does not avoid confronting the oppression that results from such violence. As the poem closes, an argument against social persecution rather than physical victimization resonates as the majority of the poem is devoted to interrogating the legal system, not the assailant. Blake places blame on the system that allows men to take advantage of women's bodies by means of physical force and social restraint. Allowing Oothoon to testify against such a travesty permits her to speak for victimized women in her culture; and when the Daughters of Albion echo her sighs and woe, readers should consider that Oothoon's impasse is not an isolated event. Other women have cried for social change and freedom, but these women either could not find the voices to argue their cases, or they tried and failed to accomplish the task. Even though Oothoon ends enchained in *VDA*, it is important to recognize the socio-political advancement that Blake has made in giving her a voice. Even if Blake, as Brenda S. Webster asserts, does not advocate 'redefining sexuality to give a more equal place to women',[81] he fosters a discourse in *VDA* that broaches the possibility of re-envisioning the unnecessary negative connection between women's sexual experience and identity. *VDA* emphasizes the misery that alleged rape victims endured when pleading their cases, mirrors the rhetoric that accused rapists used to vouch for unaccountability to the act of rape and interrogates the judicial and social systems that criminalized sexually experienced women, regardless of their resistance or consent to sexual activity.

14 THE HORROR OF THE HORNS: PAN'S ATTEMPTED RAPE OF SYRINX IN EARLY EIGHTEENTH-CENTURY VISUAL ART

Melanie Cooper-Dobbin

In a reappraisal of eighteenth-century Rococo culture, William Park shows that the period had come to identify the representation of the rapist in various cultural forms as a misfit, a character disempowered as an outmoded relic of the past.[1] Faramerz Dabhoiwala elaborated on this assessment and has described the 'cult of seduction' as one of the 'most enduring cultural innovations' of the eighteenth century.[2] Dabhoiwala's term, the 'cult of seduction', does not disregard the reality of sexual violence, rather it describes the harassment and assault so often downplayed as seduction on the assumption that all women secretly desire the attentions of their aggressors. While rape was an offence punishable by law, harassment and coercion were not in themselves considered crimes, even though such acts crossed over into forms of behaviour that would now be considered assault or abuse. Victims of seduction during the eighteenth century were those who had been coerced into consensual, illicit sex. As Dabhoiwala explains, women were particularly vulnerable to the advances of men, who likened the pursuit of women to hunting or chasing, and the consummation of their lust a triumphant victory.[3]

Diane Wolfthal demonstrates that artists from the Renaissance onwards 'glorified, sanitized and aestheticized "heroic" rape', and modern analyses of mythological imagery have consistently supported this.[4] The familiar theme of Pan's relentless pursuit of Syrinx depicted throughout the visual art of the early decades of the eighteenth century exemplifies precisely this kind of 'sanitizing' of sexual crime by artists and art historians. Syrinx's experience of terror, as an artistic subject, is seemingly at odds with the social mores and polite practices of the age. However, Pan's attempted abduction of Syrinx mirrored eighteenth-century sexual attitudes and constructions of normative sexuality. Exploring artworks produced during this period reveals that this familiar theme in art helped to define and regulate expectations of gender and correct behaviour. In addition, subsequent works adapted the theme to critique women whose misconduct aligned them with the brazen behaviour of the goat god Pan, and shaming the men who were thought emasculated by them. This lighter, even comedic treatment of assault normalized and disregarded the realities of masculine aggression, presenting women as lustful by nature and delighting in the overbearing tactics of their pursuers.

The Thrill of the Chase

The resolute virtue of the woodland nymph is described in Ovid's *Metamorphoses* as comparable with the virgin goddess, Diana. Faced with Pan's violent lust, Syrinx runs in terror from his violent pursuit until she arrives at the edge of a river, begging for help to escape. The water nymphs respond to her desperate pleas and turn her into a mass of marsh reeds, just as Pan is about to snatch her up. The metamorphosis of Syrinx represents the loss of her body and of her identity as an alternative fate to violation. Faced with Pan's relentless lust, the innocent nymph's choice insists that 'rape is worse than death'.[5]

In an ironic and cruel twist of fate, the sound of the wind blowing through the reeds so pleased Pan as he lunged after the nymph, that he determined she would remain his companion regardless of her transformation and apparent escape. Cutting the reeds down into various lengths to fashion the instrument bearing her name, the anguish of Syrinx's loss of self through metamorphosis is further compounded by the horror of her dismemberment. Yet, somewhat disturbingly, the nymph's ordeal and grisly fate is preserved as a token of artistic invention and merit, interpreted not as an act of violence, but as a cultural achievement.

Images of the myth produced during the eighteenth century have consistently been read as representations of a tale of unrequited love. For example, Jean-François de Troy's (1679–1752) *Pan and Syrinx* of 1720 (see Figure 14.1) has been described as a 'charming entertainment of love out of reach', the goat-god Pan presented as a 'handsomely featured, almost aristocratic' gentleman.[6] Obscured by shadow, the unconventional appearance of a solitary swan in the bottom left foreground of the canvas is not associated with the traditional iconography of the myth. The bird's presence in the painting as an attribute of Venus has undoubtedly contributed to the reading of the episode as one of romantic, bittersweet dalliance.[7]

The new appearance of the goat-god provides a vital clue in unravelling the eighteenth-century relevance of the theme. Alongside the sumptuous, pearly white flesh tones of Syrinx in her flight at the centre of De Troy's composition, Pan's physical features have taken on a rather more youthful appearance – one that contrasted with the mature features by which he was typically identified from antiquity onwards. Pan, it is agreed, has taken on the countenance of a gentleman. The monstrous image of a bestial rapist driven by irrational and violent lust is abandoned in favour of the imploring, wistful lover.

Figure 14.1: Jean-François de Troy, *Pan and Syrinx*, 1720. Oil on canvas, 106 x 139cm. Reproduced with permission of the Cleveland Museum of Art, Mr and Mrs William H. Marlatt Fund, no. 1973.212.

As Syrinx flees from Pan into the arms of her father, a putto steadies his arrow, holding his burning torch of love with determination towards the pair. Syrinx's expression of scorn supports the observation that in Ovid's *Metamorphoses*, the 'sexual desirability' of the victim is amplified by signs of 'discomfort and embarrassment, or by fear'.[8] Mythological images representing the objections of women against the unwelcome attempts of their assailants were considered sexually exciting, and had been used as a means to arouse desire in viewers from antiquity onwards.[9] The link between images of sexual violence and ideals of love and pleasure underscores Susan Griffin's assertion that 'heterosexual love finds an erotic expression through male dominance and female submission'.[10]

In marked contrast to visions of romantic pursuit, an anonymous French print dated to between 1650 and 1700 offers a more realistic imagining of Syrinx's terror on the cusp of her transformation.[11] Here, the minute figures of Pan and Syrinx are locked in battle within an airless landscape. Pan clutches at the nymph's waist as she throws her arms in the air, her frantic struggle among the tangle of reeds signifying both her suspension between the states of transformation and the fact that she is overwhelmed by her assailant. Swallowed whole by the enormity of her surroundings or overcome by the ferocity of Pan's lust, the nymph's ordeal within the lonely woodland setting reinforces the association between hunter and prey. Clearly, the motif of a woman in flight from her attacker underscores the feminine imperative to retain her chastity while at the same time highlighting the concept of 'sexual relations as a kind of hunt'.[12]

This idea applies outside the reference of visual mediums as well. The libertine Constant d'Hermenches confessed that he saw 'the seduction of women as a hunt', explaining in letters to his friend, Isabelle de Charrière, that 'With regard to women, my heart and mind are what a hound is with regard to its game in the field; he pursues and devours it'.[13] While men were expected to display assertive masculinity via sexual and social domination, women were to defend their reputations built on loyalty and virtue at all costs, resisting the temptations of inappropriate desire outside the lawful sanctity of marriage. Masculine honour was premised on the authority and control of feminine sexuality, while feminine honour depended on the preservation of chastity.

While assertive masculinity and masculine sexuality were promoted by equating metaphors of military conquest with amorous triumph in erotic fiction, the brutality of actual rape was usually associated with the depravity of elite, aristocratic men.[14] As the term 'satyr' remains in current use to describe the licentious 'pervert', the very term 'satyriasis' is used to describe abnormal and excessive sexual desire in men, while 'nymphomania' describes the feminine equivalent of the disorder.[15] The unfortunate characteristics of 'lascivious' men and women marked by excessive sexual craving and lecherous behaviour concerned moralists and the medical profession alike. The contemporary example of the natural Wildman or *Homo ferus*, alongside the mythical figures of Pan and satyrs, were marked by assumptions of irrepressible sexual urges and a violent lack of restraint.[16] As Richard Nash explains, satyrs and other wild figures of nature and wilderness metaphorically threaten 'to carry off those women and children who do not participate in their own domestication'.[17]

Penned with the intention of providing sound medical and moralistic advice, Nicolas Venette's *Tableau de l'amour conjugal* (1712, The Mysteries of Conjugal Love Reveal'd) warned against the dangers of 'inordinate Passions' which threatened to control the imagination.[18] Given free reign, these dangerous inflammations were associated with a disorderly life of ruin. Venette's words of caution recall the notorious sexuality of Pan, whose 'Desire is in Arms against his Reason, and overcomes it at every moment'.[19] In a word, 'tis an habitual infirmity, which commonly seizes foolish Souls only; that are dazzled by the Beauty of Women'.[20] When Venette insists that 'God must work a wonder, to make such a Man abandon his amorous Humour', his words summon the relentless figure of the goat-god whose volatile lust is endlessly repulsed.[21]

From antiquity onwards, the hybrid bodies of both satyrs and fauns signified their hyper-sexuality and lack of control. While the satyr's 'almost permanent state of erection' inspired both laughter and contempt, it also highlighted his bestiality further evidenced by his obscene behaviour.[22] Rather than signifying potent virility, the physical evidence of abnormal, excessive sexuality and misconduct identify Pan with the lascivious man described in the *Tableau de l'amour conjugal*. While Venette stipulated that conditions of climate and country contributed to lecherous behaviour, he also insisted that men of this character could be identified through their physical features.[23] He instructed the reader to:

> consider the outward Carriage of this Man, he seems to fly when he walks, his fat does not trouble him, it suffices he is fleshy and nervous, to be both nimble and lascivious. He is of a middle size, has a large Breast, big and Strong Voice. The Colour of his countenance is brown and swarthy, mix'd with a little red; and if you uncover him, his skin will not appear very white ... his skin is so rough and dry ... The Hair of his Head is hard, black and curl'd. His beard is a sign of his admirable ability in getting Children, and betokens the strength and vigour of his Complexion, it being thick, black, and hard.[24]

Venette repeatedly emphasized the dangers of the over-zealous type of man he describes as a,

> satyr, who seeks everywhere without stop or stay to assuage his passion; All women are agreeable to him in the Dark; he refuses none, tho' never so ugly, and is always in a Condition to satisfy them; his reason not being able to bridle his Amorous eagerness, and his Constitution too hot to suffer him to be Subject to its Rules.[25]

The unruly appetites of the lewd provoked more serious concerns with regards to the dangers of fornication outside legally sanctioned marriage. Promiscuity was equated with the pollution and the contagion of sin, and was seen as a direct cause of sterility and the spread of infectious disease. In the interests of the preservation of family lineage, for instance, it was considered the responsibility of elder males to educate younger men in preparation of manhood, promoting the happy pleasures of marriage while urging caution against the 'inconstancy' of women.[26]

Pierre Mignard (1612–95) painted the theme of Pan and Syrinx a number of times, and it has been observed that this subject was of some personal significance to the artist. Between 1688 and 1690, Mignard produced the first painting from which subsequent works evolved. This first version (see Figure 14.2) has been described as burdened by a 'mood of sorrow and regret'.[27] While the cool clarity of the painter's palette and open, natural setting frame the composition, the viewer's eye is resolutely drawn in towards the trio of figures at the centre of the canvas, where Syrinx's form begins to fuse with the reeds.

Arms stretched out in flight, the panic-stricken nymph looks back at her aggressor, the pearly white softness of her flesh and her fluttering drapery in direct contrast with Pan's burly musculature and darker hairiness. The marked difference between the physiognomy of Syrinx and Pan, as well as the movement of the nymph's robes and hair is, for one writer, 'symbolic both of her terror ... and of his brutality'.[28] As Pan is about to snatch Syrinx up in his rough arms, the river god, Ladon, opens his arms to his daughter. A single cherubim by Syrinx's heel holds out love's flame, clutching at her robe while her sisters to the left behind Ladon's shoulder quietly and silently observe the scene unfolding before them.

The placement of Syrinx between her would-be rapist and father in this first composition is not only striking, but also highly significant. The arrangement of figures presents a clearly distinct group embroiled in the unfolding conflict aside from the water nymphs, so that Syrinx's predicament is played out between men, to the exclusion of feminine bystanders. As a figure simultaneously pursued and safeguarded, the figure of Syrinx has become a potential token of exchange with access to her person granted or denied by paternal authority.

The subsequent version of Mignard's first painting was intentionally produced for the artist's son, Charles (see Figure 14.3). This second painting replicates the triangular arrangement of Syrinx between her father and Pan in close-up. In removing the details of landscape and the water nymphs present in the first painting, Mignard's second composition strictly emphasizes the group formation of Syrinx between two men. Here, Syrinx's body represents femininity itself, lost in the imperative to define and promote the values of patriarchy around and against the image of woman. The consequences of Pan's lust are reflected in the putto's response of extinguishing love's flame, while two of the chubby infants in the foreground of the painting scorn the outcome of misguided desire.

The Horror of the Horns 169

Figure 14.2: Pierre Mignard, *Pan and Syrinx*, 1688–90. Oil on canvas, 71 × 96cm. Reproduced with permission of the Sarah Campbell Blaffer Foundation, Houston, Texas.

Figure 14.3: Pierre Mignard, *Pan and Syrinx*, 1690. Oil on canvas, 116 x 90cm. Reproduced with permission of the Musee du Louvre, Paris. RF1979-19. Photo credits: © RMN – Grand Palais (muse du Louvre) / Michel Urtado.

It has already been acknowledged that the second painting was intended to fulfil an instructive purpose, supported by the fact that Mignard also presented its pendant, *Apollo and Daphne* (believed to be lost), to his youngest son, Rodolphe. Both paintings draw on themes of sexual pursuit and rejection, and this conscious presentation of works addressing the dangers of spontaneous passion are understood as 'an injunction not to marry without parental approval'.[29] Used as a means of communicating the moral concern of a father for his son, *Pan and Syrinx* and its pendant became tools for the education of youths in preparation for manhood.[30] Not entirely a man or goat, the hybrid image of Pan provided an example against which ideal masculinity ought to be constructed and maintained.

As we have seen, an anxious concern for the virtue and healthy generation of society fuelled the writing of those keen to promote the pleasures of lawfully sanctioned sex and desire between married couples as a means to avoid the disasters of sterility and unhealthy or malformed offspring.[31] Lust and illicit fornication were viewed as the 'frustration of what nature intended', and the parameters of marriage were promoted as a virtuous and natural way of safeguarding the survival of humanity through procreation, as well as providing a means to both gratify and regulate sexual desire.[32] The yoke of wedlock, however, was not immune to the dangers of fornication, and husbands were cautioned against indulging too often in marital sexual pleasures for fear of becoming distracted and unfit for the 'more serious Occupations' of masculine duty.[33]

Turning the Tables: The Lascivious Woman

Mignard's original version of *Pan and Syrinx* was later meticulously reproduced and even ironically reversed by virtue of the mechanics of print production. Produced and circulated from 1718, Edmé Jeurat's satirical print compositionally and metaphorically reverses the intended meaning and function associated with Mignard's first painting executed almost thirty years earlier.[34] Jeurat's print altered the reception and context of the image simply by applying a verse beneath it which in part reads:

> Once such horns were considered hideous ... But how things have changed! There is hardly a beauty today who has any difficulty in contemplating them, be they ten feet high, and she can see them on her husband and still laugh.[35]

While Mignard's earlier painting presses the need for masculine restraint and legally sanctioned marriage, Jeurat's print addresses the grave consequences for misguided victims of love and lust, focusing on the image of the cuckolded man. Here, the dangers of immoderate behaviour are tied to the treachery of unfaithful women. The immodest wife who indulges in extra-marital sex proves that the domestic authority of her husband has been compromised, signalling both 'sexual betrayal and failed masculinity'.[36] As has been shown, early eighteenth-century conventions of polite society, 'exposed women to constant sexual interest and engagement, whilst tending to absolve men of responsibility for their supposedly natural rapacity'.[37]

At the mercy of their perceived voracious appetites, women required the steady guidance and authority of husbands and fathers to safeguard their chastity and family honour. While enjoying an abundance of marital sex carried effeminizing risks and distractions for men, the most dangerous feminine behaviour was thought to lay outside of the marriage matrix. Disobedient or lascivious women presented an even greater threat to masculine privilege and codes of honour, which were sustained via the 'integrity of patriarchal inheritance'.[38] The shame of illegitimate offspring presented a troubling threat to legitimate heirs.

As ruling head of the marital couple, a cuckolded husband must bear the burden and 'wear the Horns, by the Law of Nature' when the shame of his humiliation was found out.[39] Anton Blok confirms that the shame of wearing the horns comes from the perceived inability of the husband to 'control and monopolize his wife, to ensure her chastity and thus to guarantee the immunity of his domain'.[40] In analysing the symbolism of the horn gesture within Mediterranean cultures, Blok points out that references to animals have often been used to 'represent the internal differentiation of [their] society'.[41] Therefore, the sign of the horns or *cornuto* remain firmly associated with disgrace and the theft of honour. The goat was notorious for the demeaning manner in which it permitted sexual access to partners by rival males, and so the insult of being 'given the horns' aligns the deceived husband with the shameful conduct of billy-goats who permit their own disgrace.[42] Francisco Vaz da Silva elaborates that the rival or seducer 'transfers his own horns of virility onto the cheated husband's head even as he asserts male supremacy over the cuckold'.[43] The opposition of cuckold and gallant were often described in terms of seduction and conquest versus inadequate impotence, and therefore, the horns of the cuckold are worn as a token of emasculation and domestic authority undermined by wife and rival.[44]

The titles of popular plays, comedies and novels ridiculing the contented, 'merry cuckold' who wore the 'fashionable horns' reflected an anxiety common amongst men in ages past and present.[45] Popular cuckold humour appeared to soften the blow of humiliation shared between men, even as they 'laye(s) in each other's nests'.[46] Diderot and d'Alembert's *Encyclopédie* came to define '*adultère*' as the 'most cruel of all thefts', an 'irregular union' directly contributing to the 'ruin of fertility and the opprobrium of society'.[47] Children borne of unlawful unions threatened to pollute the populace with their own lack of morality inherited from their mothers.[48]

Through the bodies of women, acts of sexual assault and transgression became offences committed against and between men.[49] As writers including

Jean-Jacques Rousseau later in the century would insist, the 'new virtuous republic' was vulnerable to the perilous threat of women who abandoned their duties as wives and mothers.[50] Women discovered to be unfaithful to their husbands were severely punished, incarcerated in convents, stripped of their dowries and matrimonial rights as their husbands saw fit.[51]

Bearing this in mind, the repeated representations of Syrinx between her father and rejected attacker in Mignard's painting and Jeurat's print take on altered meanings. Mignard's deliberate framing of the nymph between two men – to the exclusion of all else – in his second painting cautions against the consequences of thoughtless passion and illicit sexuality. This may also refer to the effeminizing effects of excessive pleasure, which, as libertines themselves remarked, presented the risk of distraction, degeneracy and emasculation.[52] Recalling again the notion of adultery as the 'cruellest kind of theft', the 'Ungrateful fair' embodied by Syrinx caught between two men ruptured the traditional 'model of exchange' between father and groom.[53]

The image of Pan's attempted rape of Syrinx in Jeurat's print underscores the unreliability of women, so that the image of violent masculine aggression seen in the original painting is disturbingly replaced by the image of dangerous female promiscuity. The monstrous horns of Pan have here been replaced by the horns of the domesticated beast, linking the cuckolded husband to the passive animal mastered by his rival. Similarly, popular prints from *Le Monde Renversé* were sold and widely distributed as satirical images of hierarchical inversion and reversed gender roles. While some images include representations of humans as working animals dominated by donkeys, for instance, another shows a woman beating her husband with a stick for not completing his spinning, and another presents her holding a musket and smoking pipe while her husband nurses their baby. Though the prints are noted for their tongue-in-cheek content in presenting impossible or improbable images, they also serve to reaffirm traditional gender roles by surrounding representations of incorrect behaviour by motifs of chaos and violence to reinforce the necessary subordination of woman and beast.[54]

Visual representations of Pan that followed Mignard's example emphasized the figure's shameless lust and highlighted masculine codes of honour, virility, patriarchal privilege and domestic authority. By contrast, the hybrid god's lack of restraint and unruly sexuality aligned him with the shameful and unmanly promiscuity of 'he-goats', as well as the irrational feminine.[55] Later, Jeurat's satirical print proposed a troubling inversion of Pan as yet another man 'abused' by woman, mocked as the emasculated victim of tyrannical, feminine sexuality and of the seducer who gave him the horns of the cuckold.[56]

The image of Syrinx caught between two men and slipping through Pan's urgent grasp, I propose, came to refer to the passing of horns from seducer to husband. This exchange through the body of Syrinx signals a '*transfer*' of virility

… between the two men', so that adultery, like rape, is an offence committed against or between men.[57] The love triangle is integral to the concept of cuckoldry and, I suggest, is explicitly referred to via the swan as an emblem of love hidden in the shadows of De Troy's painting. Rather than reading the episode of Pan's disappointment as one of romantic love lost, it ought to be understood that the violence inherent in Syrinx's attempted rape is not portrayed as a seduction, nor is it sanitized as Wolfthal might suggest during the early eighteenth century. The attempted rape, metamorphosis and destruction of Syrinx through mutilation was not ignored or downplayed in these visual representations – it was erased altogether.

NOTES

Greenfield, 'Introduction'

1. See Nahum Tate's adaptation, *The History of King Lear* (1680).
2. 'The Rape of the Bride; or, Marriage and Hanging go by Destiny' (London: Printed and Sold by J. Peele, 1723), p. 7.
3. For examples of this myth in the seventeenth and eighteenth centuries, see J. Sharp, *The Midwives Book. Or the Whole* Art *of Midwifry Discovered* (London, 1671), ed. E. Hobby (Oxford: Oxford University Press, 1999), p. 82; J. Brydall, *Compendious Collection of the Laws of England, Touching Matters Criminal* (London: Printed for John Bellinger, 1676), p. 53; W. Salmon, *Aristotle's Compleat and Experience'd Midwife*, 2nd edn (London, 1711), *Eighteenth-Century Collections Online* database [accessed 1 January 2013], p. 10.
4. 'Rape, n.3', *OED Online* (Oxford University Press), at http://0-www.oed.com.bianca.penlib.du.edu/view/Entry/ 158145?rskey=ER5EoL&result=1&isAdvanced=true [accessed 20 March 2012].
5. 'Rape', *Miriam-Webster Online Dictionary* (Merriam-Webster), at http://www.merriam-webster.com [accessed 20 March 2012].
6. W. Blackstone, *Commentaries on the Laws of England*, 4 vols (Oxford: Clarendon Press, 1765–9), vol. 4, p. 213.
7. S. Johnson, *A Dictionary of the English Language*, 2 vols, 8th edn (Dublin: Printed by R. Marchbank, 1798), vol. 1.
8. Brydall, *Compendious Collection of the Laws of England*, p. 53.

1 Gammon, 'Researching Sexual Violence, 1660–1800: A Critical Analysis'

1. S. Brownmiller, *Against Our Will: Men, Women and Rape* (New York: Simon and Schuster, 1975).
2. S. Griffin, 'Rape: The All-American Crime', *Ramparts* (September 1971), pp. 26–35.
3. See S. Jackson, 'Classic Review: Against Our Will', *Trouble and Strife*, 35 (1997), pp. 61–7.
4. E. Shorter, 'On Writing the History of Rape', *Signs*, 3:2 (1977), pp. 471–82, on p. 473. For a critical response to this review, see H. I. Hartmann and E. Ross, 'Comment on "On Writing the History of Rape"', *Signs*, 3:4 (1978), pp. 931–5.
5. S. D'Cruze, 'Approaching the History of Rape and Sexual Violence: Notes towards Research', *Women's History Review*, 1:3 (1993), pp. 377–97, on p. 379.

6. S. Edwards, *Female Sexuality and the Law* (Oxford: Martin Robertson, 1981), p. 22.
7. S. D'Cruze, *Crimes of Outrage: Sex, Violence and Victorian Working Women* (London: Routledge, 1998); K. Stevenson, '"Unequivocal Victims": The Historical Roots of the Mystification of the Female Complainant in Rape Cases', *Feminist Legal Studies*, 8 (2000), pp. 343–66.
8. G. Durston, *Victims and Viragos: Metropolitan Women, Crime and the Eighteenth-Century Justice System* (Bury St Edmunds: Arima, 2007), p. 172.
9. Ibid., p. 171.
10. R. Porter, 'Rape – Does it Have a Historical Meaning?' in S. Tomaselli and R. Porter (eds), *Rape: An Historical and Social Enquiry* (Oxford: Basil Blackwell, 1986), pp. 216–36, on p. 222.
11. B. S. Lindemann, '"To Ravish and Carnally Know": Rape in Eighteenth-Century Massachusetts', *Signs*, 10:1 (1984), pp. 63–82, on p. 81.
12. Ibid., p. 81.
13. M. Chaytor, '"Husband(ry)": Narratives of Rape in the Seventeenth Century', *Gender and History*, 7:3 (1995), pp. 378–407 and G. Walker, 'Rereading Rape and Sexual Violence in Early Modern England', *Gender and History*, 10:1 (1998), pp. 1–25.
14. N. Bashar, 'Rape in England between 1550 and 1700', in London Feminist History Workshop, *The Sexual Dynamics of History* (London: Pluto Press, 1983), p. 40.
15. T. Laqueur, *Making Sex: Body and Gender from Greeks to Freud* (Harvard, MA: Harvard University Press, 1990), cited in Stevenson, 'Unequivocal Victims', p. 347.
16. Durston, *Victims and Viragos*, p. 172.
17. S. Staves, 'British Seduced Maidens', *Eighteenth-Century Studies*, 14:2 (1980–1), pp. 109–34 and K. Binhammer, *The Seduction Narrative in Britain, 1747–1800* (Cambridge: Cambridge University Press, 2009).
18. W. Beatty Warner, 'Reading Rape: Marxist-Feminist Figurations of the Literal', *Diacritics*, 13:4 (1983), pp. 12–32, on p. 16.
19. T. Eagleton, *The Rape of Clarissa: Writing, Sexuality and Class Struggle in Richardson* (Minneapolis, MN: University of Minnesota Press, 1982), p. 61, cited in K. L. Steele, 'Clarissa's Silence', *Eighteenth-Century Fiction*, 23:1 (2010), pp. 1–34, on p. 13.
20. See for example A. Clark, *Women's Silence* (Pandora: London, 1987), pp. 46–58.
21. R. Trumbach, *Sex and the Gender Revolution* (Chicago, IL: University of Chicago Press, 1998), vol. 1, p. 302.
22. S. M. Constantine, '"By a Gentle Force Compell'd": An Analysis of Rape in Eighteenth-Century English Fact and Fiction' (D.Phil, University of Massachusetts, Amherst, 2006).
23. J. Pearson, *The Prostituted Muse 1642–1737* (New York: St Martins Press, 1988), p. 97, and E. Howe, *The First English Actresses: Women and Drama 1660–1700* (Cambridge: Cambridge University Press, 1992), pp. 43–7. Also: D. Hughes, 'Rape and the Restoration Stage', *Eighteenth Century*, 46:3 (2005), pp. 225–36, J. I. Marsden, *Fatal Desire: Women, Sexuality and the English Stage, 1660–1720* (New York: Cornell University Press, 2006) and J. L. Airey, *The Politics of Rape: Sexual Atrocity, Propaganda Wars, and the Restoration Stage* (Newark: University of Delaware Press, 2012).
24. P. Wagner, *Eros Revived: Erotica of the Enlightenment in England and America* (London: Secker and Warburg, 1988), p. 116.
25. Some attention is paid to the accused in my doctoral thesis: J. D. Gammon, 'Ravishment and Ruin: The Construction of Stories of Sexual Violence in England, c. 1640–1820' (PhD dissertation, University of Essex, 2001).
26. Clark, *Women's Silence*, p. 6.

27. Porter, 'Rape', p. 227.
28. S. Staves, 'Fielding and the Comedy of Attempted Rape', in B. Fowkes Tobin (ed.), *History, Gender and Eighteenth-Century Literature* (Athens, GA: University of Georgia Press, 1994), pp. 86–112, on p. 106.
29. Durston, *Victims and Viragos*, p. 165.
30. Lindemann, 'To Ravish and Carnally Know', p. 80.
31. Trumbach, *Sex and the Gender Revolution*, p. 306.
32. Durston, *Victims and Viragos*, p. 142.
33. J. M. Beattie, *Crime and the Courts in England 1660–1800* (Oxford: Oxford University Press, 1986), pp. 124–31; see also Gammon, 'Ravishment and Ruin'.
34. A. E. Simpson, 'Popular Perceptions of Rape as a Capital Crime in Eighteenth-Century England: The Press and the Trial of Francis Charteris in the Old Bailey, February 1730', *Law and History Review*, 22 (2004) pp. 27–70; also see Durston, *Victims and Viragos*, p. 153.
35. A. E. Simpson, 'The "Blackmail Myth" and the Prosecution of Rape and Its Attempt in Eighteenth-Century London: The Creation of a Legal Tradition', *Journal of Criminal Law and Criminology*, 77 (1986), pp. 101–50.
36. L. Edelstein, '"An Accusation Easily to be Made?" Rape and Malicious Prosecution in Eighteenth-Century England', *American Journal of Legal History*, 42 (1998), pp. 351–90, on p. 353.
37. M. Hale, *History of the Pleas of the Crown* (1736; Chicago, IL: Chicago University Press, 1971) p. 635.
38. Fielding's biographers M. C. and R. R. Battestin strongly refute this claim, cited in Staves, 'Fielding', p. 106.
39. See A. E. Simpson, 'Vulnerability and the Age of Female Consent: Legal Innovation and its Effect on Prosecution for Rape in Eighteenth-Century London', in G. S. Rousseau and R. Porter (eds), *Sexual Underworlds of the Enlightenment* (Manchester: Manchester University Press, 1987) and J. D. Gammon, 'A Denial of Innocence: Female Juvenile Victims of Rape and the English Legal System in the Eighteenth Century', in S. Hussey and A. Fletcher (eds), *Childhood in Question? Children, Parents and the State* (Manchester: Manchester University Press, 1999), pp. 74–95.
40. Simpson, 'Vulnerability', pp. 196–7.
41. A. E. Simpson, 'Masculinity and Control: The Prosecution of Sex Offenses in Eighteenth-Century London' (PhD, New York University, 1994).
42. See for example: N. M. Goldsmith, *The Worst of Crimes: Homosexuality and the Law* (London: Ashgate, 1999); R. Norton, *Mother Clap's Molly House: The Gay Subculture in England, 1700–1830* (Stroud: Chalford Press, 2006) and R. Trumbach, 'Londons Sodomites: Homosexual Behaviour and Western Culture in the Eighteenth Century', *Journal of Social History*, 11:1 (1977), pp. 1–33. Such authors have produced fascinating studies of the experiences of being gay in the eighteenth century but little attention has been paid to the legal treatment of sodomy trials in the way that rape trials have been discussed.
43. T. R. Forbes, *Surgeons at the Bailey: English Forensic Medicine to 1878* (New Haven, CT and London: Yale University Press, 1986), p. 21.
44. See for example: M. Clark and C. Crawford (eds), *Legal Medicine in History* (Cambridge: Cambridge University Press, 1994).
45. J. H. Langbein, 'The Criminal Trial Before the Lawyers', *University of Chicago Law Review*, 45 (1978), pp. 263–316, and P. Linebaugh, '(Marxist) Social History and

(Conservative) Legal History: A Reply to Professor Langbein', *New York University Law Review*, 60 (1985), pp. 212–44.
46. Griffin, 'Rape', p. 26.

2 Block, '"For the Repressing of the Most Wicked and Felonious Rapes and Ravishments of Women": Rape Law in England, 1660–1800'

1. There are several scholarly studies of rape law in early modern England. See A. E. Simpson, 'Vulnerability and the Age of Female Consent and its Effect on Prosecutions for Rape in Eighteenth-Century London', in G. S. Rousseau and R. Porter (eds), *Sexual Underworlds of the Enlightenment* (Chapel Hill, NC: North Carolina University Press, 1988), pp. 182–205; A. E. Simpson, 'Popular Perceptions of Rape as a Capital Crime in Eighteenth-Century England: The Press and the Trial of Francis Charteris in the Old Bailey, 1730', *Law and History Review*, 22:1 (Spring 2004), pp. 27–70; G. Durston, 'Rape in the Eighteenth-Century Metropolis: Part I', *British Journal for Eighteenth-Century Studies*, 28:2 (September 2005), pp. 167–79; G. Durston, 'Rape in the Eighteenth-Century Metropolis: Part II', *British Journal for Eighteenth-Century Studies*, 29:1 (March 2006), pp. 15–31; J. Rudolph, 'Rape and Resistance: Women and Consent in Seventeenth-Century English Legal and Political Thought', *Journal of British Studies*, 32:2 (April 2000), pp. 157–84; L. Edelstein, 'An Accusation Easily to be Made?: Rape and Malicious Prosecution in Eighteenth-Century England', *American Journal of Legal History*, 42 (October 1998), pp. 351–90; M. Chaytor, 'Husband(ry): Narratives of Rape in the Seventeenth Century', *Gender and History*, 7:3 (November 1995), pp. 378–407; G. Walker, 'Rereading Rape and Sexual Violence in Early Modern England', *Gender and History*, 10:1 (April 1998), pp. 1–25; and B. J. Baines, 'Effacing Rape in Early Modern Representation', *ELH*, 65:1 (Spring 1998), pp. 39–98. For violence against women, see, S. D. Amussen, '"Being Stirred to Much Unquietness": Violence and Domestic Violence in Early Modern England', *Journal of Women's History*, 6:2 (Summer 1994), pp. 70–89. See also, S. D'Cruze, 'Approaching the History of Rape and Sexual Violence', *Women's History Review*, 1:3 (1993), pp. 337–97; R. Porter, 'Rape – Does it have a Historical Meaning?', in S. Tomeselli and R. Porter (eds), *Rape* (Oxford: Blackwell, 1986), pp. 216–36; S. Robertson, 'What's Law Got to Do with It? Legal Records and Sexual Histories', *Journal of the History of Sexuality*, 14:1/2 (January/April 2008), pp. 161–85.
2. Statute of Westminster I, c. 13 (1275), Statute of Westminster II, c. 34 & c. 35 (1285).
3. 18 Elizabeth I, c. 7, §§1, 4 (1576).
4. *Treatise on the Laws and Customs of the Realm of England Commonly called Glanvill*, ed. and trans. G. D. G. Hall (Oxford: Oxford University Press, 2002), pp. 175–6. Sue Sheridan Walker is arguably the foremost authority on ravishment; see, 'Free Consent and Marriage of Feudal Wards in Medieval England', *Journal of Medieval History*, 8:2 (June 1982), pp. 123–34 and 'Punishing Convicted Ravishers: Statutory Strictures and Actual Practice in Thirteenth and Fourteenth-Century England', *Journal of Medieval History*, 13:3 (September 1987), pp. 237–50. See also, C. Saunders, *Rape and Ravishment in the Literature of Medieval England* (Cambridge: D. S. Brewer, 2001), pp. 20–1. T. Wood, *New Institute of the Imperial or Civil Law with Notes* (London, J. & J. Knapton, 1730), p. 280.

5. 18 Elizabeth I, c. 7, §1 (1576). Saunders, *Rape and Ravishment in the Literature of Medieval England*, p. 75. Benefit of clergy offered leniency to first time offenders who were branded or in some other way mutilated rather than hanged following conviction.
6. J. B. Post, 'Sir Thomas West and the Statute of Rapes, 1382', *Bulletin of the Institute of Historical Research*, 53 (1980), 24–30, on p. 24.
7. Ibid.
8. H. Bracton, *On the Laws and Customs of England*, trans. S. Thorne, 4 vols (Cambridge, MA: Harvard University Press, 1968), vol. 2, pp. 344, 403, 414–15. Post, 'Sir Thomas West', p. 24.
9. H. Finch, *Law, or, a Discourse Thereof*, ed. D. Pickering (London: Henry Lintot, 1759), p. 204; E. Coke, *Third Part of the Institutes of the Laws of England*, 6th edn (London: W. Rawling, 1681), p. 60.
10. W. Hawkins, *Treatise of the Pleas of the Crown*, 8th edn, 2 vols (London: Law Booksellers and Publishers, 1824), vol. 1, p. 122, §3.
11. T. Wood, *Institute of the Laws of England*, 10th rev. edn (London: W. Strahan & M. Woodfall, 1772), p. 361.
12. *Glanvill*, p. 175; W. Blackstone, *Commentaries on the Laws of England*, 4 vols (Chicago, IL: University of Chicago Press, 1979), vol. 4, p. 210; Coke, *Third Part of the Institutes*, p. 60. Emphasis mine.
13. Ibid., pp. 175–6.
14. Blackstone, *Commentaries on the Laws of England*, vol. 4, p. 210.
15. Hale, *History of the Pleas of the Crown*, p. 631.
16. Ibid. Bracton, *On the Laws*, vol. 2, p. 415, *Statutes: Great Britain*, rev. ed. vol. 1, Henry III to James II (London: George Edward Eyre & William Spottiswoode, 1870), 4 Edw. I, 'Of Coroners: Appeal of Rape', p. 27.
17. O. Hufton, *The Prospect Before Her: A History of Women in Western Europe*, vol. 1, 1500–1800 (New York, Alfred A. Knopf, 1996), pp. 29, 56–8; G. Geis, 'Lord Hale, Witches, and Rape', *British Journal of Law and Society*, 5:1 (Summer 1978), pp. 26–44; A. Fraser, *The Weaker Vessel* (New York: Vintage Books, 1984), pp. 1–4.
18. Blackstone, *Commentaries on the Laws*, vol. 4, p. 213.
19. Ibid.
20. T. Rizzo, 'Sexual Violence in the Enlightenment: The State, the Bourgeoisie, and the Cult of the Victimized Woman', *Proceedings of the Annual Meeting of the Western Society for French History*, 15 (November 1987), pp. 122–9; R. H. Bloch, 'Untangling the Roots of Modern Sex Roles: A Survey of Four Centuries of Change', *Signs*, 21:4 (Winter 1978), pp. 241–7.
21. Sharpe, *Crime in Early Modern England*, pp. 40–1.
22. J. H. Langbein, *Origins of the Adversary Criminal Trial* (New York: Oxford University Press, 2003), pp. 2, 10–12; Blackstone, *Commentaries on the Laws of England*, vol. 4, p. 310.
23. Langbein, *Origins of the Adversary Criminal Trial*, pp. 10–17, 21, 24.
24. Durston, 'Rape in the Eighteenth-Century Metropolis: Part I', p. 168.
25. *Britton: An English Translation and Notes*, trans. F. M. Nichols (Washington, DC: John Byrne, 1901), pp. 46, 96. The book was published c. 1530. Scholars debate who this writer was, but we are only concerned with what he wrote.
26. M. Dalton, *The Countrey Justice* (London: Adam Islip, 1618), p. 256; T. Laqueur, *Making Sex: Body and Gender from the Greeks to Freud* (Cambridge, MA: Harvard University Press, 1990), pp. 46–9, 52–4; Saunders, *Rape and Ravishment*, pp. 29–30, 73–4.

27. Hale, *History of the Pleas of the Crown*, p. 631.
28. Wood, *Institute of the Laws of England*, pp. 361–2.
29. Hawkins, *Pleas of the Crown*, vol. 1, p. 122, §§3, 8.
30. Ibid.
31. Ibid.
32. S. Farr, *Elements of Medical Jurisprudence* (London: T. Becket, 1788), p. 42–3.
33. Ibid.
34. O. W. Bartley, *Treatise on Forensic Science, or Medical Jurisprudence* (Bristol: Barry & Son, 1815), pp. 42–5.
35. Ibid.
36. Ibid.
37. Finch, *Law, or, a Discourse Thereof*, p. 204.
38. Coke, *Third Part of the Institutes*, p. 60.
39. Ibid.
40. Wood, *Institute of the Laws of England*, p. 361.
41. Hawkins, *Pleas of the Crown*, vol. 1, p. 122, §3.
42. Hale, *History of the Pleas of the Crown*, p. 628.
43. East, *Treatise of the Pleas of the Crown*, pp. 439–40.
44. George IV (1828), c. 31, §18.
45. Ibid.

3 Barclay, 'From Rape to Marriage: Questions of Consent in the Eighteenth-Century Britain'

1. 'An Excellent New Ballad from Ireland: Or, the True En—sh D—n to be Hang'd for a Rape', in *The Case of Mr Daniel Kimberly, Attorney at Law, Executed at Dublin, May, 27, 1730. For Assisting Bradock Mead to Marry an Heiress* (Dublin, [c. 1730]), p. 23.
2. M. Legates, 'The Cult of Womanhood in Eighteenth-Century Thought', *Eighteenth-Century Studies*, 1 (1976), pp. 21–39.
3. S. Dickie, *Cruelty and Laughter: Forgotten Comic Literature and the Unsentimental Eighteenth Century* (Chicago, IL: University of Chicago Press, 2011), p. 200.
4. 'Rape', in Society of Gentlemen, *A New and Complete Dictionary of the Arts and Sciences*, 4 vols (London: W. Owen, 1764), vol. 4, p. 2708.
5. H. Gally, *Some Considerations upon Clandestine Marriages* (London: J. Hughes, 1750), p. 100.
6. 'Conclusion of the Humble Remonstrance and Petition of Mary Mouthwater', *Newcastle Courant* (5 January 1754); W. M. Morrison, *The Decisions of the Court of Session*, 42 vols (Edinburgh: Bell & Bradfute, 1804), vol. 16, pp. 13912–13.
7. 'Conclusion of the Humble Remonstrance and Petition of Mary Mouthwater'; J. Marishall, *A Series of Letters*, 2 vols (Edinburgh: the Author, 1789), vol. 1, p. 133.
8. J. Gregory, *A Father's Legacy to His Daughters* (Dublin, 1774), p. 67.
9. For extended discussion see K. Barclay, *Love, Intimacy and Power: Marriage and Patriarchy in Scotland, 1650–1850* (Manchester: Manchester University Press, 2011).
10. L. Richardson, '"Who Shall Restore my Lost Credit?": Rape, Reputation and the Marriage Market', *Studies in Eighteenth-Century Culture*, 32 (2003), pp. 19–44; J. Rudolph, 'Rape and Resistance: Women and Consent in Seventeenth-Century English Legal and Political Thought', *Journal of British Studies*, 39 (2000), pp. 157–84.

11. The legal position of married women varies across the United Kingdom, see: Barclay, *Love, Intimacy*, pp. 48–52; A. Erickson, *Women and Property in Early Modern England* (London: Routledge, 1993).
12. G. Frost, *Promises Broken: Courtship, Class and Gender in Victorian England* (Charlottesville, VA: University Press of Virginia, 1995); M. Luddy, *Matters of Deceit: Breach of Promise to Marry Cases in Nineteenth- and Twentieth-Century Limerick* (Dublin: Four Courts Press, 2011).
13. R. Perry, *Novel Relations: The Transformation of Kinship in English Literature and Culture* (Cambridge: Cambridge University Press, 2004), pp. 190–287.
14. Hudibras, quoted in G. Wright, *The Unfortunate Lovers: A Story Founded on Facts* (London: C. Stalker, 1792), p. 56.
15. D. Defoe, *A Treatise Concerning the Use and Abuse of the Marriage Bed* (London: T. Warner, 1727), p. 198; 'Mr Spectator', *Spectator* (22 February 1712).
16. F. Dabhoiwala, *The Origins of Sex: A History of the First Sexual Revolution* (Oxford: Oxford University Press, 2012), pp. 158–60.
17. *The Memoirs of Miss Arabella Bolton*, 2 vols (London: J. Fell, 1770).
18. 'Trial for Seduction', *Hampshire Chronicle* (13 December 1790).
19. Ibid.
20. M. Chaytor, 'Husband(ry): Narratives of Rape in the Seventeenth Century', *Gender & History*, 7:3 (1995), pp. 378–407; G. Walker, 'Rereading Rape and Sexual Violence in Early Modern England', *Gender & History*, 10 (1998), pp. 1–25.
21. National Records of Scotland (hereafter, NRS), CC8/6/15/47 Elizabeth Lining a. Alexander Hamilton, 1747.
22. H. Swinburne, *A Treatise of Spousals or Matrimonial Contracts* (London: Daniel Brown, 1711), p. 19.
23. A. Clark, 'Rape or Seduction? A Controversy Over Sexual Violence in the Nineteenth Century', in London Feminist History Group (ed.), *The Sexual Dynamics of History: Men's Power, Women's Resistance* (London: Pluto Press, 1983), pp. 13–27.
24. Dickie, *Cruelty and Laughter*, pp. 190–235.
25. These numbers were compiled by Katie Barclay and Maria Luddy as part of the AHRC-funded project, 'Marriage in Ireland, 1660–1925'. They are based on crime records, newspaper reports in the Irish press and occasional references in other sources. The figure provided reflects the number of individual women abducted. See also: J. Kelly, 'The Abduction of Women of Fortune in Eighteenth-Century Ireland', *Eighteenth-Century Ireland*, 9 (1994), pp. 7–43.
26. See the cases of Clementina Clerke (1791); Maria Withers (1800); Mrs Lee (1804); Maria Glenn (1818); Ellen Turner (1826); Miss Row (1827); Miss Bramwell (1828); Eliza Hickson (1829).
27. See, for example, the abduction, called rape, in *The Trial of Frederick Calvert, Esq ... for a Rape on the Body of Sarah Woodcock* (Edinburgh: John Balfour, [c. 1768]); another example: 'Seduction', *Caledonian Mercury*, 21 April 1798.
28. Kelly, 'Abduction of Women'.
29. *Glasgow Journal* (14 May 1750); J. Wilson et al., *Decisions of the First and Second Division of the Court of Session from November 1819 to November 1822* (Edinburgh: Manners and Miller, 1825), pp. 478–84.
30. See for example the abduction of Clementina Clerke: *The Trial of Richard Vining Perry, Esq. For Forcible Abduction, or Stealing an Heiress, from the Boarding-School of Miss Mills* (Bristol, [c. 1794]).

31. NRS, CC8/6/19/58 Thomas Gray a. Mrs Jacobina Moir, 1751.
32. M. Lee, *The Heiresses of Buccleuch: Marriage, Money and Politics in Seventeenth-Century Britain* (East Linton: Tuckwell Press, 1996); NRS CC8/6/13/27 Captain James Dalrymple a. Mary Gainer, 1739; NRS CC8/6/19/65 Elizabeth Duncan a. Malby Brabson, 1753.
33. *An Act to Declare Void the Alleged Marriage Between Ellen Turner, an Infant, and Edward Gibbon Wakefield*, 7 & 8 Geo. 5, c. 66.
34. *The Trial of Edward Gibbon Wakefield, William Wakefield, and Frances Wakefield* (London: John Murray, 1827).
35. Dickie, *Cruelty and Laughter*, pp. 200–1.
36. Mr Ramondon, *In Heriot's Walks &c, A New Song* (Edinburgh, 1715). For an extended discussion see: K. Barclay, 'Love and Courtship in Eighteenth-Century Scotland', in K. Barclay and D. Simonton (eds), *Women in Eighteenth-Century Scotland: Intimate, Intellectual and Public Lives* (Aldershot: Ashgate, 2013), pp. 37–54.
37. Clark, 'Rape or Seduction?', p. 18.
38. NRS, CC8/6/40/171 Mary McLaughan a. Archibald McDonald, 1782.
39. Ibid.
40. L. Leneman, *Promises, Promises: Marriage Litigation in Scotland, 1698–1830* (Edinburgh: N.M.S. Enterprises, 2003).
41. NRS, CC8/5/40 Marion Meikle a. Robert McGhie, 1822.
42. Ibid.
43. 'Seduction', *Caledonian Mercury*, 21 April 1798.
44. Trial of Barton Dorrington, 10 September 1788 (t17880910-46), *Old Bailey Proceedings, London Lives, 1690–1800*, at http://www.londonlives.org [accessed 5 February 2013].
45. NRS, CC8/5/25 Margaret Kennedy a. Andrew McDowall, 1796.
46. NRS, CC8/5/40.
47. NRS, CC8/6/162 Janet Colquhoun a. Alexander Walker, 1828.
48. G. Durston, 'Rape in the Eighteenth-Century Metropolis, Part 1', *British Journal of Eighteenth-Century Studies*, 28 (2005), pp. 167–79.
49. M. Durey, 'Abduction and Rape in Ireland in the Era of the 1798 Rebellion', *Eighteenth-Century Ireland*, 21 (2006), pp. 27–47.
50. J. Kelly, '"A Most Inhuman and Barbarous Piece of Villainy": An Exploration of the Crime of Rape in Eighteenth-Century Ireland', *Eighteenth-Century Ireland*, 10 (1995), pp. 78–107.
51. A.-M. Kilday, 'The Barbarous North? Criminality in Early Modern Scotland', in T. M. Devine and J. Wormald (eds), *The Oxford Handbook of Modern Scottish History* (Oxford: Oxford University Press, 2012), pp. 386–403, on p. 396.
52. C. Brown, *Religion and Society in Scotland since 1707* (Edinburgh: Edinburgh University Press, 1997), pp. 70–2.
53. 'Edinburgh', *Caledonian Mercury*, 20 March 1732; for discussion in the medieval context see: C. Dunn, *Damsels in Distress or Partners in Crime? The Abduction of Women in Medieval England* (PhD dissertation, Fordham University, 2007), p. 133.
54. 'House of Commons', *Hampshire Chronicle*, 27 January 1794.
55. See for example, *Dublin Gazette*, 22 May 1729; *Finn's Leinster Journal*, 29 August 1770; 'Singular Termination of a Trial for Rape', *Coventry Herald*, 13 August 1824. See discussion in Kelly, 'Crime of Rape', p. 98.
56. Durey, 'Abduction and Rape', p. 37.

57. *Ballina Impartial*, 21 September 1829.
58. Ibid.
59. Ibid.
60. Ibid.
61. J. Marishall, *A Series of Letters*, 2 vols, vol. 1, p. 134.
62. Ibid.

4 Gollapudi, 'The Disordered Fundament: Sexual Violence on Boys and Sodomy Trial Narratives in the *Old Bailey Proceedings*'

1. Trial of William Williams, July 1757 (t17570713–35), *Old Bailey Proceedings Online*, at www.oldbaileyonline.org, version 7.0 [accessed 19 February 2013].
2. Trial of William Williams, July 1757 (t17570713–35), *Old Bailey Proceedings Online*, at www.oldbaileyonline.org, version 7.0 [accessed 19 February 2013].
3. Trial of William Williams, July 1757 (t17570713–35), *Old Bailey Proceedings Online*, at www.oldbaileyonline.org, version 7.0 [accessed 19 February 2013].
4. This age corresponds with boys reaching puberty at about fifteen in the eighteenth century. See R. Trumbach, 'Sodomitical Assaults, Gender Role, and Sexual Development in Eighteenth-Century London', *Journal of Homosexuality*, 16:1 (1988), pp. 407–29.
5. *The Proceedings of the King's Commission of the Peace and Oyer and Terminer, and Gaol-Delivery of Newgate, held for the City of London and the County of Middlesex, at Justice-Hall, in the Old Bailey*. Now available at www.oldbaileyonline.org.
6. Trial of Charles Hitchin, April 1727 (t17270412–41), *Old Bailey Proceedings Online*, at www.oldbaileyonline.org, version 7.0 [accessed 19 February 2013].
7. For details of the complex circumstances and processes that went into a sodomy trial from filing initial charges to a court verdict, see N. Goldsmith, *The Worst of Crimes: Homosexuality and the Law in Eighteenth-Century London* (Brookfield, VT: Ashgate, 1998).
8. R. B. Shoemaker, 'The Old Bailey Proceedings and the Representation of Crime and Criminal Justice in Eighteenth-Century London', *Journal of British Studies*, 47.3 (2008), pp. 559–80, on p. 565.
9. H. Gladfelder, *Criminality and Narrative* (Baltimore, MD: Johns Hopkins University Press, 2001), p. 22.
10. A. E. Simpson, *Masculinity and Control: The Prosecution of Sex Offenses in Eighteenth-Century London* (New York: New York University, 1984), p. 433, at http://search.proquest.com/docview/303307196?accountid=10223 [accessed 19 February 2013].
11. Trial of John Deacon Thomas Blair, January 1743 (t17430114–31), *Old Bailey Proceedings Online*, at www.oldbaileyonline.org, version 7.0 [accessed 19 February 2013].
12. Simpson, *Masculinity and Control*, p. 127.
13. Trial of Gilbert Laurence, August 1730 (t17300828–24), *Old Bailey Proceedings Online*, at www.oldbaileyonline.org, version 7.0 [accessed 19 February 2013].
14. Goldsmith, *The Worst of Crimes*, p. 55.
15. Trial of Gilbert Laurence, August 1730 (t17300828–24), *Old Bailey Proceedings Online*, at www.oldbaileyonline.org, version 7.0 [accessed 19 February 2013].
16. Trial of Christopher Samuel Graff, December 1721 (t17211206–67), *Old Bailey Proceedings Online*, at www.oldbaileyonline.org, version 7.0 [accessed 19 February 2013].

17. See, for instance, S. Landsman, 'One Hundred Years of Rectitude: Medical Witnesses at the Old Bailey, 1717–1817', *Law and History Review*, 16:3 (1998), pp. 445–94; and T. Forbes, *Surgeons at the Old Bailey: Forensic Medicine to 1878* (New Haven, CT: Yale University Press, 1985).
18. A. Gilbert, 'Sodomy and the Law in Eighteenth- and Early Nineteenth- Century Britain', *Societas*, 8 (1978), pp. 225–41, on p. 228.
19. Trial of Henry Hambleton, January 1729 (t17290116–11), *Old Bailey Proceedings Online*, at www.oldbaileyonline.org, version 7.0 [accessed 19 February 2013].
20. Trial of Henry Hambleton, January 1729 (t17290116–11), *Old Bailey Proceedings Online*, at www.oldbaileyonline.org, version 7.0 [accessed 19 February 2013].
21. Trial of Gilbert Laurence, August 1730 (t17300828–24), *Old Bailey Proceedings Online*, at www.oldbaileyonline.org, version 7.0 [accessed 19 February 2013].
22. P. Wagner, 'The Pornographer in the Courtroom: Trial Reports about Cases of Sexual Crimes and Delinquencies as a Genre of Eighteenth-Century Erotica', in P. G. Boucé (ed.), *Sexuality in Eighteenth-Century Britain* (New Jersey: Manchester University Press, 1982), pp. 120–39, on p. 123.
23. Trial of Gilbert Laurence, August 1730 (t17300828–24), *Old Bailey Proceedings Online*, at www.oldbaileyonline.org, version 7.0 [accessed 19 February 2013].
24. A. Müller, *Framing Childhood in Eighteenth-Century English Periodicals and Prints, 1689–1789* (Vermont: Ashgate, 2009), pp. 67, 43.
25. R. D. Egan and G. Hawkes, *Theorizing the Sexual Child in Modernity* (New York: Palgrave Macmillan, 2010), p. 23.
26. Egan and Hawkes, *Theorizing the Sexual Child*, p. 19.
27. *The Infants' Lawyer: or, The Law (Ancient and Modern) relating to Infants* (London, 1697), p. 2.
28. Simpson, *Masculinity and Control*, p. 199.
29. H. Brewer, *By Birth or Consent: Children, Law, and the Anglo-American Revolution in Authority* (Chapel Hill, NC: University of North Carolina Press, 2005), p. 3.
30. Ibid., p. 158.
31. Ibid., p. 165.
32. W. Blackstone, *Commentaries on the Laws of England*, ed. W. Jones, 2 vols (San Francisco: Bancroft-Whitney, 1916), vol. 2, p. 213.
33. Trial of Charles Atwell, October 1779 (t17791020–5), *Old Bailey Proceedings Online*, at www.oldbaileyonline.org, version 7.0 [accessed 19 February 2013].
34. Trial of Charles Atwell, October 1779 (t17791020–5), *Old Bailey Proceedings Online*, at www.oldbaileyonline.org, version 7.0 [accessed 19 February 2013].
35. Trial of Charles Atwell, October 1779 (t17791020–5), *Old Bailey Proceedings Online*, at www.oldbaileyonline.org, version 7.0 [accessed 19 February 2013].
36. *Commentaries on the Laws of England*, vol. 1, p. 213.
37. Ibid.
38. The other very similar eighteenth-century case in which the defendant was deemed guilty despite the lack of physical evidence was that of Michael Levi, accused of buggering twelve-year-old Benjamin Taylor. Levi's conviction had probably much to do with the fact that he was a Jew and that his alleged victim's friends seemed to suggest that he had also attacked them. However, he too was pardoned after being convicted, probably because the judge, who might not have been in agreement with the jury, interceded on his behalf. For a transcript of the case see Trial of Michael Levi, May 1751 (t17510523–

35), *Old Bailey Proceedings Online*, at www.oldbaileyonline.org, version 7.0 [accessed 20 February 2013].
39. R. Norton, 'The First Public Debate about Homosexuality in England: The Case of Captain Jones, 1772', *The Gay Subculture in Georgian England* (19 December 2004, updated 3 April 2007), at http://rictornorton.co.uk/eighteen/jones1.htm [accessed 25 February 2013].
40. R. Norton (ed.), 'The First Public Debate about Homosexuality in England: News Reports concerning the Case of Captain Jones, 1772', *Homosexuality in Eighteenth-Century England: A Sourcebook* (19 December 2004, updated 7 September 2008), at http://rictornorton.co.uk/eighteen/jones3.htm [accessed 25 February 2013].
41. R. Norton (ed.), 'The State of the Case of Captain Jones, 1772', *Homosexuality in Eighteenth-Century England: A Sourcebook* (3 April 2007), at http://rictornorton.co.uk/eighteen/jones9.htm [accessed 25 February 2013].
42. R. Norton (ed.), 'The First Public Debate about Homosexuality in England: Letters and Editorials in the *Morning Chronicle* concerning the Case of Captain Jones, 1772', *Homosexuality in Eighteenth-Century England: A Sourcebook* (19 December 2004), at http://rictornorton.co.uk/eighteen/jones5.htm [accessed 25 February 2013].
43. R. Norton (ed.), 'The First Public Debate about Homosexuality in England: News Reports concerning the Case of Captain Jones, 1772', *Homosexuality in Eighteenth-Century England: A Sourcebook* (19 December 2004, updated 7 September 2008), at http://rictornorton.co.uk/eighteen/jones3.htm [accessed 25 February 2013].
44. R. Norton (ed.), 'The State of the Case of Captain Jones, 1772', *Homosexuality in Eighteenth-Century England: A Sourcebook* (3 April 2007), at http://rictornorton.co.uk/eighteen/jones9.htm [accessed 25 February 2013].
45. R. Norton (ed.), 'The First Public Debate about Homosexuality in England: Letters and Editorials in the *Morning Chronicle* concerning the Case of Captain Jones, 1772', *Homosexuality in Eighteenth-Century England: A Sourcebook* (19 December 2004), at http://rictornorton.co.uk/eighteen/jones5.htm [accessed 25 February 2013].
46. R. Norton (ed.), 'The State of the Case of Captain Jones, 1772', *Homosexuality in Eighteenth-Century England: A Sourcebook* (3 April 2007), at http://rictornorton.co.uk/eighteen/jones9.htm [accessed 25 February 2013].
47. Simpson, *Masculinity and Control*, p. 31.

5 Greenfield, 'The Titillation of Dramatic Rape, 1660–1720'

1. For more on the popularity of these productions, see D. Hughes, 'Rape on the Restoration Stage', *Eighteenth Century: Theory and Interpretation*, 46:3 (Fall 2005), pp. 225–36; J. Marsden, *Fatal Desire: Women, Sexuality, and the English Stage, 1660–1720* (Ithaca, NY: Cornell University Press, 2006); E. Howe, *The First English Actresses, Women and Drama 1660–1700* (Cambridge: Cambridge University Press, 1992).
2. Marsden, *Fatal Desire*, p. 76.
3. Hughes, 'Rape on the Restoration Stage', pp. 232, 227.
4. The term 'erotica' is used broadly in this chapter to refer to texts that portray sexual activity and that were designed (to a significant degree) to elicit sexual responses in readers.
5. K. Harvey, *Reading Sex in the Eighteenth Century: Bodies and Gender in English Erotic Culture* (Cambridge: Cambridge University Press, 2004), pp. 195–6.
6. *The Practical Part of Love* (London, 1660), p. 71.
7. Ibid., pp. 71–2.

8. Ibid., p. 72.
9. Ibid., p. 76.
10. G. Perry, *Spectacular Flirtations: Viewing the Actress in British Art and Theatre 1768–1820* (New Haven, CT: Yale University Press, 2007), pp. 87–103.
11. W. Mountfort, *The Injur'd Lovers: or, The Ambitious Father* (London: Printed for R. Bentley and M. Haynes, 1679), p. 40. *The Injur'd Lovers* and several other plays to follow are cited according to their page numbers, as they derive from editions that do not demarcate act, scene and line numbers.
12. It should be noted that dishevelled hair was not solely associated with sexual violation on the English stage. This motif was attached to heroines in various states of disorder. For example, in John Dryden and Nathaniel Lee's *Oedipus* (1678), Jocasta's dishevelled hair is associated with her madness (rather than with a sexual violation): '*Scene Draws, and Discovers* Jocasta *held by her Women, and stabb'd in many places of her bosom, her hair dishevel'd; her Children slain upon the Bed*' (J. Dryden and N. Lee, *Oedipus*, in V. Dearing [ed.], *The Works of John Dryden*, 20 vols [Berkeley, CA: University of California Press, 1994], vol. 13, pp. 113–215, V.i.412+). However, despite the fact that dishevelled hair was used to depict scenarios aside from rape, rape was rarely depicted without referencing the victim's dishevelled hair.
13. Harvey, *Reading Sex in the Eighteenth Century*, p. 165.
14. S. Toulalan, *Imagining Sex: Pornography and Bodies in Seventeenth-Century England* (Oxford: Oxford University Press, 2007), p. 1.
15. Harvey, *Reading Sex in the Eighteenth Century*, p. 193.
16. P. Wagner, *Eros Revived: Erotica of the Enlightenment in England and America* (London: Secker & Warburg, 1988), p. 117.
17. For more on the presence of sexual crimes in erotic literature derived from trial transcripts, see Peter Wagner's 'The Pornographer in the Courtroom: Trial Reports about Cases of Sexual Crimes and Delinquencies as a Genre of Eighteenth-Century Erotica, in *Sexuality in Eighteenth-Century Britain*, pp. 120–40 and Wagner's 'Trial Reports and "Criminal Conversation" Literature', in Wagner, *Eros Revived*, pp. 113–32.
18. The title page of *The Tryal and Condemnation of Mervin, Lord Audley Earl of Castlehaven* describes the defendant's crimes as follows: 'For Abetting a *Rape* upon his *Countess*, Committing *Sodomy* with his Servants, and Commanding and Countenancing the Debauching his Daughter' (*The Tryal and Condemnation of Mervin, Lord Audley Earl of Castle-haven* [London, 1699]).
19. The full title reads, 'The Case of Seduction: Being, An Account of the Late Proceedings at *Paris*, as well *Ecclesiastical* as *Civil*, Against the Reverend Abbée, Claudius Nicholas des Rues, for Committing RAPES upon 133 VIRGINS' (*The Case of Seduction: Being, An Account of the Late Proceedings at Paris ... Against the Reverend Abbee, Claudius Nicholas des Rues*, trans. Mr Rogers [London: Printed for E. Curll, 1726]).
20. Wagner, *Eros Revived*, pp. 114, 116.
21. E. Ward, *The London-Spy Compleat*, 2 vols (London: J. How, 1703), vol. 1, pp. 135–7.
22. J. Beattie, *Policing and Punishment in London, 1660–1750: Urban Crime and the Limits of Terror* (Oxford: Oxford University Press, 2001), p. 268+.
23. See Thomas Shadwell's *The Virtuoso* (1676), act 5, scene 1 (T. Shadwell, *The Virtuoso*, in M. Summers (ed.), *The Complete Works of Thomas Shadwell*, 5 vols [New York: Benjamin Blom, 1968], vol. 3, pp. 95–182), and Thomas Otway's *Venice Preserv'd* (1682), act 3, scene 1 (T. Otway, *Venice Preserv'd, or, A Plot Discover'd*, in M. Summers (ed.), *The Complete Works of Thomas Otway*, 3 vols [New York: AMS Press, 1967], vol. 3, pp. 1–83),

for examples of characters who are aroused by sexual flagellation in Restoration drama. Samuel Pepys's famous guilt-ridden and masturbatory reading of *L'escholle des Filles* falls into the last category listed above, the whore dialogue (S. Pepys, *The Diary of Samuel Pepys*, 11 vols, ed. R. Latham and W. Matthews [Berkeley, CA: University of California Press, 1974], vol. 9, p. 58).

24. J. Dryden, *Aureng-Zebe*, in V. Dearing (ed.), *The Works of John Dryden*, 20 vols (Berkeley, CA: University of California Press, 1994), vol. 12, pp. 147–250, II.i.165–8.
25. N. Lee, *Mithridates, King of Pontus*, in T. Stroup and A. Cooke (eds), *The Works of Nathaniel Lee*, 2 vols (Scarecrow: Metuchen, 1968), vol. 1, pp. 287–365, IV.i.180–4.
26. J. Dryden, *The Conquest of Granada by the Spaniards, Part II*, in J. Loftis and D. Rodes (eds), *The Works of John Dryden*, 20 vols (Berkeley, CA: University of California Press, 1978), vol. 11, pp. 102–218, IV.iii.225.
27. Dryden, *The Conquest of Granada by the Spaniards, Part II*, IV.iii.274–7.
28. T. Porter, *The Villain, a Tragedy* (London: Printed for Henry Herringman, 1663), p. 10.
29. R. Boyle, Earl of Orrery, *The Generall*, in W. S. Clark, II (ed.), *The Dramatic Works of Roger Boyle, Earl of Orrery*, 2 vols (Cambridge: Harvard University Press, 1937), vol. 2, pp. 108–64, II.ii.145–8.
30. N. Rowe, *Tamerlane* (London: Printed for Jacob Tonson, 1702), p. 50.
31. R. Porter, 'Rape – Does it Have a Historical Meaning?', in S. Tomaselli and R. Porter (eds), *Rape: An Historical and Social Enquiry* (Oxford: Basil Blackwell, 1986), pp. 216–36, on p. 235.
32. G. Walker, 'Rereading Rape and Sexual Violence in Early Modern England', *Gender & History*, 10:1 (April 1998), pp. 1–25, on p. 16.
33. R. Steele, 'Prologue', in D. Manley, *Lucius, the First Christian King of Britain* (London: Printed for John Barber, 1717).
34. J. Dennis, *Original Letters, Familiar, Moral and Critical*, 2 vols (London: Printed for W. Mears, 1721), vol. 1, pp. 63–4.
35. D. Manley, *The Royal Mischief* (London: Printed for R. Bentley, F. Saunders and J. Knapton, 1696), p. 4.
36. The belief that women pretended to hate rape, but actually enjoyed it can also be seen in John Vanbrugh's *The Relapse; or, Virtue in Danger* (1696). Here, Berinthia is portrayed as merely an ostensible resistor to the 'rape' that follows: as Loveless carries her away, she protests ironically 'very softly' (stage directions), 'Help, help, I'm Ravish'd, ruin'd, undone' (J. Vanbrugh, *The Relapse or Virtue in Danger*, in B. Dobrée (ed.), *The Complete Works of Sir John Vanbrugh* (New York: AMS Press, 1967), pp. 1–101, on p. 69).
37. *Thesaurus Dramaticus*, 2 vols (London: Printed for Thomas Butler, 1724), vol. 2, p. i.
38. Quoted in *Thesaurus Dramaticus*, vol. 2, p. 177.
39. Ibid., vol. 2, p. 177.
40. Ibid., vol. 2, p. 178.
41. This is not the case in other entries on other negative subjects, like 'Adultery' and 'Arbitrary Power', which also have numerous passages devoted to them, but which are *always* referred to in negative ways.
42. J. Collier, *A Short View of the Immorality and Profaneness of the English Stage: Together with the Sense of Antiquity upon this Argument* (London: Printed for S. Keble, 1698), p. 21.
43. J. Wright, *Country Conversations: Being an Account of Some Discourses* (London: Printed for Henry Bonwicke, 1694), p. 11.

6 Byrd, 'Violently Erotic: Representing Rape in Restoration Drama'

1. J. Dennis, 'To Judas Iscariot, Esq; On the present State of the Stage', in E. Hooker (ed.), *The Critical Works of John Dennis*, 2 vols (Baltimore: Johns Hopkins Press, 1943), vol. 2, p. 166.
2. J. Vanbrugh, *The Relapse* (London, 1698).
3. Ibid., p. 46.
4. Ibid.
5. Ibid.
6. W. Congreve, *Love for Love*, in *The Comedies of William Congreve*, 2 vols (London, 1895), vol. 2, p. 52.
7. Ibid., vol. 2, p. 53.
8. W. Wycherley, *The Plain Dealer* (London, 1676), pp. 104–5.
9. A. Behn, *The City Heiress*, in *The Plays, Histories and Novels of the Ingenious Mrs. Aphra Behn*, 2 vols (London: John Pearson, 1871), vol. 2, pp. 237–8.
10. Ibid., p. 240.
11. Ibid.
12. Ibid., pp. 255–61.
13. J. Crowne, *City Politiques* (London, 1688), p. 25.
14. J. Dryden, *Sir Martin Marall*, in J. Loftis and V. A. Dearing (eds), *The Works of John Dryden*, 9 vols (Berkley, CA: University of California Press, 1966), vol. 9, II.i.53–70.
15. T. Otway, *Venice Preserved*, ed. J. H. Wilson, in *Six Restoration Plays* (Boston, MA: Houghton Mifflin, 1959), p. 279.
16. J. Wilmot, *Valentinian* (London, 1685), *Early English Books Online* database <http://eebo.chadwyck.com/home>, [accessed 30 January 2013], p. 46.
17. Ibid., p. 47.
18. Ibid., p. 48.
19. Ibid.
20. Ibid., pp. 49–50.
21. Ibid., p. 50.
22. Ibid., p. 52.
23. Ibid., p. 53.
24. Ibid., p. 81.
25. M. Pix, *Ibrahim* (London, 1696), *Early English Books Online* database at http://eebo.chadwyck.com/home, [accessed 30 January 2013], p. 24.
26. Ibid.
27. Ibid., p. 25.
28. Ibid., p. 28.
29. Ibid., p. 38.
30. Ibid., p. 40.
31. N. Brady, *The Rape* (London, 1692), *Early English Books Online* database http://eebo.chadwyck.com/home [accessed 30 January 2013], p. 27.
32. Ibid., p. 21.
33. Ibid.

34. Ibid.
35. Ibid., p. 25.
36. Ibid.
37. Ibid., p. 26.
38. Ibid., p. 55.
39. Ibid.
40. N. Rowe, *The Fair Penitent* (London, 1703), *Eighteenth-Century Collections Online* database, at http://eebo.chadwyck.com/home [accessed 30 January 2013], p. 44.
41. Ibid., p. 46.
42. Ibid., p. 54.
43. Ibid., p. 60.
44. Ibid., p. 62.
45. Ibid., Prologue.

7 Pfeiffer, '"A Most Obedient Wife": Passive Resistance and Tory Politics in Eliza Haywood's *A Wife to Be Lett*'

1. For more on Haywood's work as an actress, see M. Heinemann, 'Eliza Haywood's Career in the Theatre', *Notes and Queries*, n. s. 20:1 (1973), pp. 9–13. For more on Haywood's varied roles in the theatre, as well as the argument that her theatrical experience provides insight into her novels, see C. Ingrassia, '"The Stage Not Answering My Expectations": The Case of Eliza Haywood', in B. Nelson and C. Burroughs (eds), *Teaching British Women Playwrights of the Restoration and Eighteenth Century* (New York: Modern Languages Association, 2010), pp. 213–22. E. Haywood, *A Wife to Be Lett*, in M. Rubik and E. Mueller-Zettelmann (eds), *Eighteenth-Century Women Playwrights, Vol. I: Delarivier Manley and Eliza Haywood* (London: Pickering & Chatto, 2001), pp. 165–214, on p. 170.
2. Haywood, *A Wife to Be Lett*, p. 170.
3. Ibid., p. 211.
4. P. Stevens Fields, 'Manly Vigor and Woman's Wit: Dialoguing Gender in the Plays of Eliza Haywood', in K. L. Cope (ed.), *Compendious Conversations* (Frankfurt: Peter Lang, 1992), pp. 257–66; E. A. Wilputte, 'Wife Pandering in Three Eighteenth-Century Plays', *Studies in English Literature, 1500–1900*, 38:3 (1998), pp. 447–64.
5. M. Kvande, 'The Outsider Narrator in Eliza Haywood's Political Novels', *Studies in English Literature, 1500–1900*, 43:3 (2003), pp. 625–43; M. Mowry, 'Eliza Haywood's Defense of London's Body Politic', *Studies in English Literature, 1500–1900*, 43:3 (2003), pp. 645–65.
6. T. Bowers, *Force or Fraud: British Seduction Stories and the Problem of Resistance, 1660–1760* (New York: Oxford University Press, 2011).
7. In *Patriarcha* (1680), Robert Filmer makes such a way of authorizing kingly authority explicit. So thoroughly did Filmer's text shape the late seventeenth-century conversation about authority that even Whigs who opposed the patriarchal theory of government spent much energy repudiating this theory; indeed, the first of John Locke's *Two Treatises of Government* (1690) famously works to refute Filmer's claims.
8. J. Rudolph, 'Rape and Resistance: Women and Consent in Seventeenth-Century English Legal and Political Thought', *Journal of British Studies*, 39:2 (2000), pp. 157–84.

9. G. Burnet, 'An Enquiry into the Measures of Submission ... ' (Edinburgh, 1688), p. 15, *Early English Books Online* database at <http://eebo.chadwyck.com/home> [accessed 15 January 2013].
10. Haywood, *A Wife to Be Lett*, p. 190.
11. Ibid.
12. Ibid., p. 191.
13. Church of England, *The Boke of the Common Praier* (1549), *Early English Books Online* database, at <http://eebo.chadwyck.com/home> [accessed 29 August 2012].
14. R. Greaves, 'Concepts of Political Obedience in Late Tudor England: Conflicting Perspectives', *Journal of British Studies*, 22:1 (1982), pp. 23–34.
15. G. Burgess, 'Regicide: The Execution of Charles I and English Political Thought', in R. von Friedeburg (ed.), *Murder and Monarchy: Regicide in European History, 1300–1800* (New York: Palgrave Macmillan, 2004), pp. 212–36.
16. M. Zook, *Radical Whigs and Conspiratorial Politics in Late Stuart England* (University Park, PA: Pennsylvania State University Press, 1999).
17. J. Rudolph, *Revolution by Degrees: James Tyrrell and Whig Political Thought in the Late Seventeenth Century* (New York: Palgrave Macmillan, 2002).
18. Haywood, *A Wife to Be Lett*, p. 190.
19. Ibid., p. 191.
20. Ibid., p. 192.
21. Ibid., p. 171.
22. Ibid., p. 210.
23. Ibid.
24. Ibid.
25. Ibid., p. 211.
26. Ibid.
27. Ibid.
28. Ibid.
29. A. Behn, *The Lucky Chance*, in J. Spencer (ed.), *The Rover and Other Plays* (Oxford: Oxford University Press, 1998), pp. 183–270, on pp. 263, 264.
30. Behn, *The Lucky Chance*, pp. 264, 264–5.
31. Ibid., p. 265.
32. For more on the concept of passive obedience, as well as John Milton's role in laying the groundwork for the Whig rejection of the concept, see G. Sensabaugh, 'Milton and the Doctrine of Passive Obedience', *Huntington Library Quarterly*, 13:1 (1949), pp. 19–54.
33. M. Goldie, 'The Political Thought of the Anglican Revolution', in R. Beddard (ed.), *The Revolutions of 1688* (Oxford: Clarendon Press, 1991), pp. 102–36.
34. R. Markley, '"Be Impudent, Be Saucy, Forward, Bold, Touzing, and Leud": The Politics of Masculine Sexuality and Feminine Desire in Behn's Tory Comedies', in D. J. Canfield and D. C. Payne (eds), *Cultural Readings of Restoration and Eighteenth-Century English Theatre* (Athens, GA: University of Georgia Press, 1995), pp. 114–40; S. Owen, 'Sexual Politics and Party Politics in Behn's Drama, 1678–83', in J. Todd (ed.), *Aphra Behn Studies* (Cambridge: Cambridge University Press, 1996), pp. 15–29; L. Pfeiffer, '"Some For This Faction Cry, Others For That": Royalist Politics, Courtesanship, and Bawdry in Aphra Behn's *The Rover*, Part II', *Restoration: Studies in English Literary Culture, 1660–1700*, forthcoming.
35. C. Harol, 'The Passion of *Oroonoko*: Passive Obedience, The Royal Slave, and Aphra Behn's Baroque Realism', *English Literary History*, 79:2 (2012), pp. 447–75, on p. 448.

36. M. Zook, 'Contextualizing Aphra Behn: Plays, Politics, and Party, 1679–1689', in H. L. Smith (ed.), *Women Writers and the Early Modern British Political Tradition* (Cambridge: Cambridge University Press, 1998), pp. 75–94.
37. A. Pacheco, 'Reading Toryism in Aphra Behn's Cit-Cuckolding Comedies', *Review of English Studies*, 55:222 (2004), pp. 690–708.
38. Ibid., 706–7.
39. Ibid., 707.
40. For more on Tory and Whig responses to the Assassination Plot, see S. Pincus, *1688: The First Modern Revolution* (New Haven, CT: Yale University Press, 2009), esp. ch. 14, 'Assassination, Association, and the Consolidation of Revolution'.
41. Anglican clergyman Abednego Seller was the best known advocate for passive obedience in the period following the Glorious Revolution, making a case for the doctrine in his two books on the subject, *A History of Passive Obedience since the Reformation* (1689) and *A Continuation of the History of Passive Obedience since the Reformation* (1690). Arthur Mainwaring suggests that the resurgence of public support for passive obedience began in 1704–5. A. Mainwaring, *Four Letters to a Friend in Great Britain* (1710), p. 4, as quoted in G. Holmes, *The Trial of Doctor Sacheverell* (London: Eyre Methuen, 1973), p. 33.
42. G. J. Warnock, 'On Passive Obedience', *History of European Ideas*, 7:6 (1986), pp. 555–62.
43. For more on party politics during Anne's reign, see G. Holmes, *British Politics in the Age of Anne* (New York: St Martin's Press, 1967).
44. For more on Tory politics during proscription, see L. Colley, *In Defiance of Oligarchy: The Tory Party, 1714–60* (New York: Cambridge University Press, 1982).
45. Haywood, *A Wife to Be Lett*, p. 170.
46. Ibid., pp. 173, 174, 180–1.
47. Ibid., p. 170.
48. Ibid., p. 174.
49. Ibid., p. 192.
50. Ibid.
51. Interestingly, Ann Minton's 1802 adaptation of *A Wife to Be Lett* excises all of the evidence of Mrs Graspall's affection for Beaumont. In Minton's adaptation, Beaumont is a less gallant character than he is in Haywood's original, and Mrs Graspall's emotional responses to Beaumont are gone. A. Minton, *The Comedy of A Wife to be Lett, or, The Miser Cured: Compressed into Two Acts* (London: A. Seale, 1802).
52. Haywood, *A Wife to Be Lett*, p. 213.
53. Ibid.
54. The most widely discussed eighteenth-century wife panderer was Theophilus Cibber. When, in 1738, Cibber attempted to bring a lawsuit against his wife's lover, William Sloper, it emerged at trial that Cibber had, in fact, rented her to him. For a detailed examination of this case, its coverage in the press, and similar lawsuits of the period, see T. Lockwood, introduction to H. Fielding, *The Modern Husband*, in T. Lockwood (ed.), *The Wesleyan Edition of the Works of Henry Fielding: Plays, Vol. 2 (1731–4)* (Oxford: Oxford University Press, 2007), pp. 181–207.

8 Airey, 'Staging Rape in the Age of Walpole: Sexual Violence and the Politics of Dramatic Adaption in 1730s Britain'

1. C. Forman, *Protesilaus: or, The Character of an Evil Minister* (London, 1730), p. 15. An Irish Catholic Jacobite, Forman spent much of the 1720s writing political pamphlets critical of the government before reaching a brief truce with Walpole's administration in 1734. Several years later, he was arrested for seditious libel, and spent some months in prison for writing against the Treaty of Seville.
2. Ibid., p. v.
3. Ibid., p. 15.
4. Ibid., p. vi.
5. Anon., *Claudian's Rufinus: or, The Court-Favourite's Overthrow* (London, 1730), p. 19.
6. Anon., *Are These Things So? The Previous Question, from an Englishman in his Grotto, to a Great Man at Court* (London, 1740), p. 7.
7. For discussions of early modern rape law, see N. Bashar, 'Rape in England between 1550 and 1700', in The London Feminist History Group (ed.), *The Sexual Dynamics of History: Men's Power, Women's Resistance* (London: Pluto Press, 1983), pp. 28–42, and M. Chaytor, 'Husband(ry): Narratives of Rape in the Seventeenth Century', *Gender and History*, 7:3 (1995), pp. 378–407.
8. L. Bertelsen, 'The Significance of the 1731 Revisions to *The Fall of Mortimer*', *Restoration and Eighteenth-Century Theatre Research*, 2:2 (1987), pp. 8–25, on pp. 19–20.
9. C. D'Anvers, *Craftsman*, 9 (London, 1737), p. 267. For historical discussions of *The Craftsman*, see S. Varey, '*The Craftsman*', *Prose Studies*, 16:1 (1993), pp. 58–77; A. Pettit, 'Propaganda, Public Relations, and the *Remarks on The Craftsman's Vindication of His Two Honble [sic] Patrons, in His Paper of May 22, 1731*', *Huntington Library Quarterly*, 57:1 (1994), pp. 45–59; A. Pettit, 'Revitalizing Bolingbroke's "Remarks on the History of England": *The Craftsman* in Folio', *Library Chronicle of Texas*, 25:3 (1995), pp. 6–29.
10. D'Anvers, *Craftsman*, 9 (1737), p. 131. For other references to Walpole's economic rapine, see also Anon., *Verres and his Scribblers; A Satire in Three Cantos* (London, 1732), and Anon., *Authentick Memoirs of the Life and Infamous Actions of Cardinal Wolsey* (London, 1732).
11. Anon., *A Letter From the People to Caleb D'Anvers Esq* (London, 1729), pp. 11–12.
12. The rumours of William III's affairs with men also allowed images of male ravishment to take on a particularly physical cast. For in-depth discussion of the political uses of rape imagery in the seventeenth century, along with discussions of the tropes of the ravished monarch, debauched Cavalier and poisonous Catholic bride also discussed in this chapter, see J. Airey, *The Politics of Rape: Sexual Atrocity, Propaganda Wars, and the Restoration Stage* (Newark, DE: University of Delaware Press, 2012).
13. R. Ferguson, *A Brief Account of some of the late Incroachments and Depredations of the Dutch upon the English* (London, 1695), pp. 2, 22.
14. R. Ferguson, *A Letter to Mr. Secretary Trenchard, Discovering a Conspiracy against the Laws and Ancient Constitution of England* (London, 1694), p. 7.
15. C. Blount, *King William and Queen Mary Conquerors* (London, 1693), sig. a3r.
16. R. Ferguson, *Whether the Preserving the Protestant Religion was the Motive unto, or the End, that was Designed in the Late Revolution?* (London, 1695), pp. 30–1.
17. Beinecke Osborn Shelves f. c. 58, p. 125.

18. For further reading of *Eovaai*'s political content, see also J. C. Beasley, who calls the novel 'a vicious attack on the court': 'Portrait of a Monster: Robert Walpole and Early English Prose Fiction', *Eighteenth-Century Studies*, 14:4 (1981), pp. 406–31, on p. 421.
19. E. Haywood, *The Adventures of Eovaai* (Orchard Park: Broadview Press, 1999), p. 94.
20. Beasley, 'Portrait of a Monster', p. 423.
21. Haywood, *The Adventures of Eovaii*, p. 94.
22. For discussion of other texts featuring Walpole as rapist, see also Belsey, who has usefully surveyed the many texts that treated Walpole as a sexually violent, avaricious, self-obsessed monster. Such texts were designed 'to portray the prime minister as a grotesque, even bestial figure, a creature of enormous excesses: he is variously a wicked Eastern vizier, a dastardly criminal, an evil magician or avaricious usurer, a rapist of virgins, a disease-ridden whoremonger' (Beasley, 'Portrait of a Monster', p. 419).
23. S. Dickie, 'Fielding's Rape Jokes', *Review of English Studies*, 61:251 (2010), pp. 572–90, on p. 574.
24. Antony Simpson has provided the fullest modern overview and analysis of the Charteris trial and its depiction in the popular press. See A. Simpson, 'Popular Perceptions of Rape as a Capital Crime in Eighteenth-Century England: The Press and the Trial of Francis Charteris in the Old Bailey, February 1730', *Law and History Review*, 22:1 (2004), pp. 27–70.
25. Anon., *On Colonel Francisco, Rape-Master General of Great Britain* (London, 1730), p. 1.
26. D'Anvers, *Craftsman*, 6 (1731), p. 223.
27. B. Goldgar, 'The Politics of Fielding's *Coffee-House Politician*', *Philological Quarterly*, 49 (1970), p. 426. For other pamphlets featuring Walpole as Charteris, see also W. Pulteney, *An Answer to One Part of a late Infamous Libel* (London, 1731).
28. Anon., *A Wicked Resolution of the Cavaliers* (London, 1642), p. 1.
29. W. Cartwright, *The Game at Chesse* (London, 1643), p. 7.
30. G. Lawrence, *The Debauched Cavalleer: or The English Midianite* (London, 1642), p. 7. As I argue in *The Politics of Rape*, Roundhead authors frequently linked the dangers of sexual violence with the perceived evils of Roman Catholicism. Here, Lawrence's Cavaliers shift between acts of physical atrocity and displays of spiritual evil. See Airey, *The Politics of Rape*, for further discussion of the links between anti-Catholicism and rape rhetoric.
31. J. Goodwin, *Anti-Cavalierisme, or, Truth Pleading as well the Necessity, as the Lawfulness of this Present War* (London, 1642), p. 5.
32. According to Goldgar, 'in 1730, Fielding was fairly nonpartisan' (Goldgar, 'The Politics of Fielding's *Coffee-House Politician*', p. 424). For discussion of Fielding's theatre and politics, see also J. A. Downie, 'Walpole, "the Poet's Foe"', in J. Black (ed.), *Britain in the Age of Walpole* (New York: St Martin's Press, 1984), pp. 171–88; T. Lockwood, 'Fielding and the Licensing Act', *Huntington Library Quarterly*, 50:4 (1987), pp. 379–93.
33. In this, I differ fundamentally from Goldgar, who claims, 'there is not the slightest scrap of evidence which suggests that [*Rape Upon Rape* was] read or viewed at the time as satirizing Walpole, though it was obviously not a time when public comment was lacking about plays considered politically suspect': *Walpole and the Wits: The Relation of Politics to Literature, 1722–1742* (Lincoln, NE: University of Nebraska Press, 1976), p. 102. The Charteris affair itself became a media sensation. According to Simon Dickie, 'The Charteris case was accompanied by an extended silly season in the London press: there were ballads, bawdy verses, pantomimes and commemorative prints. Anything remotely related would do' (Dickie, 'Fielding's Rape Jokes', p. 574).

34. H. Fielding, *The Coffee-House Politician; or, The Justice Caught in His Own Trap*, in W. Henly (ed.), *The Complete Works of Henry Fielding, Esq*, 5 vols (New York: Barnes and Noble, 1967), vol. 2, pp. 73–158, on p. 91.

35. Such assumptions made it very difficult for rape victims to prosecute their attackers, as they often had to explain why they found themselves vulnerable to assault. For further discussion of the difficulties women faced in navigating the court system, see also A. Clark, *Women's Silence, Men's Violence: Sexual Assault in England, 1770–1845* (London: Pandora, 1987) and S. D'cruze, 'Approaching the History of Rape and Sexual Violence: Notes towards Research', *Women's History Review*, 1:3 (1997), pp. 377–97. For further readings of the gender politics of Fielding's rape jokes, see Dickie, along with J. Campbell, *Natural Masques: Gender and Identity in Fielding's Plays and Novels* (Stanford, CA: Stanford University Press, 1995); A. Smallwood, *Fielding and the Woman Question: The Novels of Henry Fielding and Feminist Debate, 1700–1750* (New York: St Martin's Press, 1989); and S. Staves, 'Fielding and the Comedy of Attempted Rape', in B. Fowkes Tobin (ed.), *History, Gender & Eighteenth-Century Literature* (Athens, GA: University of Georgia Press, 1994), pp. 86–112.

36. Fielding, *The Coffee-House Politician*, p. 88.

37. Here once again I disagree with Goldgar, who argues, 'Fielding's satire is directed not at the rake, Ramble, but at the hypocritical justice, Squeezum' (Goldgar, *Walpole and the Wits*, p. 108). While Squeezum is indeed the main target of the satire, Fielding's deliberate invocation of Cavalier imagery bespeaks his discomfort with contemporary libertine behaviour as well.

38. Historically, of course, what Antony Simpson calls the 'Blackmail myth', the belief that women would frequently cry rape either to cover up consensual relations or to extort money, was extremely culturally prevalent. See A. Simpson, 'The "Blackmail Myth" and the Prosecution of Rape and Its Attempt in 18th Century London: The Creation of a Legal Tradition', *Journal of Law and Criminology*, 77:3 (1986), pp. 101–50. For further discussion of the eighteenth-century preoccupation with false rape charges, see also L. Edelstein, 'An Accusation Easy to be Made? Rape and Malicious Prosecution in Eighteenth-Century England', *American Journal of Legal History*, 42:4 (1998), pp. 351–90. For a more general discussion of malicious prosecution in the eighteenth-century courts, see D. Hay, 'Prosecution and Power: Malicious Prosecution in the English Courts, 1750–1850', in D. Hay and F. Snyder (eds), *Policing and Prosecution in Britain 1750–1850* (Oxford: Oxford University Press, 1989), pp. 343–95.

39. Fielding, *The Coffee-House Politician*, p. 128.

40. Goldgar, 'The Politics of Fielding's *Coffee-House Politician*', p. 428. Dickie conversely argues, 'these are not Walpole and his favourites so much as the "trading justices" of the age' (Dickie, 'Fielding's Rape Jokes', p. 575).

41. According to Malcolm G. Largmann, Walpole 'appears as Sejanus, Wolsey, Macheath, and Lockit. Of course, such attacks, often quite blatant, upon Sir Robert's character, invited libel proceedings against members of the Opposition press. Nevertheless, a dramatic parallel proved occasionally so effective that the name of the dramatic character became pinned to Walpole in a series of satiric articles': 'Stage References as Satiric Weapon: Sir Robert Walpole as Victim', *Restoration and Eighteenth-Century Theatre Research*, 9:1 (1970), pp. 35–43, on p. 37. See also Maynard Mack, who writes that Walpole was linked 'with the name of every corrupt favourite and vice-regent in English and Roman history: Gaveston, Dudley, Wolsey, Villiers, Sejanus, Clodius, Verres (not to mention an assortment of tyrants and would-be tyrants ...)'. *The Garden and the City:*

Retirement and Politics in the Later Poetry of Pope, 1731–1743 (Toronto: University of Toronto Press, 1969), p. 133.

42. D'Anvers, *The Craftsman*, 9 (1737), p. 131. For other references to Edward II's court in the political tracts of the 1730s, see also Anon., *An Essay upon Rewards and Punishments, According to the Practice of the Present Times* (London, 1733) and Anon., *The Sly Subscription: On the Norfolk Monarch, &c.* (London, 1733).
43. Anon., *A Bloody Tragedie, or Romish Maske. Acted by Five Iesuites, and Sixteene Young German Maides* (London, 1607), sig. b3r.
44. J. Bancroft, *King Edward the Third, with The Fall of Mortimer* (London, 1691), p. 24. The rape of the chaste matron Lucrece by the degenerate Prince Tarquin precipitated the foundation of the Roman Republic and it served throughout the early modern era as a powerful symbol of the relationship between rape and monarchical tyranny. For further discussion of the Lucrece myth, see Airey, Bashar or Chaytor.
45. Ibid., p. 20.
46. Ibid.
47. S. Staves, *Players' Scepters: Fictions of Authority in the Restoration* (Lincoln, NE: University of Nebraska Press, 1979), pp. 103–4.
48. W. Hatchett, *The Fall of Mortimer. An Historical Play* (London, 1731), p. 11.
49. That Walpole's mistress was coincidentally also named Maria would likely have added a scandalous frisson for contemporary audiences.
50. Bancroft, *King Edward the Third*, p. 8.
51. Hatchett, *The Fall of Mortimer*, p. 35.
52. Ibid., p. 36.
53. Anon., *The Great Eclipse of the Sun, or, Charles His Waine* (London, 1643), p. 3.
54. Anon., *The English Pope* (London, 1643), p. 12.
55. Bancroft, *King Edward the Third*, p. 2.
56. Anon., *A Nest of Nunnes Egges, Strangely Hatched* (London, 1680), p. 1.
57. E. Stephen, *Popish Policies and Practices Represented in the Histories of the Parisian Massacre; Gun-powder Treason; Conspiracies against Queen Elizabeth and Persecutions of the Protestants in France* (London, 1674), pp. 21, 49.
58. Ibid., p. 27.
59. For other dramatic representations of the poisonous Catholic bride, see, for instance, Elkanah Settle's *The Empress of Morocco* and *Love and Revenge*, Mary Pix's *Ibrahim* and Lee's *Lucius Junius Brutus*.
60. Hatchett, *The Fall of Mortimer*, p. 53.
61. Ibid.
62. Ibid.
63. Ibid., p. 52.
64. Mack, *The Garden and the City*, p. 129. Mack is not here speaking of *The Fall of Mortimer*, but the play represents a similar form of attack against Caroline.
65. Caroline, cited in C. Hibbert, *George III: A Personal History* (New York: Basic Books, 1998), p. 3.

9 Runia, '"What Do You Take Me For?": Rape and Virtue in *The Female Quixote*'

1. C. Lennox, *The Female Quixote*, ed. E. Dalziel (New York: Oxford University Press, 1989), p. 20.
2. Ibid., p. 20.
3. See E. Rothstein, 'Woman, Women and *The Female Quixote*', in A. J. Rivero (ed.), *Augustan Subjects* (Newark, DE: University of Delaware Press, 1997), pp. 249–75. Rothstein has also argued on behalf of Arabella's intellectual agency in the novel, seeing resemblances between the generic and gender conflicts presented in the novel.
4. See K. Levin, '"The Cure of Arabella's Mind": Charlotte Lennox and the Disciplining of the Female Reader', *Women's Writing*, 2:3 (1995), pp. 271–90. Levin argues that the eighteenth century's positive critical reception of the novel hinged upon the submission of Arabella to patriarchal authority, the very elements responsible for the unease of many feminist critics. I am arguing here that reading Arabella's relationship to patriarchy as a qualification, as opposed to annihilation, of women's intellectual agency provides an alternative middle ground.
5. See L. Langbauer, 'Romance Revised: Charlotte Lennox's *The Female Quixote*', *Novel: A Forum on Fiction* (Fall 1984), pp. 29–49, on p. 49. Langbauer maintains the opposition of romance and the real throughout the novel. She writes: 'Whether Lennox is emphasizing the link between romance and women's sexuality or romance and women's power, the structural parallel between romance and women remains. Each is the name for qualities the status quo finds transgressive and threatening and attempts to dispel by projecting into a separate genre or gender'. While Arabella's assertions in this first encounter with Mr Hervey could be read as an acknowledgement of female sexuality, as we will see, later encounters suggest a much more complicated relationship between women's sexuality and empowerment or its lack. See also C. Roulston, 'Histories of Nothing: Romance and Femininity in Charlotte Lennox's *The Female Quixote*', *Women's Writing*, 2:1 (1995), pp. 25–42. Roulston complicates Langbauer's argument, concluding that even if feminine romance does not overcome the unified subject position claimed by masculine realist discourse, it does disrupt it. See also C. Gallagher, *Nobody's Story: The Vanishing Acts of Women Writers in the Market-place, 1670–1820* (Berkeley, CA: University of California Press, 1994). Gallagher engages Langbauer but focuses on the generic consequences of defining fiction.
6. See E. Zimmerman, 'Personal Identity, Narrative and History: *The Female Quixote* and *Redgauntlet*', *Eighteenth-Century Fiction*, 12:2–3 (January–April 2000), pp. 369–90, on p. 379. Zimmerman acknowledges *The Female Quixote*'s engagement with and complication of standards for female behaviour. Pitting a dominant masculine history against feminine romance, he concludes: 'To a degree, then, *The Female Quixote* suggests that history has negotiable boundaries and that fiction is not without a capacity to negotiate'. See also H. Thompson, 'Charlotte Lennox and the Agency of Romance', *Eighteenth-Century: Theory and Interpretation*, 43:2 (2002), pp. 91–114. Thompson also acknowledges the significance of Arabella's status as subject but attributes it to the impossibility of reconciling realist and romance values. See also A. Paul, 'Feminine Transformations of the *Quixote* in Eighteenth-Century England: Lennox's *Female Quixote* and Her Sisters', in *The Cervantean Heritage: Reception and Influence of Cervantes in Britain* (Leeds: Legenda, 2009), pp. 166–75. Paul similarly sees romance, in its opposition to realism, as a source of female empowerment, but she also reads the novel's end as a denial of such

potentiality. See also P. Spacks, 'The Subtle Sophistry of Desire: Dr. Johnson and *The Female Quixote*', *Modern Philology*, 85:4 (1988), pp. 532–42. Spacks similarly insists on Arabella's agency. See also Z. Watson, 'Desire and Genre in *The Female Quixote*', *Novel: A Forum on Fiction*, 44:2 (Spring 2011), pp. 31–46, on p. 32. In contrast, Watson has identified 'important assumptions underpinning both genres', but he restricts his examination of the reading's impact upon desire to an abstract instrumentality.

7. See S. Gordon, 'The Space of Romance in Lennox's *The Female Quixote*', *SEL*, 38 (1998), pp. 499–516. Gordon articulates this opposition as values of disinterestedness versus instrumentality in defence of Arabella's 'madness'. I submit, in contrast, that both eighteenth-century society and the world of romance presented in the novel allow the possibility of both value sets. In both worlds, Arabella is a pawn in the schemes of others. The novel dramatizes this struggle and Arabella's solution.
8. Lennox, *The Female Quixote*, p. 94.
9. Ibid., p. 95.
10. Ibid.
11. Ibid., pp. 95, 99, 100.
12. Ibid., pp. 101, 107. See also J. Lynch, 'Romance and Realism in Charlotte Lennox's *The Female Quixote*', *Essays in Literature*, 14 (Spring 1987), pp. 51–63, on p. 51. The repetition of both real and imagined scenes of near-rape corresponds to James Lynch's conclusion: 'Lennox demonstrates that the codes of behavior conventional to eighteenth-century realism are not all that far removed from the romance behavior which most eighteenth-century novels condemn as improbable'.
13. Lennox, *The Female Quixote*, p. 71, emphasis added.
14. Ibid., p. 72.
15. Ibid., p. 71.
16. Ibid., pp. 73, 74.
17. Ibid., p. 77.
18. Ibid., p. 89.
19. Ibid.
20. Ibid., p. 90.
21. Ibid., pp. 155, 157.
22. Ibid., p. 259.
23. Ibid.
24. Ibid., p. 300.
25. Ibid.
26. Ibid., pp. 361, 362.
27. Ibid., pp. 362, 363.
28. Ibid., p. 366.
29. Ibid.
30. Ibid.
31. Ibid.
32. Admittedly, such a reading of this conversation complicates the nearly universal critical consensus that has repeatedly affirmed that the Learned Divine ultimately 'cures' Arabella's absurdity. See D. Marshall, 'Writing Masters and "Masculine Exercises" in *The Female Quixote*', *The Frame of Art: Fictions of Aesthetic Experience, 1750–1815* (Baltimore, MD: Johns Hopkins University Press, 2005), pp. 147–75. Marshall assesses Arabella's and Lennox's reading of the Learned Divine as Samuel Johnson. He argues that the doctor's 'cure' of Arabella betrays the rejection of authority necessary for any but cross-dressed

women. However, important recent scholarship and a close reading of the text itself support a revised reading. Lennox, *The Female Quixote*, p. 366.
33. See E. Gardiner, 'Writing Men Reading in Charlotte Lennox's *The Female Quixote*', *Studies in the Novel*, 28 (Spring 1996), pp. 1–11, on p. 4. Gardiner acknowledges the power of Arabella's 'superior critical judgment' to work 'influentially within the public sphere'.
34. O. Brack and S. Carlile, 'Samuel Johnson's Contributions to *The Female Quixote*', *Yale University Library Quarterly* (April 2003), pp. 166–73, on p. 171.
35. A. Udden, 'Narratives and Counter-Narratives-Quixotic Hermeneutics in Eighteenth-Century England: Charlotte Lennox, *The Female Quixote*', *Partial Answers: Journal of Literature and the History of Ideas*, 6:2 (June 2008), pp. 443–57, on p. 446.
36. S. Carlile and R. Perry, 'Introduction', in *Henrietta* (Lexington, KY: University Press of Kentucky, 2008), pp. iiv–xxix, and on p. xv.
37. N. Schürer (ed.), *Charlotte Lennox: Correspondence and Miscellaneous Documents* (Lewisburg, PA: Bucknell University Press, 2012), p. 432. See also A. Bailey, 'Charlotte Lennox's *The Female Quixote*: The Reconciliation of Enlightenment Philosophies', *Tennessee Philological Bulletin*, 38 (2001), pp. 9–18, on p. 14. Bailey's reading of the novel as a reconciliation of rationalism and empiricism also observes the poor reasoning of the clergyman and his reliance upon emotional appeal within the argument of the last chapter. However, her conclusion that Arabella's sudden conversion corresponds to his desperate appeals reflects the history of critical dissatisfaction. She writes: 'Lennox might have appropriately entitled the final book of *The Female Quixote* "The Conclusion in Which Nothing Is to Be Concluded", for the apparent textual resolution, Arabella's decision to marry Mr. Glanville, merely pays "lip service" to the stereotypical concluding formula for an eighteenth-century novel, a formula that dictates that the heroine must either marry or die'.
38. This reading challenges, in multiple ways, many who would see Arabella's cure in the Doctor's conversation. See J. Lamb, '"Lay Aside My Character": The Personate Novel and Beyond', *Eighteenth-Century Theory and Interpretation*, 52:3–4 (2011), pp. 271–87, on p. 283. Lamb argues that Arabella is 'forced into a forensic conjecture', a point which is not proved by the text and 'overwhelmed by instrumental untruth'. See also Wendy Motooka, 'Coming to a Bad End: Sentimentalism, Hermeneutics and *The Female Quixote*', *Eighteenth-Century Fiction*, 8:2 (January 1996), pp. 251–70, on p. 251. Motooka concludes: 'The final scenes of the novel, however, depict her as defeated, humiliated and subordinated by a dogmatic clergyman'. I am arguing, in contrast, that Arabella is at no point overwhelmed in the argument by the Learned Divine's reasoning, which leads him through a process under which she has already gone herself.
39. Lennox, *The Female Quixote*, p. 368.
40. Ibid., p. 369.
41. Ibid., p. 371.
42. Ibid.
43. Ibid.
44. Ibid, pp. 372, 374.
45. Ibid., p. 374.
46. Ibid. See S. Augustin, 'Charlotte Lennox – *The Female Quixote*', *Eighteenth-Century Female Voices* (New York: Peter Lang, 2005), pp. 53–76, on p. 76. Arabella's shaping of the discourse would seem to complicate claims, like Sabine Augustine's that, 'Lennox silently submits to the constraints of the patriarchal society within which both she and

her heroine must live'. Those constraints do indeed shape Arabella's world, but she is not silent.
47. Lennox, *The Female Quixote*, p. 375.
48. Ibid.
49. Ibid., p. 377.
50. Ibid.
51. Ibid., p. 379.
52. Ibid.
53. Ibid., p. 380.
54. Ibid.
55. See R. Mack, 'Quixotic Ethnography: Charlotte Lennox and the Dilemma of Cultural Observation', *Novel: A Forum on Fiction* (Spring/Summer 2005), pp. 193–213. Mack's interesting reading of Arabella's ability to maintain multiple perspectives allows Arabella a kind of agency, but I would argue, in contrast to her claim that Arabella is not assimilated and that her redefinition of female virtue exchanges romantic definitions for a Christian ethic. Her ultimate substitution of piety as the definition of female virtue – as opposed to romance – reveals the necessity of assimilation for those who would cling to the kind of limited autonomy promised by romance. Arabella's exchange reveals her refusal to assimilate.
56. Lennox, *The Female Quixote*, p. 381.
57. Ibid.
58. See P. Hamilton, 'Arabella Unbound: Wit, Judgment and the Cure of Charlotte Lennox's *Female Quixote*', in S. Carlile (ed.), *Masters of the Marketplace: British Women Novelists of the 1750s* (Bethlehem, PA: Lehigh University Press, 2011), pp. 108–27, on p. 117. Hamilton has observed, Arabella's reformation involves a genuine embrace of the 'Christian ethic to which she has paid lip service all along', but while Hamilton sees the Learned Divine's 'verbal shock therapy' as necessary to this behavioural shift, we will see how Arabella's contributions to the Doctor's 'cure' prove she has already done the heavy lifting necessary to transform herself from a sexual object to a pious agent.
59. Lennox, *The Female Quixote*, p. 381.
60. Ibid., p. 377.
61. See the eponymous heroines in *Henrietta* (1758) and *Sophia* (1762), who preserve their piety against threats to their reputations. See also Carlile and Perry, 'Introduction', in *Henrietta*, p. xxiii. This ascendancy of piety over intellect also corresponds to Carlile and Perry's observation in their introduction to *Henrietta* that 'Lennox often exhibits ambivalence about learning in women', pitting her well-read heroines against contemptible female pedants.
62. Lennox, *The Female Quixote*, p. 383, emphasis added.

10 Nawrot, '"Nothing But Violent Methods Will Do": Heterosexual Rape and the Violation of Female Friendship'

1. N. Armstrong, *Desire and Domestic Fiction: A Political History of the Novel* (Oxford: Oxford University Press, 1987), pp. 98, 21, 133.
2. Ibid., p. 21.
3. Ibid., p. 134.

4. J. Locke, *Two Treatises of Government* (1689), ed. T. I. Cook (New York: Hafner Press, 1947), p. 123.
5. Ibid., p. 166.
6. Ibid., pp. 128, 169.
7. Ibid., p. 128.
8. A. Silver, 'Friendship in Commercial Society: Eighteenth-Century Social Theory and Modern Sociology', *American Journal of Sociology*, 95:6 (1990), pp. 1474–504, on pp. 1476, 1475. I agree with Silver that it is important to differentiate between familial and extra-familial relationships because individuals and the female literary characters I discuss choose to participate in these associations unlike the hierarchical familial relationships that men and women are generally born into or marry into.
9. Aristotle, '*Nicomachean Ethics: Book VIII and IX*', in M. C. Bradley and P. Blosser (eds), *Of Friendship: Philosophical Selections on a Perennial Concern* (Wolfeboro, NH: Longwood Academic, 1989), p. 66.
10. M. Friedman, *What are Friends For? Feminist Perspectives on Personal Relationships and Moral Theory* (Ithica, NY: Cornell University Press, 1993), p. 211.
11. Silver, 'Friendship in Commercial Society', p. 1477.
12. Aristotle, *Nicomachean Ethics*, p. 67.
13. Ibid., p. 65.
14. Ibid., p. 62.
15. Ibid., pp. 64–5.
16. Ibid., p. 62.
17. M. Astell, *A Serious Proposal to the Ladies* (1701; New York: Source Book Press, 1970), p. 33.
18. J. Broad, 'Mary Astell on Virtuous Friendship', *Parergon*, 26:2 (2009), pp. 65–86, on p. 69.
19. Astell, *A Serious Proposal to the Ladies*, p. 37.
20. S. Johnson, 'Friend', in *A Dictionary of the English Language* (Edinburgh: Brown, Ross, and Symington, 1797).
21. H. Fielding, 'Of the Remedy of Affliction for the Loss of our Friends', in L. Stephen (ed.), *The Works of Henry Fielding* (London: Smith, Elder & Company, 1882), pp. 257–70, p. 259.
22. Ibid., p. 259.
23. Ibid., p. 269.
24. A. Smith, *The Theory of Moral Sentiments*, 1759 (Amherst, NY: Prometheus Books, 2000), p. 27.
25. Ibid.
26. Astell, *A Serious Proposal to the Ladies*, p. 32.
27. Ibid.
28. D. Hume, 'An Enquiry Concerning the Principles of Morals', in M. C. Bradley and P. Blosser (eds), *Of Friendship: Philosophical Selections on a Perennial Concern* (Wolfeboro, NH: Longwood Academic, 1989), pp. 236–50, on p. 243.
29. Ibid., p. 243.
30. Ibid., p. 248.
31. E. Haywood, 'Book Eighteen', *The Female Spectator*, Volume 3 (London: T. Garner, 1755), pp. 322–3.
32. Ibid., p. 323.
33. Ibid., p. 317.

34. Ibid.
35. H. Fielding, *Tom Jones* (1749), ed. J. Bender and S. Stern (Oxford: Oxford University Press, 1996), p. 698.
36. Ibid., p. 134.
37. E. Jacques, 'Fielding's Tom Jones and the Nicomachean Ethics', *English Language Notes*, 30 (1992), pp. 20–32, on p. 20–1.
38. Ibid., pp. 20–1.
39. W. Jones, *Consensual Fictions: Women, Liberalism, and the English Novel* (Toronto: University of Toronto Press, 2005), p. 4.
40. Ibid., p. 5.
41. Ibid.
42. Fielding, *Tom Jones*, p. 306.
43. Ibid., p. 538.
44. Ibid.
45. Ibid., p. 608.
46. Aristotle, *Nicomachean Ethics*, p. 68.
47. Fielding, *Tom Jones*, p. 646.
48. Ibid.
49. Ibid.
50. Ibid., p. 688.
51. Ibid., p. 691.
52. Ibid., p. 694.
53. Ibid., p. 697.
54. A. J. Cahill, 'Sexual Violence and Objectification', in R. J. Heberle and V. Grace (eds), *Theorizing Sexual Violence* (New York: Routledge, 2009), pp. 14–30, on p. 25.
55. Ibid.
56. C. Mui, 'A Feminist Sartrean Approach to Understanding Rape Trauma', *Sartre Studies International*, 11:1–2 (2005), pp. 153–65, on p. 158.
57. Mui, 'A Feminist Sartrean Approach to Understanding Rape Trauma', p. 158.
58. Fielding, *Tom Jones*, p. 695.

11 Weizenbeck, 'Bringing Sentimental Fiction to its (Anti-)Climax: Sterne's *A Sentimental Journey*'

1. J. Hagstrum, *Sex and Sensibility: Ideal and Erotic Love from Milton to Mozart* (Chicago, IL: University of Chicago Press, 1980), p. 248; J. Todd, *Sensibility: An Introduction* (London: Methuen, 1986), p. 7.
2. Hagstrum, *Sex and Sensibility*, p. 259.
3. M. New, 'Proust's Influence of Sterne: Remembrance of Things to Come', in M. New's (ed.), *Critical Essays on Laurence Sterne* (London: G. K. Hall, 1998) pp. 177–97, on p. 184.
4. D. Fairer, 'Sentimental Translation in Mackenzie and Sterne', *Essays in Criticism: A Quarterly Journal of Literary* Criticism, 49:2 (1999), pp. 132–51, on p. 135. Sterne was not alone in writing upon this newer definition of sentiment and sensibility; George Cheyne, David Hartley and William Smith amongst others developed theories surrounding this body/mind connection.

5. L. Sterne, *A Sentimental Journey through France and Italy* (Peterborough: Broadview Press, 2010), p. 58.
6. Ibid.
7. G. J. Barker-Benfield claims one of sensibility's goals was literally to rewrite the masculine ideal. He argues, 'There was an obvious relationship between the idealization in sentimental fiction of men capable of virtuous suffering and the "feminized" figure of Christ, elevated by the campaign for the reformation of manners'. G. J. Barker-Benfield, *The Culture of Sensibility: Sex and Society in Eighteenth-Century Britain* (Chicago, IL: University of Chicago Press, 1992), p. 247.
8. As Todd so aptly highlights, men cannot lose their power and male characters are not raped and abandoned (Todd, *Sensibility*, p. 89). I would go on to argue that men can also not be truly 'feminized'. They may have feminine qualities but always retain the hierarchical position of male and therefore retain an inherent – even if compromised by their sensibility – masculinity. As witnessed in *A Sentimental Journey*, Yorick is always in the position of possible predator yet is saved by his sentiment and is never in danger of becoming the victim because of it.
9. Robert Markley maintains 'The ideology of sentiment also explicitly promotes narrowly conservative and essentialist views of class relations, implicitly identifying the victims of social inequality – men, women, and children – with "feminine" powerlessness'. R. Markley, 'Sentimentality as Performance: Shaftesbury, Sterne, and the Theatrics of Virtue', in M. New (ed.), *Critical Essays of Laurence Sterne* (London: G. K. Hall, 1998), pp. 270–91, on p. 271. Whereas Mark Loveridge sees an othering of society's less fortunate (for example, beggars, the mad, the forgotten), I would argue that Sterne is using the 'feminine' quality of 'weakness', which is also attributed to powerlessness, as a loaded term to deride the very notion that human empathy, sympathy and pity are 'weak'. See *Laurence Sterne and the Argument about Design* (Totowa: Barnes and Noble, 1982), pp. 167–209.
10. Sterne, *A Sentimental Journey*, p. 85.
11. Ibid., p. 169.
12. Ibid., p. 75; Todd states, 'in sentimental men tears are mainly a response to a victim' (*Sensibility*, p. 99). While the majority of instances of male weeping in the novel seem to conform to this paradigm, Sterne nevertheless challenges such a model in *A Sentimental Journey*; the Monk has actively renounced the material goods of the world and is working to better humankind – not the traditionally abandoned victim.
13. Ibid.
14. Maria would be another strong example of Yorick's heartfelt grief for another's anguish caused by a sordid world.
15. Theirs in an association so deep that it radiates outside of the text; in this scene the Monk is named for the first time as Father Lorenzo, which according to Katherine Turner 'is the Italianate rendering of Sterne's own first name', *A Sentimental Journey*, fn 1, p. 75. Considering that Yorick has been deemed by some to be Sterne's alter-ego, this may mean that Sterne felt an immense personal interest in humanity and that it affected him in a profoundly personal way. Or, it may be proof that Sterne is simply a narcissist.
16. Jean Hagstrum asserts that in the 1760s 'thanks mostly to Sterne, [sentiment] described refined, tender emotions that often involve amatory feelings', *Sex and Sensibility*, p. 7. Paradoxically, he later maintains that 'Sterne is careful to elevate the sentimental above the sensual', and that 'Sterne could be said to be taking the side of friendship against love' (Hagstrum, *Sex and Sensibility*, pp. 248, 256). Further there remains another possible

reading that 'though the physical may be properly present in love, it must be transcended by the truly sentimental and moral', but Hagstrum finds this to be 'too solemn, too categorical for so sensual, so subtle, so noncommittal an author' (Hagstrum, *Sex and Sensibility*, p. 257). Todd, on the other hand, believes the conflation between sexuality and sensibility to have appeared in an earlier work with La Mettrie, who saw the 'mind and body as different forms of the same substance' (Todd, *Sensibility*, p. 8). Todd also notes, however, that after Sterne, the noun 'sentimental' was applied 'to sensibility and to its emotional and physical manifestations, and to indicate the heart rather than the head' (Todd, *Sensibility*, p. 9).

17. Sterne, *A Sentimental Journey*, p. 80.
18. Ibid., p. 101.
19. Ibid., p. 65.
20. Ibid., pp. 83–4.
21. Todd, *Sensibility*, p. 6.
22. New, 'Proust's Influence', p. 191.
23. Sterne, *A Sentimental Journey*, p. 146.
24. Katherine Turner maintains that the men Sterne admired – Isaac Barrow, John Tillotson and Samuel Clark – popularized the belief that the 'passions' 'were implanted by God to make us act virtuously', and, indeed, Yorick continually overcomes his carnal passions allowing both Yorick and the women to remain virtuous. See the introduction to Laurence Sterne's *A Sentimental Journey through France and Italy* (Peterborough: Broadview Press, 2010), pp. 11–46, on p. 27.
25. Sterne, *A Sentimental Journey*, p. 159.
26. As noted by Hagstrum, when the traveller (Yorick) finds the moment 'he is kindled by love, he is also all "generosity"', *Sex and Sensibility*, p. 249.
27. Sterne, *A Sentimental Journey*, p. 62.
28. Ibid., p. 131.
29. New, 'Proust's Influence', p. 179.
30. Patricia Meyer Spacks sees the denial of climax during an erotic experience to be a pattern within the genre of the sentimental novel: *Desire and Truth: Functions of Plot in Eighteenth-Century English Novels* (Chicago, IL: University of Chicago Press, 1990), p. 128. Suggestively, Hagstrum asks how Sterne's apparently inexplicable venereal disease and his subsequent rage (protesting he has had no sexual commerce with women, not even his wife) affected the work (Hagstrum, *Sex and Sensibility*, pp. 249–50). Additionally, Turner claims that Sterne's frustrated correspondence with Elizabeth Draper helped to fuel the composition of *A Sentimental Journey* (Turner, 'Introduction', p. 16).
31. She again interrupts him at their parting, arguably playing on the idea of *coitus interruptus*.
32. Sterne, *A Sentimental Journey*, p. 73.
33. According to Madeleine Descargues, the women in a *Sentimental Journey* 'are dispensers of pleasures and the means of moral reflection as well, mediators between human and the divine, consolers and redeemers'. M. Descargues, 'A Sentimental Journey, or "The Case of (In)delicacy"', in New (ed.), *Critical Essays on Laurence Sterne*, pp. 243–56, on p. 250.
34. Sterne, *A Sentimental Journey*, p. 76.
35. Ibid., p. 77.
36. Ibid., p. 57.
37. Ibid., p. 80.

38. While attempting to pass the Marquesina di F— in a doorway, they both prevent the other from moving forward. As much as this seems to resemble Sterne's trope of stasis, there remains a tantalizing possibility of a successful conclusion to the episode as he relates to her: 'I made six efforts to let you go out', and she replies that she made six attempts to let him enter. He retorts, 'I wish to heaven you would make a seventh', to which she answers, 'With all my heart ... Life's too short to be long about the forms of it'. It ends with them going to her house, and 'the connection which arose out of that translation, gave me more pleasure than any one I had the honor to make in Italy' (Sterne, *A Sentimental Journey*, p. 111). New views this as a moment of 'fulfillment ... of unfettered actualization' (New, 'Proust's Influence', p. 184). I would add that it is worthy to note it is the Marquesina who is the aggressor; Yorick allows her to 'carry' him away.
39. Sterne, *A Sentimental Journey*, p. 108.
40. Susan Lamb maintains that the one convention Sterne preserves in this scene of *A Sentimental Journey* 'underlies the centrality to the work of free-ranging erotic encounters with foreign women'. S. Lamb, *Bringing Travel Home to England; Tourism, Gender, and Imaginative Literature in the Eighteenth Century* (Newark, DE: University of Delaware Press, 2000), p. 155.
41. Sterne, *A Sentimental Journey*, p. 121. So, too, does Yorick envision a familial rather than sexual relationship with Maria as she should 'not only eat of my bread and drink of my own cup, but Maria should lay in my bosom, and be unto me as a daughter', Sterne, *A Sentimental Journey*, p. 168.
42. Barker-Benfield notes that Hume and Smith believed 'the company of women ... would "melt" and "soothe" the ferocious and forbidding aspects of male behavior' (Barker-Benfield, *The Culture of Sensibility*, p. 248).
43. Many critics believe this incident to be ambiguous or proof of Yorick's sexuality based on the following chapter's title, 'The Conquest', but given Sterne's ironic allusions to closure, locking, security, etc., I read this as another example of Yorick's lack of performance. Other critics have also argued that 'the conquest' is his triumph over impure thoughts.
44. Sterne, *A Sentimental Journey*, p. 151.
45. Markley asserts, 'If sentimentality is not a dead end, it is a discrete moment that can provide the impetus only for reflection, not action' (Markley, 'Sentimentality as Performance', p. 287).
46. Interestingly, the Monk also blushes in their exchange.
47. Fairer, 'Sentimental Translation is Mackenzie and Sterne', p. 137.
48. Because Yorick is able to overcome his desires yet remain sensual, Lamb argues, '*A Sentimental Journey* provided a model for a publicly acceptable erotic, sexually charged male tourist' (Lamb, *Bringing Travel Home*, p. 153).
49. Sterne, *A Sentimental Journey*, p. 70.
50. Yorick builds the Lady from Brussels's face in his imagination, *Fancy* supplying the missing details at which point he exclaims his imagination to be a 'seduced and seducing slut' (Sterne, *A Sentimental Journey*, p. 71). Not only do hands prove a dangerous gateway to lascivious temptations; so, too, does imagination.
51. Sterne, *A Sentimental Journey*, p. 146.
52. Pointedly, Lamb cites Sterne's own reference to France as 'foutre-land', or 'fuckland' (Lamb, *Bringing Travel Home to England*, p. 157).
53. Sterne, *A Sentimental Journey*, p. 137.
54. Markley, 'Sentimentality as Performance', p. 282.

55. Spacks proposes that sentimental novels' plotlessness, their protagonists' striking passivity and their peculiar treatment of sexuality are all ways to 'deny separation among people, the power of the self, the existence of the Other – ways, in short, to close the gap' (Spacks, *Desire and Truth*, p. 121).
56. Yorick responds to the Hotelier's accusations that 'the girl is no worse – and I am no worse – and you will be just as I found you', p. 149.
57. Sterne, *A Sentimental Journey*, p. 150.
58. New, 'Proust's Influence', p. 180.
59. Hagstrum, *Sex and Sensibility*, p. 250.
60. Barker-Benfield, *The Culture of Sensibility*, p. 231.

12 Olsson, '"Violence that's Wicked for a Man to Use": Sex, Gender and Violence in the Eighteenth Century'

1. For the discrepancy between the law and its practical application in a courtroom setting, see N. Bashar, 'Rape in England between 1550 and 1700', in The London Feminist History Group (eds), *The Sexual Dynamics of History: Men's Power, Women's Resistance* (London: Pluto Press, 1983), pp. 28–42, esp. pp. 29, 40. See also A. E. Simpson, who describes the legal background of eighteenth-century rape cases as 'an unhappy clash between the interests of a legal system undergoing modernization and the values of a popular culture' ('The "Blackmail Myth" and the Prosecution of Rape and Its Attempt in 18th Century London: The Creation of a Legal Tradition', *Journal of Criminal Law & Criminology*, 77 [1986], pp. 101–50, on p. 102).
2. See, for instance, M. Hale, *The History of the Pleas of the Crown*, 2 vols (London: F. Gyles, T. Woodward and C. Davis, 1736), vol. 1, pp. 635, 636; H. Dagge, *Considerations on Criminal Law* (London: T. Cadell, 1772), p. 376.
3. M. Dawes, *An Essay on Crimes and Punishments* (London: C. Dilly and J. Debrett, 1782), p. 97.
4. According to Gregory Durston, in addition to being severely underreported, the conviction rate for rape during the eighteenth century was very low, approximately 16 per cent (G. Durston, 'Rape in the Metropolis: Part 2', *British Journal for Eighteenth-Century Studies*, 29 [2006], pp. 15–31, on p. 15). Simpson establishes the conviction rate for rape at the Old Bailey between the years 1730–1830 to have been 17 per cent ('Vulnerability and the Age of Female Consent: Legal Innovation and Its Effect on Prosecutions for Rape in Eighteenth-Century London', in G. S. Rousseau and R. Porter (eds), *Sexual Underworlds of the Enlightenment* [Chapel Hill, NC: University of North Carolina Press, 1988], pp. 181–232, on p. 188).
5. W. Eden, *Principles of Penal Law* (London: B. White and T. Cadell, 1771), p. 236; Dagge, *Considerations on Criminal Law*, p. 374. See also G. Durston, 'Rape in the Metropolis: Part 1', in *British Journal for Eighteenth-Century Studies*, 28 (2005), pp. 167–79, on p. 168. The reliance on the victim's testimony was complicated by the fact that women were commonly believed to be untrustworthy, illogical and vindictive (see, for example, Durston, 'Rape in the Metropolis: Part 1', p. 168 and S. Dickie, 'Fielding's Rape Jokes', *Review of English Studies*, 61 [2010], pp. 572–90, on p. 582).
6. L. Gowing, *Common Bodies: Women, Touch and Power in Seventeenth-Century England* (New Haven, CT: Yale University Press, 2003), pp. 101, 90.

7. For the prevalence of this myth, see Durston, 'Rape in the Metropolis: Part 2', p. 25; Dickie, 'Fielding's Rape Jokes', p. 583; G. Vigarello, *A History of Rape: Sexual Violence in France from the 16th to the 20th Century* (Cambridge: Polity Press, 2001), pp. 93–4; J. Bourke, *Rape: A History from 1860 to the Present* (London: Virago, 2007), pp. 24–8. It should be noted that the unspoken implication of this belief is that the woman needs to be resolute because she otherwise risks giving in, not to fear or violence, but to the sexual pleasure that is assumed to be a given in any sexual act, no matter the circumstances.
8. W. Hawkins, *A Treatise of the Pleas of the Crown*, 2nd edn, 2 vols (London: J. Walthoe and J. Walthoe, Jr, 1724), vol. 1, p. 108. For a definition of the term 'rape myth', see K. A. Lonsway and L. F. Fitzgerald, 'Rape Myths', *Psychology of Women Quarterly*, 18 (1994), pp. 133–64, on p. 134: 'attitudes and beliefs that are generally false but are widely and persistently held, and that serve to deny and justify male sexual aggression against women'.
9. Dickie, 'Fielding's Rape Jokes', p. 583.
10. J. Cleland, *Memoirs of a Woman of Pleasure* (1748–9), ed. P. Sabor (Oxford: Oxford University Press, 1985), p. 103.
11. A. Smith, *The School of Venus: or, Cupid Restor'd to Sight*, 2 vols (London: J. Morphew and E. Berington, 1716), vol. 1, p. 148.
12. A. G., *The Impetuous Lover: or The Guiltless Parricide*, 2 vols (London: E. Ross, 1757), vol. 2, pp. 249–50.
13. Anon., 'On the Taking St. Maries: A Poem', in *The Beau's Miscellany* (London: A. Moore, [c. 1731]), pp. 46–53, on p. 48. The poem was originally published in 1703.
14. Anon., 'On the Taking St. Maries', pp. 53, 50. From a legal perspective, sexual intercourse was considered rape if consent had been obtained under duress; see Hawkins, *A Treatise of the Pleas of the Crown*, vol. 1, p. 108. However, the depiction of the men making sure to secure the women's (forced) consent supports Gowing's claim about the differing understandings of rape in popular culture and legal literature, and in a real-life courtroom such a precaution may well have persuaded a jury to find in favour of a rapist, whatever the letter of the law.
15. A. G., *The Impetuous Lover*, vol. 2, pp. 250–1. Original italics.
16. Smith, *The School of Venus*, vol. 1, pp. 148–9. Original italics.
17. S. Richardson, *Pamela: or, Virtue Rewarded* (1740), ed. T. Keymer and A. Weekly (Oxford: Oxford University Press, 2001), p. 203.
18. H. Fielding, *Joseph Andrews* and *Shamela* (1742 and 1741), ed. D. Brooks-Davies (Oxford: Oxford University Press, 1999), pp. 328, 329. Susan Staves has suggested that this mysterious method for avoiding rape involves 'squeezing or pulling the assailant's penis as hard as possible'; see S. Staves, 'Fielding and the Comedy of Attempted Rape', in *History, Gender & Eighteenth-Century Literature*, ed. B. Fowkes Tobin (Athens, GA: University of Georgia Press, 1994), pp. 86–112, on p. 91.
19. Whereas Shamela cares little for preserving her 'vartue', she is, of course, determined not to give in until she has at least acquired a settlement from Squire Booby.
20. E. Haywood, *The Lucky Rape*, in *Cleomelia: or, The Generous Mistress* (London: J. Millan, 1727), pp. 79–94, on p. 89.
21. Anon., *Genuine Memoirs of the Celebrated Miss Maria Brown*, 2 vols (London: I. Allcock, 1766), vol. 1, p. 111.
22. Anon., *The Memoirs of Miss Arabella Bolton* (London: I. Fell, 1770), vol. 1, pp. 25–6.
23. Ibid., vol. 1, p. 27.

24. S. Richardson, *Clarissa: or, The History of a Young Lady* (1747–8), ed. A. Ross (London: Penguin, 1985), pp. 897, 896. Original italics.
25. Ibid., p. 1011.
26. Smith, *The School of Venus*, vol. 2, pp. 47–8.
27. Ibid., p. 48.
28. Ibid., p. 40.
29. Ibid., p. 48.
30. Anon., *The Case of the Ld. John Drummond* (London: J. Roberts, 1715), p. 3.
31. G. Mauquest de la Motte, *A General Treatise of Midwifry* (London: James Waugh, 1746), p. 263.
32. J. F. Faselius, *Elements of Medical Jurisprudence* (London: T. Becket, 1788), p. 42.
33. J. L. Baudelocque, *A System of Midwifery*, 3 vols (London: the Author, 1790), vol. 1, p. 218.
34. Dawes, *An Essay on Crimes and Punishments*, p. 97.
35. J. Bourke, 'Sexual Violence, Bodily Pain, and Trauma: A History', *Theory Culture Society*, 29 (2012), pp. 25–51, on p. 34.
36. Anon., *Captain Leeson's Case* (London: J. Roberts, 1715), p. 18. The author of this work notes that Leeson was a mere 5 foot 6 inches tall (approx. 168 cm), p. 13.
37. Anon., *The Trial of Frederick Calvert, Esq; Baron of Baltimore* (London: W. Owen, and J. Gurney, 1768), p. 48.
38. G. Walker, 'Rereading Rape and Sexual Violence in Early Modern England', *Gender & History*, 10 (1998), pp. 1–25, on p. 8; E. Foyster, *Manhood in Early Modern England: Honour, Sex and Marriage* (London: Longman, 1999), p. 30; K. Harvey, *Reading Sex in the Eighteenth Century: Bodies and Gender in English Erotic Culture* (Cambridge: Cambridge University Press, 2004), p. 133.
39. Harvey, *Reading Sex in the Eighteenth Century*, p. 193 (original italics). The emphasis on the victim's resistance in rape trials may be explained by the need for proving two of the necessary requirements for an act to be defined as rape: 'by force' and 'against her will'.
40. Walker identifies screaming and running away as the two behaviours typically emphasized in women's testimonies in rape trials ('Rereading Rape and Sexual Violence in Early Modern England', pp. 10–11).
41. Gowing suggests that an exception to this is when women relate stories of successfully resisting assault, which enabled them to speak from a position of having retained, not lost, their sexual reputations (*Common Bodies*, pp. 96–7).
42. Foyster, *Manhood in Early Modern England*, p. 41; J. Skipp, 'Masculinity and Social Stratification in Eighteenth-Century Erotic Literature, 1700–1821', *British Journal for Eighteenth-Century Studies*, 29 (2006), pp. 253–69, on pp. 257–8.
43. See, for instance, A. K. Clark, 'Rape or Seduction? A Controversy over Sexual Violence in the Nineteenth Century', in The London Feminist History Group (eds), *The Sexual Dynamics of History: Men's Power, Women's Resistance* (London: Pluto Press, 1983), pp. 13–27, on pp. 17–19; Durston, 'Rape in the Metropolis: Part 2', p. 23; Gowing, *Common Bodies*, p. 99; J. Hurl-Eamon, *Gender and Petty Violence in London, 1680–1720* (Columbus, OH: Ohio State University Press, 2005), p. 37; Walker, 'Rereading Rape and Sexual Violence in Early Modern England', p. 16.
44. A. Clark, *Women's Silence, Men's Violence: Sexual Assault in England 1770–1845* (London: Pandora, 1987), pp. 34, 39; Foyster, *Manhood in Early Modern England*, p. 10; E. Foyster, *Marital Violence: An English Family History, 1660–1857* (Cambridge: Cambridge University Press, 2005), p. 37.

208 Notes to pages 147–52

45. Gowing, *Common Bodies*, p. 92; Walker, 'Rereading Rape and Sexual Violence in Early Modern England', pp. 5, 8.
46. See, for instance, Dagge, *Considerations on Criminal Law*, p. 377; Dawes, *An Essay on Crimes and Punishments*, p. 87.
47. Hurl-Eamon, *Gender and Petty Violence in London*, p. 40.
48. Simpson, 'Blackmail Myth'.

13 Krueger, 'The Rhetoric of Rape: William Blake's *Visions of the Daughters of Albion* as Eighteenth-Century Rape Trial'

1. See D. Aers, 'William Blake and the Dialectics of Sex', *ELH*, 44:3 (1977), pp. 500–14; N. M. Goslee, 'Slavery and Sexual Character: Questioning the Master Trope in Blake's Visions of the Daughters of Albion', *ELH*, 57:1 (1990), pp. 101–28; C. Jackson-Houlston, '"The Lineaments of Gratified Desire": Blake's *Visions of the Daughters of Albion* and Romantic Literary Treatments of Rape', in H. P. Bruder and T. Connolly (eds), *Queer Blake* (New York: Palgrave, 2010), pp. 153–62; S. Matthews, 'Blake, Hayley and the History of Sexuality', in S. Clark and D. Worrall (eds), *Blake, Nation and Empire* (New York: Palgrave, 2006), pp. 83–101; A. Mellor, 'Sex, Violence, and Slavery: Blake and Wollstonecraft', *Huntington Library Quarterly*, 58:3–4 (1996), pp. 345–70; and A. Ostriker, 'Desire Gratified and Ungratified: William Blake and Sexuality', in N. Hilton (ed.), *Essential Articles for the Study of William Blake, 1970–1984* (Hamden, CT: Archon, 1986), pp. 211–36.
2. M. Hale, *Historia Placitorum Coronae*, 2 vols (London: J. R. and J. Hazard, 1736), vol. 1, p. 628.
3. R. and J. Burn, *A New Law Dictionary*, 2 vols (London: A. Strahan and W. Woodfall, 1792), p. 267.
4. Hale, *Historia Placitorum Coronae*, vol. 1, p. 628.
5. J. Giles, *Every Man His Own Lawyer* (London: J. R. and J. Hazard, 1736), p. 442.
6. Hale, *Historia Placitorum Coronae*, vol. 1, p. 628.
7. W. Blackstone, *Commentaries on the Laws of England*, 11th edn, 4 vols (London: A. Strahan and W. Woodfall, 1791), vol. 4, p. 212.
8. Hale, *Historia Placitorum Coronae*, vol. 1, p. 635.
9. Ibid., p. 633.
10. Ibid.
11. Ibid.
12. Giles, *Every Man His Own Lawyer*, p. 443.
13. Blackstone, *Commentaries on the Laws of England*, vol. 4, p. 211.
14. Giles, *Every Man His Own Lawyer*, p. 442.
15. Hale, *Historia Placitorum Coronae*, vol. 1, p. 633.
16. M. Durey, 'Abduction and Rape in Ireland in the Era of the 1798 Rebellion', *Eighteenth-Century Ireland*, 21 (2006), p. 27–47, on p. 37.
17. A. Clark, *Women's Silence, Men's Violence: Sexual Assault in England 1770–1845* (London: Pandora, 1987), pp. 47, 58.
18. Hale, *Historia Placitorum Coronae*, vol. 1, p. 636.
19. Durey, 'Abduction and Rape in Ireland', p. 37
20. F. Ferguson, 'Rape and the Rise of the Novel', *Representations*, 20 (1987), pp. 88–112, on p. 88. See A. E. Simpson's use of 'second assault' in 'The Blackmail Myth and the

Prosecution of Rape and Its Attempt in 18th Century London: The Creation of a Legal Tradition', *Journal of Criminal Law & Criminology*, 77:1 (1986), pp. 101–50.
21. Trial transcripts show that adolescent and unmarried prosecutrices either were asked first to state their age, or volunteered this information. The ages of the prosecutrices I studied ranged from eight to twenty-one years of age.
22. *Proceedings of the Old Bailey, 1674–1913* (2012), at http://www.oldbaileyonline.org [accessed 4 January 2013].
23. *Cuckold's Chronicle*, 2 vols (London: H. Lemoin, 1793), vol. 1, p. 285.
24. *Proceedings of the Old Bailey*.
25. Giles, *Every Man His Own Lawyer*, p. 460, confirms this belief. Also see K. Harvey, *Reading Sex in the Eighteenth Century* (Cambridge: Cambridge University Press, 2004) and S. Toulalan, *Imagining Sex: Pornography and Bodies in Seventeenth-Century England* (Oxford: Oxford University Press, 2007).
26. T. Bowers, *Force or Fraud: British Seduction Stories and the Problem of Resistance 1660–1760* (Oxford: Oxford University Press, 2011), p. 22.
27. *Proceedings of the Old Bailey*.
28. Ibid.
29. For studies on propriety and sensibility see M. Poovey's *The Proper Lady and the Woman Writer* (Chicago, IL: University of Chicago Press, 1984) and G. J. Barker-Benfield's *The Culture of Sensibility: Sex and Society in Eighteenth-Century Britain* (Chicago, IL: University of Chicago Press, 1992).
30. *Proceedings of the Old Bailey*.
31. Ibid.
32. *Cuckold's Chronicle*, vol. 1, pp. 45–92.
33. J. Gurney, *The Trial of John Motherhill for Committing a Rape on the Body of Miss Catharine Wade* (London: G. Kearley, 1786), p. 10.
34. Clark, *Women's Silence, Men's Violence*, p. 35. As Clark explains, women professed Motherhill a hero, and other accused rapists were awarded such titles as 'Rape-master General'.
35. *Cuckold's Chronicle*, vol. 1, pp. 66–7.
36. J. Motherhill, *The Case of John Motherhill* (London: R. Randall, 1786).
37. Clark, *Women's Silence, Men's Violence*, p. 23.
38. Ibid., p. 24.
39. See D. G. Burks, *Horrid Spectacle: Violation in the Theater of Early Modern England* (Pittsburgh, PA: Duquesne University Press, 2003) and B. Swan, 'Clarissa Harlowe, Pleasant Rawlins, and Eighteenth-Century Discourses on Law', *Eighteenth-Century Novel*, 1 (2001), pp. 71–93.
40. See *Bloody Register* (London: E. and M. Viney, 1764); *British Tribunal: For 1789* (London: J.S. Barr, 1790); and *Tyburn Chronicle* (London: J. Cook, 1768).
41. Giles, *Every Man His Own Lawyer*, p. 442.
42. *Proceedings of the Old Bailey*.
43. Ibid.
44. Ibid.
45. Ibid.
46. Ibid.
47. I refer to Copy G in W. Blake, *The Complete Illuminated Books* (New York: Thames & Hudson, 2000), pp. 142–52, on p. 142.
48. Gurney, *The Trial of John Motherhill*, p. 10.
49. Blake, *The Complete Illuminated Books*, pp. 147–8.

50. Ibid., p. 144.
51. Ibid., p. 145.
52. Ibid.
53. Ibid. 144–5.
54. Ibid., p. 145.
55. Mellor, 'Sex, Violence, and Slavery', p. 358.
56. *Oxford English Dictionary* (2012), at http://www.oed.com [accessed 4 January 2013].
57. Blake, *The Complete Illuminated Books*, p. 146
58. Ibid., p. 145.
59. Ibid.
60. M. L. Johnson and J. E. Grant (eds), *Blake's Poetry and Designs* (New York: W.W. Norton & Company, 1979).
61. Blake, *The Complete Illuminated Books*, p. 145.
62. Ibid.
63. Clark, *Women's Silence, Men's Violence*, p. 35.
64. Blake, *The Complete Illuminated Books*, p. 146.
65. Ibid.
66. Ibid.
67. Ibid.
68. Ibid.
69. Clark, *Women's Silence, Men's Violence*, p. 24.
70. Blake, *The Complete Illuminated Books*, p. 147.
71. Ibid.
72. Ibid., p. 146.
73. Ibid., p. 149.
74. Ibid.
75. Ibid., p. 150.
76. Ibid.
77. Ibid.
78. Ibid.
79. Ibid., p. 151.
80. T. Eagleton, *Sweet Violence: The Idea of the Tragic* (Malden, MA: Blackwell, 2003), p. xi.
81. B. S. Webster, 'Blake, Women, and Sexuality', in D. Punter (ed.), *William Blake* (New York: St Martin's, 1996), pp. 188–206, on p. 190.

14 Cooper-Dobbin, 'The Horror of the Horns: Pan's Attempted Rape of Syrinx in Early Eighteenth-Century Visual Art'

1. W. Park, *The Idea of Rococo* (Newark, DE: University of Delaware Press; London, Cranbury, NJ: Associated University Presses, 1992), p. 32.
2. F. Dabhoiwala, *The Origins of Sex: A History of the First Sexual Revolution* (London, England; New York, NY: Allen Lane, 2012), p. 144.
3. Ibid., pp. 142–8.
4. D. Wolfthal, *Images of Rape: The 'Heroic' Tradition and its Alternatives* (Cambridge; New York; Melbourne: Cambridge University Press, 1999), p. 27
5. H. Hazen, *Endless Rapture: Rape, Romance, and the Female Imagination* (New York: Scribner, 1983), p. 74.

6. W. Talbot, 'Jean-François De Troy: Pan and Syrinx', *Bulletin of the Cleveland Museum of Art*, 61:8 (1974), pp. 250–9, on p. 254.
7. J. Hall, *Dictionary of Subjects and Symbols in Art* (London: John Murray Publishers, 1996), p. 294.
8. L. Curran, cited in Wolfthal, *Images of Rape: The 'Heroic' Tradition and Its Alternatives*, p. 21.
9. Wolfthal, *Images of Rape*, p. 21.
10. S. Griffin, *Rape: The Power of Consciousness* (San Francisco, CA: Harper & Row, 1979), p. 8; cited in E. Rooney, 'Criticism and the Subject of Sexual Violence', *MLN*, 98:5 (December 1983), pp. 1269–78, fn 13, p. 1278.
11. This image can be found online at <http://www.britishmuseum.org/research/search_the_collection_database/search_object_details.aspx?objectid=3308697&partid=1&IdNum=F%2c1.72&orig=%2fresearch%2fsearch_the_collection_database%2fmuseum_number_search.aspx>.
12. Wolfthal, *Images of Rape*, p. 12.
13. D'Hermenches, cited in A. Clark, *Desire: A History of European Sexuality* (New York and London: Routledge, 2008), p. 118.
14. J. Skipp, 'Masculinity and Social Stratification in Eighteenth-Century Erotic Literature, 1700–1821', *British Journal for Eighteenth Century Studies*, 29 (2006), pp. 253–69, on p. 263.
15. F. Lissarague, 'The Sexual Life of Satyrs', in D. M. Halperin, J. J. Winkler and F. I. Zeitlin (eds), *Before Sexuality: The Construction of Erotic Experience in the Ancient Greek World* (Princeton, NJ: Princeton University Press, 1990), pp. 53–82, on p. 53; C. Groneman, 'Nymphomania: The Historical Construction of Female Sexuality', in J. Terry and J. Urla (eds), *Deviant Bodies: Critical Perspectives on Difference in Science and Popular Culture* (Bloomington and Indianapolis, IN: Indiana University Press, 1995), pp. 219–51, on p. 221. See also pp. 231–2.
16. J. V. Douthwaite, '*Homo ferus*: Between Monster and Model', *Eighteenth-Century Life*, 21:2 (1997), pp. 176–202, on p. 195.
17. R. Nash, *Wild Enlightenment: The Borders of Human Identity in the Eighteenth Century* (Charlottesville, VA: University of Virginia Press, 2003), p. 29.
18. N. Venette, *The Mysteries of Conjugal Love Reveal'd*, 3rd edn (London, 1712), p. 92, at www.gender.amdigital.co.uk.proxy.library.adelaide.edu.au/contents/documents-detail.aspx?sectionid=58872 [accessed 8 June 2012].
19. Venette, *The Mysteries of Conjugal Love Reveal'd*, p. 92.
20. Ibid.
21. Ibid.
22. Lissarague, 'The Sexual Life of Satyrs', pp. 55–8.
23. Venette gives the example of Naples and Seville as areas particularly prone to lascivious characteristics in inhabitants of 'places where monsters are often born, which are the effects of abominable love'. *The Mysteries of Conjugal Love Reveal'd*, p. 89.
24. Venette, *The Mysteries of Conjugal Love Reveal'd*, pp. 90–1.
25. Ibid., p. 88.
26. Ibid., pp. 61–9.
27. C. B. Bailey, *The Loves of the Gods: Mythological Painting From Watteau to David* (Fort Worth: Kimball Art Museum; New York: Rizzoli International Publications, 1992), p. 102.

Notes to pages 168–72

28. C. B. Bailey (ed.), *The First Painters of the King – French Royal Taste from Louis XIV to the Revolution* (New York: Stair Sainty Matthies, 1985), pp. 58–9.
29. Bailey, *The Loves of the Gods: Mythological Painting from Watteau to David*, pp. 100–2.
30. I acknowledge with gratitude the vital information provided by Bailey's *Loves of the Gods* catalogue, imperative to understanding these works.
31. H. Roodenburg, 'Venus Minsieke Gasthuis: Sexual Beliefs in Eighteenth-Century Holland', in J. Bremmer (ed.), *From Sappho to de Sade – Moments in the History of Sexuality* (London; New York: Routledge, 1989), pp. 84–107, on p. 94.
32. R. Porter, '"The Secrets of Generation Display'd: *Aristotle's Masterpiece* in Eighteenth-Century England', in R. P. Maccubbin (ed.), *'Tis Nature's Fault: Unauthorized Sexuality During the Enlightenment* (New York: Cambridge University Press, 1987), pp. 1–21, on p. 1; R. Porter, 'Spreading Carnal Knowledge or Selling Dirt Cheap? Nicolas Venette's Tableau de l'Amour Conjugal in Eighteenth Century England', *Journal of European Studies*, 14:233 (1984), pp. 233–55, on p. 239.
33. Venette, *The Mysteries of Conjugal Love Reveal'd*, p. 69. See also p. 80.
34. This image can be found online at http://britishmuseum.org/research/search_the_collection_database/search_object_details.aspx?objectid=1438445&partid=1&searchText=pan+and+syrinx+&fromADBC=ad&toADBC=ad&numpages=10&orig=%2fresearch%2fresearch_the_collection_database.aspx&currentPage=1>.
35. Translated and cited in Bailey, *The Loves of the Gods: Mythological Painting from Watteau to David*, p. 102.
36. D. M. Turner, *Fashioning Adultery: Gender, Sex, and Civility in England, 1660–1740* (Cambridge; New York: Cambridge University Press, 2002), pp. 101–2.
37. Dabhoiwala, *The Origins of Sex: The History of the First Sexual Revolution*, p. 186.
38. R. A. Nye, *Masculinity and Male Codes of Honor in Modern France* (New York and Oxford: Oxford University Press, 1993), pp. 29–30.
39. *The British Apollo*, 1:2 (18 February 1708), cited in Turner, *Fashioning Adultery: Gender, Sex, and Civility in England, 1660–1740*, p. 87.
40. A. Blok, 'Rams and Billy-Goats: A Key to the Mediterranean Code of Honour', *Man*, 16:3 (September 1981), pp. 427–40, on p. 431.
41. Ibid.
42. Blok, 'Rams and Billy-Goats: A Key to the Mediterranean Code of Honour', pp. 427–8.
43. F. Vaz da Silva, 'Sexual Horns: The Anatomy and Metaphysics of Cuckoldry in European Folklore', *Comparative Studies in Society and History*, 48:2 (April 2006), pp. 396–418, on p. 399.
44. Turner, *Fashioning Adultery: Gender, Sex, and Civility in England, 1660–1740*, pp. 101–2.
45. These terms appear within titles by popular authors including Aphra Behn, Joseph Harris and Reuben Bourne.
46. Anon., *The Horn Exalted, or Room for Cuckolds. Being a Treatise Concerning the Reason and Original of the Word Cuckold, and Why Such are Said to Wear horns. Also an Appendix Concerning Women and Jealousie* (London, 1661), pp. 2–3.
47. F. V. Toussaint, Y. Claude and D. Diderot (ascribed). 'Adultery'. *The Encyclopedia of Diderot and d'Alembert Collaborative Translation Project*, trans. N. Andrews (Ann Arbor, MI: MPublishing, University of Michigan Library, 2007), http://hal.handle.net/2027/spo.did2222.0000.328 [accessed 18 June 2012]. Originally published as 'Adultère', *Encyclopèdie ou Dicctionnarie raisonné des sciences, des artes at des metiers*, 1:150 (Paris, 1751).
48. Toussaint, 'Adultery', p. 150.

49. Wolfthal, *Images of Rape: The 'Heroic' Tradition and Its Alternatives*, p. 9. Wolfthal draws on the example of Poussin's *Rape of the Sabines* to demonstrate the concept of *raptus* in Roman law as theft or violation of property rights committed against the woman's husband or other male relative. Wolfthal further explains how the story of the Sabines was viewed in Roman history as central to family life and nation building, p. 8.
50. J. J. Rousseau, cited in C. Roulston, 'Separating the Inseperables: Female Friendship and Its Discontents in Eighteenth Century France', *Eighteenth Century Studies*, 32:2 (1998–9), pp. 215–31, on p. 221.
51. P. Mainardi, *Husbands, Wives and Lovers: Marriage and its Discontents in Nineteenth-Century France* (New Haven, CT: Yale University Press, 2003), pp. 7–8.
52. Dabhoiwala, *The Origin of Sex: The History of the First Sexual Revolution*, p. 150.
53. Ovid, *Metamorphoses*, trans. S. Garth et al. (Amsterdam, 1732); reprint (London and New York: Garland Publishing Inc., 1976), p. 36. Again I acknowledge my debt to Wolfthal's study with regards to the 'model of exchange'.
54. M. Bellhouse, 'Visual Myths of Female Identity in Eighteenth Century France', *International Political Science Review/Revue Internationale de Science Politique*, 12:2 (1991), *Political Theory By Other Means. La politique sous d'autres formes* (April 1991), pp. 117–35, on p. 122.
55. Vaz da Silva, 'Sexual Horns: The Anatomy and Metaphysics of Cuckoldry in European Folklore', p. 400.
56. Anon., *The Horn Exalted*, p. 4.
57. Vaz da Silva, 'Sexual Horns: The Anatomy and Metaphysics of Cuckoldry in European Folklore', pp. 399, p. 402.

INDEX

A Bloody Tragedie, 102
abduction
   bride, 39–44
accomplice
   rapist's need for an, 119–20, 125–9, 141–8
Addison, Joseph
   Cato, 66
Adventures of Eovaai, Princess of Ijaveo, 98
age of consent *see* age of discretion
age of discretion, 6, 20, 25, 28, 45, 48, 52
Amboyna, 60, 78
Anon., *A Bloody Tragedie*, 102
Anon., *Captain Leeson's Case*, 146
Anon., *Claudian's Rufinus: or, The Court-Favourite's Overthrow*, 95–6
Anon., *Genuine Memoirs of the Celebrated Miss Maria Brown*, 144
Anon., *The Memoirs of Miss Arabella Bolton*, 38, 144
Anon., *The Practical Part of Love*, 59
Anon., *The Trial of Frederick Calvert, Esq; Baron of Baltimore*, 146
anti-Catholicism, 61, 62, 101–5
see also poisonous Catholic bride
Apollo, 171
An Apology for the Life of Mrs. Shamela Andrews, 143
Aristotle, 121, 122–3, 125, 126, 127
Armstrong, Nancy, 119, 120
arteries
   related to sensibility, 132, 136, 137
Astell, Mary, 120, 122, 123, 124
Aureng-Zebe, 62
autonomy
   female, 3, 36–8, 44, 113, 119, 120, 125, 126, 128–9

Bancroft, John
   King Edward the Third, With the Fall of Mortimer, 101–4
Barker-Benfield, G. J., 131, 139
Barry, Elizabeth, 69
Bartley, O. W., 30–1
Bashar, Nazife, 15
Baudelocque, Jean Louis, 146
Behn, Aphra, 1, 74, 78, 89, 96, 99, 100, 101
   The City Heiress, 72–3
   The Lucky Chance, 87–9
   The Rover Part 1, 1, 96, 99–100, 101
Berkeley, George, 90
Bertelsen, Lance, 96
Binhammer, Katherine, 15–16
blackmail myth, 19–21, 27, 101, 148, 151
Blackstone, Sir William, 6, 26, 27, 30, 52, 53, 150, 151, 155
Blake, William
   Visions of the Daughters of Albion, 149–62
Blok, Anton, 172
Blount, Charles, 97
blushing, 90, 116, 132, 136, 137, 138
Bolton, Arabella *see* Anon., *The Memoirs of Miss Arabella Bolton*
Bond, Anne, 19, 98
Bowers, Toni, 84, 152
Boyle, Robert
   The Generall, 64
Bracegirdle, Anne, 69
Brack, O. M., 113
Bracton, Henri de, 26
Brady, Nicholas
   The Rape, 78–81, 96, 100
breeches roles, 69

Breval, John
    The Rape of Helen, 96
Brewer, Holly, 51–2
Broad, Jacqueline, 122
Brown, Maria *see* Anon., *Genuine Memoirs of the Celebrated Miss Maria Brown*
Brownmiller, Susan, 13–14
Brydall, John, 6
Buffon, Comte de, 51
Burnet, Gilbert, 84

Cahill, Ann, 128
Calvert, Frederick, Lord Baltimore, 146
Captain Leeson's Case, 146
Carlile, Susan, 113
Caroline of Ansbach, 104
Cartwright, William, 99
Catholicism *see* anti-Catholicism
Cato, 66
Cavalier, 97, 99–103, 105
Charles I, 85, 88, 97, 103
Charles II, 89, 99, 104
Charteris, Colonel Francis, 19, 98–101
chastity, 2–3, 5, 6–7, 16, 38, 67–8, 92, 98, 107–13, 116–17, 126–9, 155, 160, 166, 172
children
    as victims of sexual violence, 20, 24, 31, 45–56, 149
    see also age of discretion
The City Heiress, 72–3
City Politiques, 73–4
Clancy, Michael
    The Sharper, 96
Clarissa: or, The History of a Young Lady, 1, 2, 16, 38, 108, 119, 144
Clark, Anna, 15, 16, 18, 20, 39, 41, 151, 154, 159
Claudian's Rufinus: or, the Court-Favourite's Overthrow, 95–6
Cleland, John
    Memoirs of a Woman of Pleasure, 142
Coke, Edward 26, 29, 31
Collier, Jeremy
    The Immorality and Profaneness of the English Stage, 67
comedy of manners, 70–2
Congreve, William
    Love for Love, 71

The Conquest of Granada by the Spaniards, Part II, 63–4
Constantine, Stephen M., 16–17
Court of Assize, 18, 27, 32, 42
The Craftsman, 96–7
Crowne, John
    City Politiques, 73–4
crying, 55, 132, 78, 133, 138
cuckold, 89, 100, 145, 171–4
cult of seduction, 163

d'Anvers, Caleb
    The Craftsman, 96–7
Dabhoiwala, Faramerz, 163
Dawes, Manasseh
    An Essay on Crimes and Punishments, 146
Dennis, John, 65, 69
divine right *see* political obedience
doctrine of resistance *see* political resistance
drugging *see* victim, drugging of
Drummond, John, 145
Dryden, John
    Amboyna, 60, 78
    Aureng-Zebe, 62
    The Conquest of Granada by the Spaniards, Part II, 63–4
    The Rival Ladies, 66
    Sir Martin Marall, 73–4
Durston, Gregory, 14, 15, 18, 29
Dutch, 97

East, Edward Hyde, 30, 31–2
Edelstein, Laurie, 19
Eden, W.
    Principles of Penal Law, 141
Edward II, 97, 101, 103
Edward III, 105
Edwards, Susan, 14
Egan, R. Danielle, 51
ejaculation, 5, 16, 21, 31, 32, 47, 48, 150, 152
Elizabethan Statute (1576), 24, 25, 31, 33
emission *see* ejaculation
English Civil Wars, 97, 99, 103
Enlightenment, 17, 27, 46, 50–1
erotica, 2, 9, 17, 58–62

Index

fainting *see* victim, loss of consciousness
The Fair Penitent, 78, 81–2
The Fall of Mortimer, 96, 101–5
Farr, Samuel, 30, 145–6
Faselius, J. F.
   Elements of Medical Jurisprudence, 145–6
The Female Quixote, 107–17
Ferguson, Robert, 97–8
Fielding, Henry, 17, 19, 123
   An Apology for the Life of Mrs. Shamela Andrews, 143
   Joseph Andrews, 2
   Rape Upon Rape, 3, 96, 100–1, 105
   Tom Jones, 2, 10, 119, 120, 124–9
Fille de Chambre, 135, 136–8
Filmer, Robert, 84
Finch, Henry, 26, 31
First Statute of Westminster (1275), 24
Forbes, Thomas, 21
Forman, Charles
   Protesilaus: or, The Character of an Evil Minister, 95
Foucault, Michel, 49
Frederick, Prince of Wales, 104
friendship
   in rape narratives, 119–29
Friedman, Marilyn, 121

G., A.
   The Impetuous Lover: or The Guiltless Parricide, 143
Gallway, Elizabeth, 145
Ganymede figure, 46, 103
Gardiner, Ellen, 113
The Generall, 64
Genuine Memoirs of the Celebrated Miss Maria Brown, 144
George I, 90
George II, 97
Gilbert, Arthur, 49
Giles, Jacob, 150–1, 154
Glanvill, 25–6
Glorious Revolution, 85–6, 89, 97–8, 99, 102
Goldgar, Bertrand, 99
Goldie, Mark, 89
Goldsmith, Netta Murray, 21, 48
Gowing, Laura, 144
Grant, John E., 158

Greaves, Richard L., 85
Gwynn, Nell, 69

Hagstrum, Jean, 131
Hale, Sir Matthew, 19–20, 26–7, 29, 31, 149, 150, 151, 155
hands
   as a literary motif, 77, 136–7
Harol, Corrinne, 89
Harvey, Karen, 59, 60, 61, 146
Hatchett, William
   The Fall of Mortimer, 96, 101–5
Hawkes, Gail, 51
Hawkins, William, 26, 30, 31
Haywood, Eliza, 1, 120, 123, 124
   Adventures of Eovaai, Princess of Ijaveo, 98
   The History of Miss Betsy Thoughtless, 119
   The Lucky Rape, 144
   A Wife to Be Lett, 83–93
Henrietta Maria, Queen of England, 103–4
'heroic' rape, 153, 158, 163
The History of Miss Betsy Thoughtless, 119
Howe, Elizabeth, 17, 57
Hughes, Derek, 57
Hume, David, 120, 123–4
Hurl-Eamon, Jennine, 148

Ibrahim, 76–8
The Immorality and Profaneness of the English Stage, 67
The Impetuous Lover: or The Guiltless Parricide, 143
impotence, 135–9, 172
The Injured Lovers, 59

Jacobites, 90, 97–9
James II, 84, 85, 88–9, 97, 104
Jacques, Eileen, 125
Jeurat, Edmé, 171–4
Johnson, Samuel, 6, 113, 117, 122
Johnson, Mary Lynn, 158
Jones, Wendy, 125
Joseph Andrews, 2

King Edward the Third, With the Fall of Mortimer, 101–4

Langbein, John, 21
Laqueur, Thomas, 15
Lawrence, George, 99
Lee, Nathaniel
    Lucius Junius Brutus, 96, 100
    Mithridates, 1, 63
Leeson, Hugh, 146
Lennox, Charlotte
    The Female Quixote, 107–17
The Libertine (retitled *Don Jon; or, The Libertine Destroy'd*), 63, 96, 99
libertinism, 98–103, 143, 147, 158, 166, 173
Lindemann, Barbara, 15, 18
Linebaugh, Peter, 21
Locke, John, 46, 51, 55, 85, 86, 120, 121, 124, 125
Love for Love, 71
Lucius Junius Brutus, 96, 100
The Lucky Chance, 87–9
The Lucky Rape, 144

Mack, Maynard, 104
Manley, Delarivière (alternately Delarivier or de La Rivière), 1, 65, 77
    The Royal Mischief, 65
Markley, Robert, 138
marriage
    as a solution for rape, 25, 38–40, 42–4, 72, 128–9, 148
Marsden, Jean, 57
Mary II, 97, 104
Mauquest de la Motte, Guillaume, 145
May, Mary, 146
medical jurisprudence, 15, 21, 29–31, 49–50, 53–6, 142, 145–6
Medici, Catherine de, 104
Mellor, Anne, 157
Memoirs of a Woman of Pleasure, 142
Metamorphoses, 164, 166
Mignard, Pierre, 168–74
Mithridates, 1, 63
Motherhill, John, 153–4, 155
Mountfort, William
    The Injured Lovers, 59
Mui, Constance, 128

Müller, Anja, 51
myth of the 'unrapeable' woman, 10, 30, 141–8

New, Melvyn, 131, 134, 135, 139
Norton, Rictor, 54
nymphomania, 166

Old Bailey Court, 18, 27, 28, 29, 45–56, 151, 152
'On the Taking St. Maries: A Poem', 143
Orrery, Earl of *see* Boyle, Robert
Otway, Thomas
    Venice Preserv'd, 75–6, 96
Ovid
    Metamorphoses, 164, 166

Pacheco, Anita, 89
Pamela: or, Virtue Rewarded, 2, 119, 143
Pan, 163–74
    see also Ovid, *Metamorphoses*
passive obedience *see* political obedience
pedophilia/paedophilia, 46, 48
penetration, 5, 16, 21, 31–2, 47–9, 53, 54, 142, 150, 152
Perry, Gill, 59
Perry, Ruth, 113
Pix, Mary
    Ibrahim, 76–8
The Plain Dealer, 71–2
poisonous Catholic bride, 103–5
    see also anti-Catholicism
political obedience, 2, 83–93
political resistance, 2, 3, 83–93, 119–20
Pope, Alexander, 3, 98
Porter, Roy, 14, 17, 64–5
Porter, Thomas
    The Villain, 1, 64
The Practical Part of Love, 59
promiscuity, 4–5, 11, 127, 168, 172–3
propaganda, 95–105
Pulteney, William, 99

rape
    as a political symbol, 2–3, 14, 57, 75–7, 95–105, 119–20, 125, 162
    as a property crime, 3–5, 15, 26, 36–7, 40, 96, 97, 154, 155, 160

conviction rate, 13, 14–15, 18, 19, 23, 29, 42, 141, 148, 151
evidence for, 13, 16, 20, 21, 26–8, 31, 32, 40, 47–8, 50, 53–5, 150–5, 158
impossibility of *see* myth of the 'unrapeable' woman
laws regarding, 6, 14, 16–17, 19, 20, 21, 23–33, 40, 45–56, 141, 142, 146–7, 149–55, 159, 163
legal definition, 23–6, 31–3, 36, 142, 147, 149–50
myths regarding, 5, 13, 15–16, 141–8
see also myth of the 'unrapeable' woman
pregnancy resulting from, 5, 29–31, 152
rape of seduction, 36–9
The Rape, 78–81, 96, 100
The Rape of Helen, 96
Rape Upon Rape, 3, 96, 100–1, 105
Ravenscroft, Edward
Titus Andronicus, 104
ravishment, 23–6, 29, 70
The Relapse, 70–1
Richardson, Samuel
Clarissa: or, The History of a Young Lady, 1, 2, 16, 38, 108, 119, 144
Pamela: or, Virtue Rewarded, 2, 119, 143
ritualized rape *see* blackmail myth
The Rival Ladies, 66
Rochester, Earl of *see* Wilmot, John
Roundhead, 89, 97, 99
The Rover Part 1, 1, 96, 99–100, 101
Rowe, Nicholas
The Fair Penitent, 78, 81–2
Tamerlane, 64
The Royal Mischief, 65
Rudolph, Julia, 36–7, 84

Sacheverell trial, 89–90
St Bartholomew's Day massacre, 104
satyriasis, 166–7
Saunders, Corrine, 23, 29
The School of Venus: or, Cupid Restor'd to Sight, 142–3, 144
Second Statute of Westminster (1285), 24
seduction, 1, 2, 3, 7, 15–16, 36–9, 41–2, 61, 69–72, 108, 153, 163, 166, 172
see also rape of seduction
sensibility, 36, 38, 50, 111, 131–9
see also arteries

sentiment *see* sensibility
A Sentimental Journey, 131–9
Shadwell, Thomas
The Libertine (retitled *Don Jon; or, The Libertine Destroy'd*), 63, 96, 99
The Sharper, 96
she-tragedy, 75–82
Shoemaker, Robert B., 18, 47
Shürer, Norbert, 113
Silver, Allan, 121
Simpson, Anthony E., 17, 19, 20, 21, 47, 48, 51, 56, 148
Sir Martin Marall, 73–4
Smith, Adam, 123
Smith, Alexander
The School of Venus: or, Cupid Restor'd to Sight, 142–3, 144
social contract *see* political resistance
sodomite *see* sodomy
sodomy, 3, 19, 20–1, 45–56, 61
South Sea Bubble, 98
Staves, Susan, 15–16, 17, 102
Steele, Richard, 65
Sterne, Laurence
A Sentimental Journey, 131–9
surgeon *see* medical jurisprudence
swooning *see* victim, loss of consciousness

Tamerlane, 64
tears *see* crying
Thesaurus Dramaticus, 66–7
Titus Andronicus, 104
Todd, Janet, 131, 134
Tory politics, 2, 83–93
Toulalan, Sarah, 60
tragic drama
sexual violence in, 1, 57–68, 75–82
tragicomedy of intrigue, 72–4
The Trial of Frederick Calvert, Esq; Baron of Baltimore, 146
Tom Jones, 2, 10, 119, 120, 124–9
Troy, Jean-François de, 164–6, 174
Trumbach, Randolph, 17

Udden, Anna, 113
underage *see* age of discretion

Valentinian, 63, 66, 76
Vanbrugh, John
   The Relapse, 70–1
Venette, Nicolas, 167
Venice Preserv'd, 75–6, 96
victim
   drugging of, 38, 144
   loss of consciousness of, 16, 38, 78, 142, 143, 144
The Villain, 1, 64
violence
   deemed acceptable in courtship situations, 15, 35–44, 147
Visions of the Daughters of Albion, 149–62

Wade, Catharine, 153, 155, 156, 159
Wagner, Peter, 50
Walker, Garthine, 65
Walpole, Sir Robert, 95–105
Ward, Edward, 61
Webster, Brenda S., 162
Whig politics, 2, 83–93
wife pandering, 83–93
A Wife to Be Lett, 83–93
William III, 97, 102
Wilmot, John, Earl of Rochester
   Valentinian, 63, 66, 76
witnesses to sexual violence, 13, 18–19, 21, 26, 28, 47–8, 51–2, 149–55
Wolfthal, Diane, 163, 174
Wood, Thomas, 26, 29, 31
Woodcock, Sarah, 146
Wright, James
   Country Conversations, 67
Wycherley, William
   The Plain Dealer, 71–2